ATTENTION TEACHER:

IMPORTANT INSTRUCTIONS FOR ACCESSING
WRITE WITH WORLD **ONLINE TEACHER SERVICES:**

A valuable part of your *Write with WORLD* curriculum are the online teacher services. This secure, password-protected website is designed just for you – the teacher. Your first year's access is included with your purchase of the *Write with WORLD* curriculum. Subsequent years are available by subscription.

FOLLOW THESE INSTRUCTIONS TO ACCESS YOUR ONLINE TEACHER SERVICES:

1. Go to **www.writewithworld.com** and click on the link to enter the teacher services area.
2. Follow the directions to enter your unique access code and set up your password.
3. That's it! In the future, just enter your password to access your teacher services.

Your unique access code:

10I0974

YOUR ONLINE TEACHER SERVICES INCLUDE:

▶ **Student writing samples…** A great way to teach by example. Submit your student writing samples for possible publication online. Review other students' writing to use as examples in your teaching.

▶ **Teachers' forum…** You're not alone! This *Write with WORLD* members-only forum is a helpful, secure online forum where you can discuss ideas and strategies for teaching, learn what others are doing to get the best results from their students, and generally find encouragement for some of "those days."

▶ **New material, without new books…** Your *Write with WORLD* textbooks are non-consumable, but they're also slow to age. Over time you will find new lesson prompts and other content online, to keep your curriculum up-to-date without purchasing new textbooks every few years.

▶ **Teacher training…** A practical confidence-builder. The authors of *Write with WORLD* not only teach writing, they teach *teachers* of writing. Access your online teacher services to learn practical tips and techniques to encourage your student's best work, and to build your confidence in teaching and evaluating writing.

Write with WORLD I

Thinking Through Images, Developing Voice, and Crafting Narrative.

Parent/Teacher Edition

Dr. Ronald L. Pitcock
Dr. Jennifer Workman Pitcock
Dr. Rayshelle Dietrich
Contributors from *God's World News* and *WORLD Magazine*

God's World Publications, Inc.
Asheville, NC

Published by God's World Publications, Inc.

Printed in the United States of America.

ISBN: 978-0-9855957-0-8

About the authors:

Ron Pitcock, General Editor and Author, is the J. Vaughn and Evelyn H. Wilson Honors Fellow at Texas Christian University in Fort Worth, Texas. He earned his Ph.D. in English and American Literature at the University of Kentucky.

A National Writing Project Fellow, Dr. Pitcock was recently named one of the top 300 professors in the United States by The Princeton Review. Dr. Pitcock has also received the "Promising Researcher Award" from the National Council of Teachers of English and the 2010 Wassenich Award for Mentoring in the TCU Community. His approach to teaching writing has led to multiple teaching awards at the University of Kentucky, Indiana State University, and TCU, where he was named TCU's "Honors Professor of the Year" and chosen by students as the recipient of the 2009 TCU Inspirational Professor Award presented by EECU.

Each summer, Dr. Pitcock spends a month in Europe eating gelato (and teaching Honors students a little too). When he's not traveling the world, he enjoys spending time at the swimming pool with his wife and three children.

Jenny Pitcock, Associate Editor and Author, has served as a writer for *God's World News* since 2005 and currently serves as a news writer and editor. She earned her Ph.D. in American Literature at the University of Kentucky. She is a Fellow of the National Writing Project and has received teaching awards at the University of Kentucky, most notably the Chancellor's Award for Most Outstanding Teaching Assistant in the University.

A mother of three living in Fort Worth Texas, Dr. Pitcock is an avid reader and freelance writer. She loves nothing more than spending time with her family—though she occasionally sneaks away to Starbucks to relax and read a good book.

Rayshelle Dietrich, Author, lives in Fort Worth with her husband and three energetic children. She earned her Ph.D. in American Literature from Texas Christian University where she was awarded the College of Liberal Arts Graduate Teacher of the Year. When she isn't reading Dr. Seuss with her kids or sneaking veggies into their food, she enjoys doing archival work to recover the diaries and letters of local women.

Contributors from *God's World News* and *WORLD Magazine*:

Krieg Barrie, Illustrator, *WORLD Magazine*
Emily Belz, Reporter, *WORLD Magazine*
Joel Belz, Founder, *God's World News* and *WORLD Magazine*
Mindy Belz, Editor, *WORLD Magazine*
Rich Bishop, Creative Director, *God's World News*
Anthony Bradley, Correspondent, *WORLD Magazine*
Howard Brinkman, Publisher, *God's World News*
Janie B. Cheaney, Senior Writer, *WORLD Magazine*
Rebecca Cochrane, Editor, *God's World News*
Jamie Dean, News Editor, *WORLD Magazine*
Victoria Drake, Editor, *God's World News*
Megan Dunham, Writer, *God's World News*
Amy Henry, Correspondent, *WORLD Magazine*
Roy McGinnis, Writer, *God's World News*
Mickey McLean, Web Executive Editor, worldmag.com
Marvin Olasky, Editor-in-Chief, *World News Group*
Susan Olasky, Senior Writer, *WORLD Magazine*
Arsenio Orteza, Correspondent, *WORLD Magazine*
Edward Lee Pitts, Reporter, *WORLD Magazine*
Patti Richter, Writer, *God's World News*
Warren Smith, Vice President, *World News Group*
Kim Stegall, Editor, *God's World News*
James Allen Walker, Photojournalist, *WORLD Magazine*

CONTENTS

Write with WORLD I
Thinking through Images, Developing Voice, and Crafting Narrative

SUGGESTED LESSON PLANNING

Write with WORLD is organized into Units, Lessons, and Capsules. There are four Units in each volume (year) of the curriculum, with each Unit composed of four Lessons. Within each Lesson are five Capsules.

We recommend pacing the work to do three capsules one week and two the next. Students' writing improves most when they practice process writing—planning, writing, and revising. This schedule allows the time needed for process writing.

On the week you complete two capsules, the third time slot should be used as a built-in time for conferencing. You may want or need to do more conferencing, but a planned conference at least that often is a good idea. In a classroom setting, we recommend a one-on-one conference at least once a quarter.

Students will need a three-ring binder and page dividers for their writer's journal. They may use loose-leaf notebook paper, or if writing on a computer, print and three-hole punch the paper for their journal.

GENERAL INTRODUCTION

Take a minute to read the General Introduction so you understand what to expect from this curriculum and from your students.

UNIT #1: DEVELOPING CRITICAL READERS

Before beginning Unit 1, please refer to the General Overview for the Unit, and the Detailed Overview for each of the Lessons found in your Teacher's textbook at the beginning of Unit 1.

Week 1
Lesson 1: Reading Images and Advertisements
- Capsule 1: The Story Behind the Image
- Capsule 2: What a Photojournalist Sees
- Capsule 3: The Story Behind the Image

Week 2
- Capsule 4: The Message Behind the Advertisement
- Capsule 5: Style, Diction, and Revision
- Conference: Before conferencing with your student, refer to the section, "Three Ways to Help Your Student Writer in Unit 1," found in your Teacher's textbook at the beginning of Unit 1… Conference Regularly… Encourage Specificity… Use Low-stakes Evaluation Instead of High-stakes Evaluation.

Week 3
Lesson 2: Comparative Reading: Sentences
- Capsule 1: Knowing the Subject
- Capsule 2: Knowing the Subject Better
- Capsule 3: Strong Subjects Need Strong Actions

Week 4
- Capsule 4: Using Adverbs to Answer Important Questions
- Capsule 5: Sentences Can Create Images
- Conference: Before conferencing with your student, refer again to the section, "Three Ways to Help Your Student Writer in Unit 1," found in your Teacher's textbook at the beginning of Unit 1… Conference Regularly… Encourage Specificity… Use Low-stakes Evaluation Instead of High-stakes Evaluation.

Week 5
Lesson 3: Comparative and Critical Reading: Paragraphs
- Capsule 1: Starting to Think About Paragraphs
- Capsule 2: Paragraphs Help Readers Understand Your Point
- Capsule 3: Sentences Work Together to Create Focus in a Paragraph

Week 6
- Capsule 4: Transitions Help Organize Paragraphs
- Capsule 5: Evaluating Paragraphs
- Conference: Before conferencing with your student, refer again to the section, "Three Ways to Help Your Student Writer in Unit 1," found in your Teacher's textbook at the beginning of Unit 1… Conference Regularly… Encourage Specificity… Use Low-stakes Evaluation Instead of High-stakes Evaluation.

Week 7
Lesson 4: Developing Critical Readers: Essays
- Capsule 1: What is an Essay?
- Capsule 2: Reading an Essay
- Capsule 3: Reading With Skillful Judgment

Week 8
- Capsule 4: More Practice
- Capsule 5: Essay Writing Requires Practice
- Conference: Before conferencing with your student, refer again to the section, "Three Ways to Help Your Student Writer in Unit 1," found in your Teacher's textbook at the beginning of Unit 1… Conference Regularly… Encourage Specificity… Use Low-stakes Evaluation Instead of High-stakes Evaluation.

UNIT #2: DEVELOPING WRITERS: BUILDING BLOCKS AND BIOGRAPHY

Before beginning Unit 2, please refer to the General Overview for the Unit, and the Detailed Overview for each of the Lessons found in your Teacher's textbook at the beginning of Unit 2.

Week 9
Lesson 1: The Paragraph
▶ Capsule 1: Effective Paragraphing
▶ Capsule 2: Achieving Unity in a Paragraph
▶ Capsule 3: Creating the Topic Sentence

Week 10
▶ Capsule 4: Sentences Must "Talk" to Each Other in Paragraphs
▶ Capsule 5: Parallel Sentences
▶ Conference: Before conferencing with your student, refer to the section, "Three Ways to Help Your Student Writer in Unit 2," found in your Teacher's textbook at the beginning of Unit 2… Specifically Encourage… Emphasize Taking Chances Over Correctness… Provide an Audience for Student Writing.

Week 11
Lesson 2: Composing and Linking Sentences
▶ Capsule 1: Starting to Think about Sentences
▶ Capsule 2: Composing Compound Sentences
▶ Capsule 3: Crafting Complex Sentences

Week 12
▶ Capsule 4: Constructing Compound-Complex Sentences
▶ Capsule 5: More Thoughts on Sentences
▶ Conference: Before conferencing with your student, refer again to the section, "Three Ways to Help Your Student Writer in Unit 2," found in your Teacher's textbook at the beginning of Unit 2… Specifically Encourage… Emphasize Taking Chances Over Correctness… Provide an Audience for Student Writing.

Week 13
Lesson 3: Creating Focus and Arrangement
▶ Capsule 1: Topic Sentences Spark Questions
▶ Capsule 2: Arranging Ideas
▶ Capsule 3: Arranging Ideas Chronologically

Week 14
▶ Capsule 4: Arranging Ideas Spatially
▶ Capsule 5: Arranging Ideas to Argue
▶ Conference: Before conferencing with your student, refer again to the section, "Three Ways to Help Your Student Writer in Unit 2," found in your Teacher's textbook at the beginning of Unit 2… Specifically Encourage… Emphasize Taking Chances Over Correctness… Provide an Audience for Student Writing.

Week 15
Lesson 4: Linking Paragraphs: Transitions and Logic
▶ Capsule 1: Organizing the Middle of an Essay
▶ Capsule 2: Making Organizational Choices
▶ Capsule 3: Linking Paragraphs with Transitions

Week 16
▶ Capsule 4: The Logic Behind Your Organization
▶ Capsule 5: Let Go, Rethink, and Revise
▶ Conference: Before conferencing with your student, refer again to the section "Three Ways to Help Your Student Writer in Unit 2," found in your Teacher's textbook at the beginning of Unit 2… Specifically Encourage… Emphasize Taking Chances Over Correctness… Provide an Audience for Student Writing.

UNIT #3: WRITING AUTOBIOGRAPHY

Before beginning Unit 3, please refer to the General Overview for the Unit, and the Detailed Overview for each of the Lessons found in your Teacher's textbook at the beginning of Unit 3.

Week 17
Lesson 1: Reporting Facts
▶ Capsule 1: Just the Facts, Please
▶ Capsule 2: Family Facts
▶ Capsule 3: Communities

Week 18
▶ Capsule 4: Events that Define You
▶ Capsule 5: The On-Paper Me
▶ Conference: Before conferencing with your student, refer to the section, "Three Ways to Help Your Student Writer in Unit 3," found in your Teacher's textbook at the beginning of Unit 3… Foster Ownership…Provide Specific Feedback…Facilitate Revision.

Week 19
Lesson 2: Creating Character
▶ Capsule 1: World Wisdom – the Real Me
▶ Capsule 2: What Makes You You?
▶ Capsule 3: Inside Events

Week 20
▶ Capsule 4: The You of Yesterday
▶ Capsule 5: Considering Possibilities
▶ Conference: Before conferencing with your student, refer again to the section, "Three Ways to Help Your Student Writer in Unit 3," found in your Teacher's textbook at the beginning of Unit 3… Foster Ownership…Provide Specific Feedback…Facilitate Revision.

Week 21
Lesson 3: Developing Ideas
Capsule 1: What Story Should You Tell?
Capsule 2: Including the Right Details
Capsule 3: Click. Click. Click. Your Story in Pictures

Week 22
Capsule 4: Images and Storyboarding
Capsule 5: Making a Choice
Conference: Before conferencing with your student, refer again to the section, "Three Ways to Help Your Student Writer in Unit 3," found in your Teacher's textbook at the beginning of Unit 3… Foster Ownership…Provide Specific Feedback…Facilitate Revision.

Week 23
Lesson 4: Composition
Capsule 1: Writing a Beginning
Capsule 2: Avoiding a Mess in the Middle
Capsule 3: Drawing a Conclusion

Week 24
Capsule 4: Making Your Autobiographical Essay Even Better
Capsule 5: Writing Autobiography
Conference: Before conferencing with your student, refer again to the section, "Three Ways to Help Your Student Writer in Unit 3," found in your Teacher's textbook at the beginning of Unit 3… Foster Ownership…Provide Specific Feedback…Facilitate Revision.

UNIT #4: CRAFTING NARRATIVES
Before beginning Unit 4, please refer to the General Overview for the Unit, and the Detailed Overview for each of the Lessons found in your Teacher's textbook at the beginning of Unit 4.

Week 25
Lesson 1: Developing a Point of View
▶ Capsule 1: Writing from a First-person Perspective
▶ Capsule 2: Writing from a Second-person Perspective
▶ Capsule 3: Writing from a Third-person Perspective

Week 26
▶ Capsule 4: More Third-person Narrators
▶ Capsule 5: Choosing a Point of View
▶ Conference: Before conferencing with your student, refer to the section, "Helping Your Student Through Effective Feedback," found in your Teacher's textbook at the beginning of Unit 4… Effective Conferencing… Effective Grading.

Week 27
Lesson 2: Showing Versus Telling
▶ Capsule 1: Showing Versus Telling: What Does It Mean?
▶ Capsule 2: Preparing to Show
▶ Capsule 3: Strategies for Showing – Sketching a Scene

Week 28
▶ Capsule 4: Showing More Than Telling
▶ Capsule 5: When to Show, When to Tell
▶ Conference: Before conferencing with your student, refer again to the section, "Helping Your Student Through Effective Feedback," found in your Teacher's textbook at the beginning of Unit 4… Effective Conferencing… Effective Grading.

Week 29
Lesson 3: Narrative with a Purpose
▶ Capsule 1: What Story do You Want to Tell?
▶ Capsule 2: Pros and Cons of Fictionalizing Your Personal Narrative
▶ Capsule 3: Details that Convey Your Purpose

Week 30
▶ Capsule 4: The Storyboarding Test
▶ Capsule 5: Why Fictionalize Your Narrative?
▶ Conference: Before conferencing with your student, refer again to the section, "Helping Your Student Through Effective Feedback," found in your Teacher's textbook at the beginning of Unit 4… Effective Conferencing… Effective Grading.

Week 31
Lesson 4: Writing a Fictional Narrative
▶ Capsule 1: Getting Ready to Write
▶ Capsule 2: A Good Beginning
▶ Capsule 3: Show Your Story

Week 32
▶ Capsule 4: A Strong Finish
▶ Capsule 5: Making Improvements
▶ Conference: Before conferencing with your student, refer again to the section, "Helping Your Student Through Effective Feedback," found in your Teacher's textbook at the beginning of Unit 4… Effective Conferencing… Effective Grading.

Write with WORLD

WRITING CURRICULUM

GENERAL INTRODUCTION

What would happen if nationally recognized journalists and writers, award-winning college professors, and the resources of *God's World News* and *WORLD Magazine* joined forces? We asked this question and then posed an even more compelling one: What would happen if a young student learning to write had access to these journalists, writers, and professors? This curriculum is our answer.

Write with WORLD aims to produce young writers who love writing, can write effectively, and intelligently share ideas, beliefs, and their worldview. We hope to support a generation of young believers who aspire to use their writing skills in the service of God's Kingdom and explain effectively the reasons for their beliefs.

Learning to write well is one of the greatest and most important challenges students will face. Creating young writers—particularly students learning the building blocks necessary for writing with meaning—requires time, effective assignments, practice, conversation, and encouragement.

Most importantly, they need to enjoy what they are doing: to write well, young writers must develop a love and excitement for writing. Students can achieve excellence, but quality writing begins with quality teaching and a passion for and enjoyment of the composing process.

Unfortunately, many young writers learn the opposite lesson. Too many students are taught to dislike writing. They learn that writing is a trivial, rules-based skill that has little impact on their learning or future calling. They learn that writing is an either-or proposition: writing is either good or bad, right or wrong.

For these students, writing becomes a painful process shaped by regulations, busy work and "canned" assignments. They learn to regard grammar as unimportant and inconsequential—as a skill disconnected from their learning and the world. These students see writing as tedious—as a process that puts them through meaningless steps for no audience or real purpose beyond getting a grade. They learn to write in a vacuum.

Write with WORLD teaches the skills necessary for becoming an effective writer while encouraging students to step outside the vacuum. Young writers need to see models of excellent writing on a regular basis. They need to read materials produced by published authors, and they need to engage in conversations with writers. They need opportunities to practice using language with a purpose and without the stress of being graded. They need writing assignments that are timely and thought-provoking. They need readers. They need thoughtful responses to their efforts.

Clearly, parents and teachers play a major role in fostering a love for writing. A primary goal of this curriculum is to help you fulfill this most significant role. The passion shaping this writing curriculum grows from the authors' experiences and research. For nearly 20 years, we have worked with writing teachers in middle schools, high schools, and universities. As consultants, we've helped teachers develop effective teaching methods and revise their curricula to include thoughtful writing assignments. In graduate seminars on writing, we've taught aspiring middle and high school teachers how to motivate students and instill a passion for prose.

Like everyone working with this curriculum, our most influential experiences come from our own lives as students, teachers, and writers. As students, we have sat in the classroom with teachers who cared only about correctness and ignored our ideas and content; as young writers, we've learned to dislike writing because teachers assigned "canned" prompts. We know well the negative impact of poor assignments, curricula, and uninformed teaching.

Write with WORLD concentrates on developing young writers who can think and express their thoughts through writing. Students using *Write with WORLD* are connected to other writers— *God's World News* and *WORLD Magazine* journalists, celebrated writing professors, and student authors. Students will benefit from these writers' advice. They will respond to timely and thoughtful assignments that encourage them to discuss ideas and language with teachers. The potential for publication will energize students, giving them purpose and audience.

Write with WORLD replicates the processes, assignments, opportunities, and moments that taught us to love writing.

DISTINCTIVES:

- *Students belong to a community of writers and have an audience*

Students need conversations with both writers and teachers. *Write with WORLD* offers these communities. Every unit will offer relevant advice and commentary from published writers: *God's World News* and *WORLD Magazine* journalists, photojournalists, essayists, and editors. English professors who specialize in teaching writing design lessons and offer special "teaching moments" based on their experience. Students need to understand that the problems and challenges they face are the same ones published authors face. Students will strive for excellence knowing that their writing could be read and potentially published by these authors, editors, and professors.

- *Students see the curriculum as a living, up-to-date conversation*

Dull, general writing prompts will most likely produce dull, general prose and uninspired writers. *Write with WORLD* seeks to give students assignments that inspire quality writing. Assignments emphasize purpose, role, and audience. Most importantly, assignments ask writers to engage the world around them and will be updated regularly to include current topics and material covered in *WORLD Magazine* and *God's World News.*

- *Students have access to multiple assignments to choose from in many lessons*

Write with WORLD lessons sometimes focus on developing necessary skills. Other lessons build up to major writing assignments. Most of these lessons offer multiple writing assignments. Students and teachers need flexibility and choice. Sometimes, a major writing prompt can cause writer's block: a student writer simply cannot relate to the question. In such a case, it helps the writer to have other opportunities. A student who is required to choose her major writing assignment is also more likely to feel committed to her writing before she ever begins to invent ideas.

- *Students who learn to read with critical eyes are more likely to become strong writers*

Write with WORLD teaches students the art of critical reading. These lessons first use images to teach an eye-for-detail and invention; students then apply those lessons to words, sentences, and paragraphs. As students work their way through the curriculum, they continue to develop critical reading skills as they read and write about more complex essays and narratives.

- *Students will examine models—both strong and weak—to improve their writing*

Students need models of writing. They need to study models of excellence to understand the characteristics of good writing. They need to inspect models with weaknesses that can be improved. Before starting an assignment, students need models of the genre they are composing.

- *Students learn style in the context of their own writing*

Write with WORLD believes student writers need to develop their voice while they learn grammar. Grammar lessons are important. Students will not learn grammar as standalone rules. Instead, students will learn concepts and then apply the lessons to their own writings. Not only will students learn style but they will also learn to revise for correctness and style.

- *Students learn to write with a worldview*

Write with WORLD wants students to understand that all writers have a worldview. More importantly, worldview influences writing from choice of topic to the premises underlying writing. A writer who views life as a gift from God will write differently from a writer who believes life began accidentally and has no ultimate purpose. *Write with WORLD* will train students to look for "worldview clues" in writing so that they become discerning readers. The curriculum also aims to help them discover their own voice as writers with a worldview of their own which they know how to articulate. We want students to learn to join the thinkers and writers of our day, with, in the words of the Apostle Paul, "conversation . . . full of grace, seasoned with salt, so that [they] may know how to answer everyone" (Colossians 4:6).

- *Writing teachers need ideas and support*

Just as writers should not write in a vacuum, teachers should not teach in one. *Write with WORLD* offers multiple levels of support for teachers. In the teacher handbook, teachers can find rationales for assignments and approaches; they also have access to directions, teacher discussions, and suggestions. The web site will provide additional updated information and help.

Write with WORLD

GENERAL OVERVIEW

When purchasing a car, typical buyers do not walk into a store and choose their automobile of choice in a quick minute. Instead, purchasing a car requires thought. Buyers tend to compare models and makers. They compare advertisements to determine the stores in which they will shop. They pay close attention to and ask questions about details: engine size, trunk space, number of cup holders, safety record, comfort, sound system, and price. They take multiple cars for test drives, looking for which car feels the best. Buyers also tend to compare automobiles and customization packages to figure out what car set-up will meet their needs. To "buy a car" means to engage a long process of asking questions, trying options, and making educated decisions. Teaching students to write well requires a similar process.

Most students will not start this curriculum with excellent writing skills: some may have a natural talent, others may struggle putting ideas on a page, but all will need to learn to link thoughtful reading to thoughtful writing.

See, many writing curricula teach students to understand the basic building blocks of writing—sentences and paragraphs. But that requires little thought. Like many of you, we learned early on the parts of speech, that a sentence required a subject and verb, and that a sentence was an independent clause. All were important lessons, but none of them made us great writers. None taught us how to be thoughtful: we had basic tools but did not know how to use them when our seventh-grade teachers said, "Let's write your first essay."

Essentially, our teachers were asking us to produce essays in a week without engaging a process. We understood thoroughly the concept of a sentence, but did not know what made one sentence weak and another great. Same thing for paragraphs: we knew the rules for paragraphing, but no one had ever challenged us to dissect a paragraph, to comprehend why some paragraphs worked better than others. And, finally, not until the last two years of high school, did anyone ever challenge us to explain why an essay was excellent. We could put words on a page but possessed little skill for explaining the choices we made when we put pen to paper.

The lessons and capsules in Unit 1 challenge your student writer to engage a thoughtful process. We want them to understand from the very beginning that good writing begins with the thoughtful arrangement of details, ideas, and words. We want your young writers to become comparative readers: students who can not only see but also explain why one sentence is better than another, why one paragraph works and another paragraph fails, and why one essay captures a reader's interest while another essay loses the reader's interest. We want them to understand that writing is about more than putting down words: to become an excellent writer they need to engage a long process of asking questions, trying options, and making educated decisions. Discerning readers become strong writers because they see ways of using basic tools—words, sentences, and paragraphs—that other writers miss completely.

DETAILED OVERVIEW

1.1.1-5 (Unit 1, Lesson 1, Capsules 1-5): Students need to start somewhere, and this unit asks students to begin where they are comfortable—with images. Images speak to this generation of writers more than any other previous generation; more importantly, however, this generation can read images. They can explain why they like it, how it works, or even how it persuades them to purchase. The first lesson asks students to consider more carefully the process of reading images.

1.2.1-5: This lesson's capsules challenge students to extend the process they use to understand images to understanding writing—to see how great sentences function like their favorite images. More specifically, we want them to understand the importance of a well-defined subject and strong, active verbs. Adjectives and adverbs are touched upon here but only in context. Adjectives do not stand alone; they serve a function, and in this lesson we want students to see how adjectives can improve their subjects. The same holds true for adverbs: adverbs can improve the clarity of their verbs. By the end of this unit, students should begin to see and explain why one sentence is better than another.

1.3.1-5: This lesson builds on the comparative reading skills developed in the previous lesson to help students become better readers of paragraphs. We want students to see and ultimately evaluate how one paragraph is better than another. Students will learn to look for basic organizational moves—particularly logical order and transitions—that determine a paragraph's success.

1.4.1-5: Previous lessons have taught students to read sentences and paragraphs comparatively. By now students should, to a certain degree, comprehend what makes a sentence strong and see how effective paragraphs work. But why are these skills important? Most will not ask this question. The answer is clearly stated in this lesson: great sentences work together to produce strong, logical paragraphs, and those paragraphs produce essays that explain students' thinking, show their thought process, and articulate a voice. Just as an image captures a picture of a real event, an essay represents a picture of how their mind works. Great images are full of details and are intriguing to study because of the stories they tell. In a similar vein, effective essays—through detailed sentences (strong subjects and actors) and organization (logic that links sentences and places them in paragraphs)—tell a story or state an opinion.

THREE WAYS TO HELP YOUR STUDENT WRITER IN UNIT 1

CONFERENCE REGULARLY

Unit 1 asks students to produce many writing tasks that should not require teachers to assign grades beyond complete/incomplete. These writing exercises are designed as pre-writing exercises. Students need to develop specific material for writing. Your primary role as a teacher is to encourage them to produce specific answers to the questions they develop. You can encourage your writer through conferences; talk to them about their responses. Ask students to explain their answers and the choices they made, and motivate them to be specific in their answers through constant questioning.

Imagine the CWJ, their journal, as the place where the conversation begins rather than ends. This idea of conferencing—holding a meeting time where you discuss their work—is key to helping students become stronger writers. Strong writers will do more than complete and memorize The Right Word: they will think about and use the word in their speech and writing. Strong writers will be able to explain why one sentence is better than another. Ultimately, students will do this on the page; however, for now, key is their providing this explanation orally to their teacher in conferences.

ENCOURAGE SPECIFICITY

Great writers are specific. They use details to make their writing convey an image; they explain points thoroughly to persuade readers. This is a difficult skill for most students—many of our college writers experience difficulty with specificity—and your writer needs to practice specific idea development from the very beginning.

When you conference with your student, do not let them settle for simple answers. For example, when asked to compare paragraphs, many students will settle for a simple answer;

"Paragraph B is better than Paragraph A" or "I liked Paragraph B more." While the answer may be correct, the material supporting the answer is poor. Challenge your student to explain—either orally or in writing—why they believe Paragraph B is better. In short, don't let your student settle for the simple or general response. Encourage them to talk, to give reasons for their evaluations—reasons that either cite or work with specific qualities in the text. In short, let's teach them to think about writing in specific, meaningful ways.

USE LOW-STAKES EVALUATION INSTEAD OF HIGH-STAKES EVALUATION

Not all writing requires intense scrutiny or a red pencil. Sometimes, grading can be used to challenge students or ask for improvement without terrifying the writer or causing them to freeze up. How we evaluate carries significant consequences. On many occasions in his graduate seminar, "Teaching Writing," Dr. Ron Pitcock has worked with graduate students who shared a distaste for writing, and this distaste could be traced to the ways in which teachers evaluated their essays. They remember red ink bleeding on their papers, teachers who seemed more interested in sharing where writing was poor rather than effective, and getting weighty grades on seemingly minor assignments.

For this unit, we encourage you to embrace low-stakes evaluation methods over high-stakes evaluation. We are all familiar with high-stakes grading. Teachers embracing high-stakes use the red pencil repeatedly in their marking and comments system, concentrate on providing critical response, and constantly evaluate for a grade. High-stakes grading should be reserved for larger projects that complete a unit.

We believe Unit 1 is not the place for high-stakes evaluation. Unit 1 is a developmental unit: students are learning to become a discerning reader who sees quality in sentences, paragraphs, and essays. Let's use low-stakes grading to encourage writers, teach them what we are looking for in their responses, and challenge them to improve.

Low-stakes grading requires less critical evaluation and more helpful general evaluation. Instead of awarding a final grade, low-stakes grading offers students minimal grading—at most, a general evaluation (excellent, satisfactory, weak or +/-). Offer students specific and tactful ways for improving their response: explain how they can turn a weak response into a satisfactory one. Use low-stakes grading to encourage your student to develop as readers and writers who take time to practice. (For more on grading, see Unit 4 Teacher Headnote, "Helping Your Student Through Effective Feedback: Effective Grading.")

People may not consider this "writing practice." You are discussing an image but not putting pen to paper.

You are, however, working on writing; you are teaching idea development. Strong writers think about and compose essays around specific ideas. Note that in the last sentence "think" came before "compose." Students need to practice how to think specifically before they can ever write with details. Idea development is key to writing great sentences, logical paragraphs, and interesting—as well as persuasive—essays.

If your student is struggling to come up with questions, look at the picture with him. But don't come up with the questions for him. Ask him leading questions that will help him to formulate questions of his own.

▶ What do you see? (When the student begins naming things, "What does that make you curious about?)

▶ Do you like the picture? What do/don't you like about it?

▶ How does the picture make you feel?

Students could easily offer a one-word answer to the last question – happy, sad, bored. But one-word answers don't require students to interrogate why they feel a certain way.

WHAT WRITERS WILL NEED FOR THIS LESSON:

▶ Your writer's journal
▶ Dictionary
▶ Thesaurus
▶ A timer
▶ A highlighter
▶ One or more magazines with photographs, images, advertisements

CAPSULE 1

1.1.1

THE STORY BEHIND THE IMAGE

Are you a bookworm? Or are you the opposite—your library card, if you could find it, might be covered in cobwebs? No matter whether you're an **avid** reader, a reluctant reader, or something in-between, you read more than you think. A LOT more.

◀ TAKE A LOOK AT THIS PICTURE

And you started early. Whenever you look at an image and try to figure out what it means, you're reading. If you have younger brothers or sisters, you've probably seen them pick up a book and "read" it by looking at the pictures. Maybe you can even remember doing that yourself.

Take a look at this picture. A quick glance tells you it's a picture of a girl on a skateboard playing a guitar. But you see much more if you look carefully. How old would you guess the girl is? Why is she riding a skateboard while playing a guitar? What kind of day is it outside? Where do you think she might be? Is she enjoying herself? How does the picture make you feel?

When we "read" this image, we see a teenaged girl. Her facial expression seems to indicate that she's relaxed but concentrating. Her skateboard appears to be a longboard, which would make sense, because some people use this type of skateboard as transportation. She seems to be going somewhere: She's crossing a street. We know she's in a city because we can see tall buildings and city busses behind her. We can infer that the weather is warm because there are trees with green leaves in the background, and she's wearing shorts and flip-flops. Perhaps she's taking her guitar to a friend's house. Or maybe she's planning to perform on the street or in a park. We like this picture because the girl seems to be enjoying herself. It makes us wonder who she is and where she's going with that guitar.

CONVERSATIONS: YOUR WRITER'S JOURNAL

NOW IT'S YOUR TURN

▶ TAKE A CLOSE LOOK AT THIS PICTURE

IN YOUR JOURNAL ▶

What questions does this picture raise in your mind? Our first question would be, "Is the surfer in control, or is he about to wipe out?"

In your Conversations Writer's Journal (CWJ), write down your questions (at least five). Now describe the picture in writing, as we did in the example with the girl playing a guitar while riding a skateboard. Make sure you include an answer to the question, "How does the picture make you feel?"

THE RIGHT WORD:

Remember that each time you see a word in bold, you need to look up that word in the dictionary and write the definition in your journal. For 1.1.1, look up **avid** in your dictionary. Read through all the definitions. Now read through the sentence where **avid** appears again. Choose the meaning that best defines the word as it was used in the sentence and write that definition in your CWJ.

CAPSULE 2   1.1.2

WHAT A PHOTOJOURNALIST SEES

Capsule 1 demonstrated how pictures tell stories and how we read those stories. This capsule concentrates on the "author" responsible for those stories/pictures: the photojournalist. In a split second, the photojournalist makes a decision to take a photograph that can tell a story for a lifetime.

Let's look at what a photojournalist sees when he or she takes a picture and what elements make a photograph special.

Try prompting students to complete their answer with a "because" clause explaining what specific aspects of the image evoke this feeling. "This image makes me feel confident because...." In fact, whenever you come across one-word answers in the CWJ, it is a great place for you to ask questions and encourage more thinking.

This is the first time your student is encountering The Right Word. If you don't have a good dictionary, we suggest investing in any one of the collegiate style dictionaries rather than the abbreviated ones you can pick up for a dollar or so in the school supply section. One purpose of this section is to expand your student's vocabulary; a more detailed dictionary definition will show her a wider range of meanings for each word.

In this first lesson, it would be a good idea to walk through the process of looking up the word with your student. But before you open the dictionary, have her take a guess at what it means based on how it is used in the sentence. We want your student to begin learning to use context to determine word meanings.

Have her read all the definitions aloud and then look at the word in context in the sentence again. Discuss which definition is the best choice and why.

WORLD WISDOM:

James Allen Walker is a photojournalist with *WORLD Magazine*. He's taken thousands of pictures over the course of his career, but this is one of his favorites.

"Choosing one photo that I've made as my favorite is not an easy task. One reason is most of the images I make for WORLD Magazine *are often very similar. More often than not I make a portrait of someone I've just met for the first time. Getting to know that person becomes part of the task of illustrating them for the magazine story. However, in the case of this shot I made the person that I'm illustrating and I'm introducing him to the rest of the world! He's my son, Ethan at six months old. It becomes plain why it happens to be my favorite photo, but let me expound.*

I didn't make this portrait for the purpose of a magazine cover. That came later. I've been photographing Ethan since minutes after my wife, Beth gave birth to him. So, for me the picture is one example of a whole body of work and it has become about me being a dad. It's also about sharing my life with this little person whom I adore. It's also about my sharing this treasured title with many other men who have children. All of whom execute the responsibilities in their own imperfect way. It's been a life changing experience through which God has taught me many lessons, and He's made me aware of myself and how much I need Him to be a good dad. He shows me every day how I need to change my habits, and choose carefully every word in order to be a standard for Ethan. What a precious gift."

— James Allen Walker

CONVERSATIONS: YOUR WRITER'S JOURNAL

1. In your journal, list what you liked (or disliked) about James Allen Walker's picture.

2. Find a photograph that holds special meaning for you. Describe the picture. Why is it important to you?

◀ IN YOUR JOURNAL

THE STORY BEHIND THE IMAGE

They're funny. And they sell a lot of chicken. If you live in one of the 40 states that **boasts** one or more Chick-fil-A restaurants, you probably recognized these cows even before you read the signs they are wearing. If you did recognize the Chick-fil-A cows, you have seen Chick-fil-A's advertisements.

Advertisements are **ubiquitous**—whether you are driving down the street, reading a magazine, watching TV, or checking your e-mail, you can't get away from companies trying to sell you something.

Advertisers' influence begins early with advertisements, commercials, and images. Did you know that by the age of two, many toddlers recognize logos for companies and products such as McDonald's, Chuck E. Cheese's, and Cheerios?

Besides feeling annoyed when a commercial interrupts your favorite television program, you may have become so used to ads that you barely notice them. But advertisers will try all kinds of tricks to get your attention. Advertisers are particularly interested in you. Why? Kids in your age group as a whole spend about $50 billion a year.

That brings us back to the cows. Why use cows to advertise for a restaurant that doesn't even sell beef? The idea of cows making signs that promote chicken sales to save their own hides is funny. Advertisers sometimes use humor to get your attention. Creating recognizable characters helps, too. The Chick-fil-A cows are not regular cows; these cows are known for spelling words incorrectly. The cows give Chick-fil-A's brand a personality. It's hard to feel connected to a chicken sandwich. But people emotionally connect with the cow characters.

This analysis of Chick-fil-A is quick but could be performed with any number of brands. We suggest that you analyze brands regularly with your student. Discussing how advertisements work, why they use the words they do, and why they incorporate certain imagery trains your student to be a critical thinker.

They will learn to see logical flaws and become more thoughtful thinkers. Most importantly, they will learn how to wade through the media noise to discover what is true and what is false.

Since Chick-fil-A began running the cow campaign in 1995, their food sales have at least doubled. It's estimated that they spend over $20 million a year on advertising.

Companies would not spend such big money on ads if they didn't work. Do advertisements work on you? Can you think of anything you've bought (or wanted to buy) because you liked the ad?

CONVERSATIONS: YOUR WRITER'S JOURNAL

◀ IN YOUR JOURNAL

1. Do a quick survey of your house. How many visible brand names or logos can you count? (Make sure to look down at the clothes and shoes you're wearing.) Don't forget shopping bags with logos, appliances and computer equipment, and cars in your garage.

2. As you go through the rest of your day, force yourself to be aware of the number of times you're bombarded with advertisements. Keep your journal handy and note which advertisements catch your attention and why.

3. Why do you think Chick-fil-A uses cows instead of chickens in their advertisements? Make a list of reasons.

Read through your student's answers to questions 1 and 2. Do you see any patterns? Are there certain brands that you or your student tend to buy? (Nike, Apple, Honda, etc.) Discuss why you/your student are drawn to these brands. Does advertising play a role? Does experience with the products play a role? What is the main reason you buy this brand(s)?

THE RIGHT WORD:

Here's a tip. The word "boasts" has a different usage than you may think. Make sure you read the entire definition and choose the right meaning for "boasts" as it is used in the sentence.

CAPSULE 4

1.1.4

THE MESSAGE BEHIND THE ADVERTISEMENT

Whether they're drinking soda, driving cars, or mopping floors, most people in advertisements have one thing in common: They're smiling. Often, the advertisement lists all the reasons we should buy a product ("This car gets the best gas mileage in its class. Its safety rating is unbeatable."). At the same time, the beautiful, contented-looking models in the ad silently create another message: "Look at us. We're happy. If you buy this car, you'll be happy too."

You should be using the same careful eye to examine ads as you did the surfer earlier this lesson. Why? Advertisers are constantly trying to sell you something. Each company wants us to believe its product is the best. When people have lots of choices, many of them fairly similar, a company must make people believe they need (or at least really want) that company's product. If a company can't get enough customers, it'll go out of business. The company must make its product stand out.

That's why it's important to look at the **tactics** advertisers use to influence you to buy products. An ad is an image with a message. Some messages are printed right on the page. Imagine a toothpaste ad. Emblazoned across the top of the page is this motto: "Blinding White toothpaste will brighten your smile!" Below are two pictures.

In one, a yellow-toothed girl stands alone, looking sad. In the next picture, teeth now white, she's smiling and laughing with a group of friends. Which child would you rather be like? What message would you get from the pictures? If you said something like, "People will like you better if you whiten your teeth with Blinding White toothpaste," you understand the advertisement's **implicit** message.

Targeting emotions can be particularly effective with tweens and teens. When trying to sell to kids your age, advertisers often focus on worries you already have. They want to make you think you need their product to fix a particular problem—yellow teeth, acne, bad breath, and so on. Ads can make you feel even more insecure about your "flaws" if you buy into their messages.

Ads often focus on outward appearance and the things we own. It is easy to get caught up in the desire to look great and have the latest phone, mp3 player, or other gadget. In general the message of advertising is, "We can fix you. We can give you a great life. Buying stuff is fun, and it will make you happy."

If you are not carefully "reading" the ads that come your way, you're more likely to let their hidden messages influence your worldview. Everyone has a worldview. The beliefs that determine how you look at and live your life make your worldview. As Christians, we need to remember that we don't belong to this world (John 15:19). We belong to Christ. Our joy and fulfillment come through him, not through products we purchase. Believing in Christ gives meaning to our lives; products and advertisements want you to believe in their product's power to improve your life.

THE PROFESSOR'S OFFICE

Pictures, words, advertisements all have the power to make you feel. They can make you feel happy or sad, thirsty or hungry. Most importantly, they can make you feel like you need what they are selling. You need the grape-flavored drink in the ad to be stronger or you need to try that sandwich with five different types of cheese and purple ketchup to be happy.

Everywhere you go and look, advertisers are speaking to you through their messages. When you made a list of brand names and logos in your house, how many did you find? Which ones did you find? In your home—when you wake up, open your refrigerator, or go into the kitchen—advertisers are speaking to you and your family through these messages.

Knowing this is important. The people making these advertisements don't want you to think. They only want you to listen to and learn from them. Why think when you can watch television and listen to advertisements that tell you how to live? Why think when you can read a magazine in a comfortable chair and see what you need to live a happy life?

If you listen to advertisements, you will learn how a pair of jeans can make you happy, what food will make you stronger, what toothpaste will make your teeth whiter, and what computer will make you look smarter. Advertisements tell you what an ideal world could look like.

I once had a student who bought a bottle of water because advertisers claimed the water came from a tropical island in the South Pacific. This "Island" water came in a bottle that had a beautiful picture of paradise with palm trees, a shining sun, and a bright blue waterfall. My student told me the water tasted better than other bottled waters because it came from this beautiful place. In fact, my student wouldn't drink any other water—nothing tasted as good as her "Island" water.

Let's think about that. My student believed this water was ideal because the bottle implied or said it came from a beautiful waterfall on an island in the South Pacific. I had to test this student's belief.

First, I found five colored cups. In a yellow cup, I poured "Island" water. In blue, red, and green cups, I poured other bottled waters. In the orange cup, I poured tap water from the kitchen sink. My student did not know which water was in each cup. This is called a blind taste test. She took a drink from all the cups and then ranked them in terms of taste. Which water do you think she thought was best or worst?

She chose the water in the green cup—another bottled water—as the best tasting. Her second best tasting water was tap water from the kitchen sink! The "Island" water in the yellow cup came in fourth. My student even said the water in the yellow cup tasted "dirty."

What do we learn from this? Advertisers' messages and images can be very powerful. The images they use can make us believe in and want what they are selling. You and I need to read advertisements very carefully and realize they are making promises or presenting ideas that may not be true.

CONVERSATIONS: YOUR WRITER'S JOURNAL

Look through magazines until you find an advertisement that interests you. Put a copy of the advertisement into your journal.

Write a two-to-three-sentence description of the ad in your journal. (e.g. "This advertisement is for Jump-high Shoes. The picture shows a tall, sweating athlete jumping and dunking a basketball. The athlete looks happy and is wearing the shoes.")

Then answer these questions:

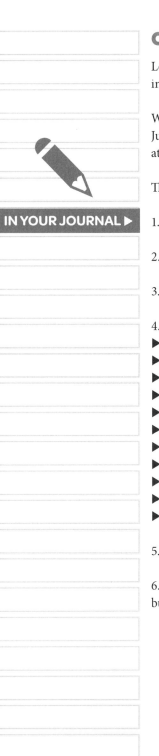

IN YOUR JOURNAL ▶

1. What is the ad selling?

2. What is the stated message?

3. Look carefully at the picture. What is its unspoken or **implicit** message?

4. What tactics does the ad use to persuade you to buy the product? Here's a list of possibilities:
▶ a famous person using the product
▶ value/price
▶ humor
▶ before/after pictures—this person looks much better after using the product
▶ image—you'll be cool if you use this product
▶ fear—if you don't use this product people will not like you
▶ facts and statistics—9 out of 10 bicyclists ride this bike
▶ top of the line or "snob" appeal
▶ scarcity or limited supply appeal—this product is made of the rarest materials
▶ adventure or fun appeal
▶ "fix-it" appeal—this product will make you prettier, younger-looking, healthier

5. Do you like this advertisement? Why or why not?

6. In this advertisement, do you think the stated or unstated message is more likely to persuade people to buy the product? (In other words, which message is stronger?) Why?

Students may have difficulty answering the third and fourth questions. It requires that they interpret the advertisement. Some student writers may have difficulty doing this. You may need to ask leading questions like, "Why do you think the athlete is super-sweaty?" or "Why do you think the sweat is colored orange? Have you ever seen orange sweat?"

This final question is a big one—a question that deserves a lot of attention. The question asks the student to take a stance and give reasons supporting his stance. This is his first argument.

Feel free to challenge your student by taking the other side of the argument. If he thinks the unstated question is more powerful, you can argue in favor of the stated message—the actual words, the image. Make your student writer dig as deep as possible to explain his claim. Doing so will help him formulate better ideas and have a clearer understanding of what he thinks and why.

CAPSULE 5 1.1.5

STYLE, DICTION, AND REVISION

STYLE TIME

i When you hear the word "grammar" what springs to mind? Pages of worksheets with sentences to correct? Notes in red all over your paper? Learning grammar is necessary to writing well. The rules are there for a reason. For instance, if you use vague pronouns all the time, your readers get confused. Knowing rules—such as how to properly construct a sentence—will improve your style. That's why we're calling this section "Style Time." The more you know about how grammar works, the more comfortable you will be experimenting with sentences and language. And people who are comfortable with language make better writers.

You'll be glad to know that research shows that students learn better in real-life situations. That's why when we work on grammar and style, we'll have you examine your own writing. We'll focus on ways that you can improve your writing in each "Style Time."

The first "Style Time" is an easy one—"its" and "it's."

People confuse the two all the time. Here's why: "its" is possessive. Often, a possessive requires an apostrophe. If I'm talking about the car that belongs to John, I would say "John's car." But some possessives—like her, his, and its—don't require an apostrophe. For example, if we were talking about a car's tire, we would write "its tire," NOT "it's tire."

"It's" is a contraction, or a way to put together the two words "it is." So if you write "it's tire," you're really writing, "it is tire," which doesn't make sense.

REVISE:

Now, take a pencil and start back at the beginning of your journal. Circle each use of *its* or *it's*. Read each sentence containing one of these words aloud. If you've written *it's* substitute the words *it is*. Does the sentence still make sense? If not, you need to change to the possessive *its* instead.

Technology tip: *If you're keeping your journal as a computer file or if you write a draft on the computer, use the "search" feature of your word-processing program to find each use of* it's *and* its *in your writing. Read each sentence containing* its *or* it's *aloud, replacing with* it is. *If* it is *doesn't make sense,* its *is the right choice. If* it is *does make sense, use the contraction* it's.

Some people may think this is a controversial move. They may say, "What . . . no grammar handouts or exercises?" Grammar is important—every writer needs to have an understanding of grammar. Research shows that students learn grammar better when there is a purpose, when the grammar occurs in the context of their own writing.

Grammar handbooks exist, and we think these can be extremely helpful when a teacher identifies a student's weakness. We would suggest you purchase a handbook for this reason. The purpose of this curriculum is to teach writing. We first focus on the process of writing: idea development, organization, drafting, etc. Then we will address common grammar mistakes and easy ways to improve a writer's style in the actual writing students produce.

◄ IN YOUR JOURNAL

IN YOUR JOURNAL ▶

CONVERSATIONS: **YOUR WRITER'S JOURNAL**

I'm sure you've noticed that the journal-writing sections are called CWJ: Conversations ... Writer's Journal. That may seem a little strange—how is writing in a journal a conversation—unless you're talking to yourself?

Ideally, it will become a place that you begin conversations. It's nice to have a place to keep information and "think" on paper a bit where no one is judging you or criticizing your ideas.

And it should be a conversation-starter. From time to time, your parents will read through your journal. When they find something interesting you've written, they may respond with a question to get you to think a bit more about what you've said and then respond to their questions. We hope you and your parents will get a dialogue going that will get you excited about some of your ideas.

It's okay to have some bad ideas in your journal. Putting your thoughts down on paper allows you to really examine them and see if they make sense or not. Just like an inventor may try lots of different formulas or designs before coming up with the one that works, writers sort through lots of ideas before they come up with a brilliant one.

Today, we want you to look back through what you've written so far. Highlight your most interesting section. Write a sentence or two telling what you like about it.

Also, now that you understand the meaning behind CWJ, we will no longer refer to the section as CWJ: Conversations ... Writer's Journal. We'll use the simple abbreviation CWJ.

THE RIGHT WORD

 For this section, you'll need your thesaurus and your dictionary. Over the course of Lesson 1, you defined five words. Here are the words in context.

1. No matter whether you're an **avid** reader, a reluctant reader, or something in-between, you read more than you think.

2. If you live in one of the 40 states that **boasts** one or more Chick-fil-A restaurants, you probably recognized these cows even before you read the signs they're wearing.

3. Advertisements are **ubiquitous**—whether you're driving down the street, reading a magazine, watching TV, or checking your e-mail, you can't get away from companies trying to sell you something.

4. That's why it's important to look at the **tactics** advertisers use to influence you to buy products.

5. If you said something like, "People will like you better if you whiten your teeth with Blinding White

The teacher's responsibility is to review the CWJ and start a conversation with the student. While a student may think the response itself is the conversation, the initial response actually provides material for discussing the CWJ prompt or exercise.

toothpaste," you're reading the **implicit** message.

Using your thesaurus, try to find the BEST word to replace the bold word in the sentence. This can be tricky. Take for instance, the word **boasts**:

In the *Concise Oxford American Thesaurus*, the word **boast** lists two different meanings for the word **boast** as a verb. The first lists as synonyms brag, crow, swagger, swank, gloat, show off, exaggerate, overstate.

The second meaning is the one we're looking for:
▶ Possess
▶ Have
▶ Own
▶ Enjoy
▶ Pride oneself/itself on.

Still, though, not all of these synonyms mean the same thing—the state may **have** a Chick-fil-A—but the state doesn't **own** it.

So in this case, we would rewrite the sentence like this: "If you live in one of the 40 states that **has** one or more Chick-fil-A restaurants, you probably recognized these cows even before you read the signs they're wearing."

There! We have done one for you. Now do the other four. You may find you need your dictionary—sometimes the synonyms may be unfamiliar words. In order to decide which one is the best fit, you should look up any words you don't already know.

Write with WORLD

DEVELOPING CRITICAL READERS

COMPARATIVE READING: SENTENCES

CAPSULE 1   1.2.1

KNOWING THE SUBJECT

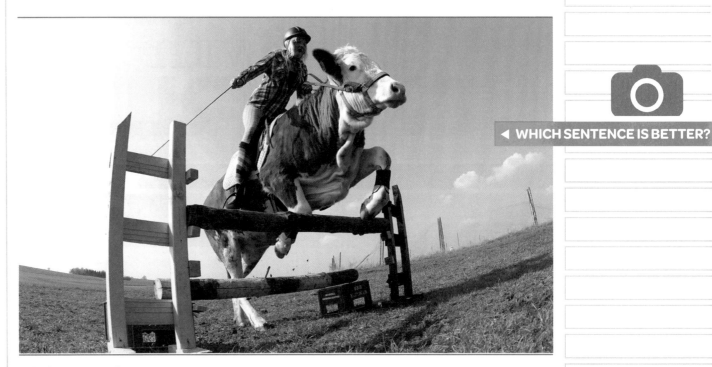

◀ **WHICH SENTENCE IS BETTER?**

Which sentence is better?

▶ The girl is on the cow.
▶ The teenaged girl riding the brown and white cow is teaching it to jump over a hurdle.

That's pretty easy, right? The first sentence doesn't give us any real idea of what's happening in the picture. But even if you couldn't see the picture, the second sentence gives enough information that you could recreate it in your mind. Your cow and girl and the hurdle it is jumping over might look different, but you'd have the basic idea.

If you understand that simple illustration of the importance of **pertinent** details in writing, congratulations! You've grasped one of the key elements of good writing. In this lesson we're going to examine ways of making sentences more descriptive.

Don't worry—we're not going to have you rush to your thesaurus and add in a bunch of smart-sounding words. We just want you to take some time to think about the words you use. Can you use more specific words that will help your readers better visualize what you're describing to them?

AKE FOR INSTANCE THIS PICTURE ▶

How would you describe this picture? Let's start with the subject of the picture. By subject we mean the central figure. The subject of the picture will also be the subject of your sentence. We could say the subject is "a child," but that does not give readers a very specific picture. What are some other nouns we could use that help the reader see in their minds what's on the page?

The child looks very young, so we could probably use one of these nouns:
▶ Toddler
▶ Preschooler

The child's hairstyle and clothing look female, so we could say:
▶ Girl

OW TAKE A LOOK AT THE SUBJECT OF THIS PICTURE ▶

The subject of this picture is a man. If we look at the details of the picture, we can be more specific. Two other nouns that are more descriptive of this subject are
▶ Artist
▶ Painter

Can you think of any others?

Effective writers work with strong subjects. The importance of this difficult concept can pose a challenge to students.

One way to help students may be to talk about sentence subjects as actors: good sentences have strong actors. If students look at their favorite stories, cartoons, or movies, they will likely find strong actors that have distinct characteristics and roles.

CWJ

◀ IN YOUR JOURNAL

PART A:

Flip through copies of *Top Story* or *WORLD Magazine* until you find an interesting photograph. DON'T let your parents see the picture you chose.

Make sure you choose a photograph that has some good visual details. We'll be coming back to it throughout the lesson as we build an effective sentence that helps your readers imagine the photograph.

1. What or who is the subject (or subjects) of the photograph?

2. What's another, more descriptive noun you can use to identify this subject?

PART B:

YOU are the subject. Come up with at least 10 nouns that describe you. I'll get you started: Student, writing scholar….

CAPSULE 2   1.2.2

KNOWING THE SUBJECT BETTER

 In the last section, we looked at the subjects of two pictures. By subject, we mean the person, animal, object, place or thing that the picture is about—the central figure. When we say a sentence has a subject, it is just like the subject in the picture: The central character or topic of the sentence. The subject is always a noun (a person, place, or thing).

In order to make writing detailed and descriptive—so that someone can actually get a mental picture of what we're talking about—we need to be as specific as possible when we choose each word in a sentence. "Cougar" is more descriptive than "animal." "Cookie" is more descriptive than "snack." "Writer" is more specific than "person."

When someone says "cookie," we want to know what kind. Is it a *chocolate chip* cookie, *peanut butter* cookie, or *Snickerdoodle* cookie? The italicized words in the last sentence describe or **modify** the noun "cookie"; they are called adjectives. Well-chosen adjectives are of utmost importance when it comes to good description. I should warn you, though, it is easy to get carried away. Let's look back at our pictures from yesterday:

Which is a better description?
▶ A fascinated blonde toddler

▶ A cherubic, blonde-haired, blue-eyed, purple-clad female toddler

The second one gives more information, but it seems forced. No one talks that way. You've overwhelmed your reader with too much information even before you even get to the subject. You can include some of those details later in the sentence. A **surfeit** of adjectives will create lots of detail. But some of that detail is unnecessary and distracting.

What about the second picture? There's lots of detail to choose from here—the artist is male, he's middle-aged, he's wearing a hat and a jacket. He's holding a palate and brush, and he's got a goatee. Remember that the entire description doesn't have to come in adjectival form.

We would probably start off with details that describe the artist himself:
▶ A goateed, middle-aged artist

How would you describe him?

THE PROFESSOR'S OFFICE:

Adjectives can make your writing more specific and help people see a picture. Adjectives are one feature that can turn good writing into great writing.

However, did you know that adjectives can be dangerous? A sentence can have too many adjectives. Look at the example in this capsule:

▶ A cherubic, blonde-haired, blue-eyed, purple-clad female toddler

This writer uses eight—yes, eight—adjectives to describe a child. When people talk, they use adjectives, but rarely do they use eight. This writer is forcing adjectives into this part of her sentence and, as a result, creates a phrase that is forced. Too many adjectives will cause your audience to stop listening before they ever finish reading the sentence.

I once had a student who wrote a paper describing a summer trip through Italy. The student loved her trip, but she was really excited about gelato. Gelato is an Italian ice cream; it is richer, creamier, and tastier than ice cream in the United States. Even I love gelato, but this student was crazy about it.

When the time came for this student to write about gelato, she wrote a lot. Sadly, she wrote a lot of adjectives—too many adjectives. Here is one sentence from her paper:

▶ When we got to Florence, the first thing we did was buy gelato. We found a gelato shop, and I looked at the counter. They had chocolate gelato, lemon gelato, lime gelato, hazelnut gelato, pistachio gelato, vanilla gelato, cream gelato, cappuccino gelato, raspberry gelato, chocolate chip gelato, banana gelato, peach gelato, pineapple gelato, coffee gelato, blackberry gelato, fig gelato, strawberry gelato, dark chocolate

We are introducing the concept of balance here. Students will need time to develop their own sense of balance, and it will come as they compose their own sentences, paragraphs, and essays. If a student believes the second sentence is better, they are not necessarily wrong. That sentence provides a lot of detail, but the author has said everything they can in a beginning phrase.

gelato, peanut butter gelato, champagne gelato, and many other types of gelato.

Do you see the problem? I understand that the shop sold many flavors of gelato, but this sentence actually fails to make this point. I stopped paying attention at "hazelnut." This writer feels it is necessary to tell me every flavor the shop sold, and she uses adjectives to do this. In other words, this sentence has too many adjectives.

This student could use fewer, smarter adjectives to create a better picture of all the gelato this shop sold. For example, she might write:

▶ When we got to Florence, the first thing we did was buy gelato. We found a gelato shop, and I looked at the counter. This shop sold over 28 exciting flavors of gelato.

I like this revision: It tells me that the shop had a lot of gelato and lets me know that the author is excited about all the gelato. More importantly, I know this and am ready to move to the next sentence.

You want to use adjectives in your sentences, but you should use them carefully. Use adjectives to encourage your readers to read more, to see what you are describing. Do not overload sentences with adjectives or force them on your readers. Using a few well-chosen adjectives can improve a sentence more than a large number of adjectives.

CWJ

PART A:
Take another look at the picture you chose in Capsule 1.
Make a list of all the adjectives you can think of to describe the subject of the picture
Write a short description (e.g., A goateed, middle-aged artist). Choose the adjectives that best describe the subject without overdoing it. Remember, you'll have other opportunities later.

PART B:
List at least 10 adjectives that describe you.

◀ IN YOUR JOURNAL

This is a great exercise for students to practice over and over with different images. Developing strong subjects/actors will help them avoid writing overgeneralized sentences.

CAPSULE 3
1.2.3

STRONG SUBJECTS NEED STRONG ACTIONS

In the first two sections, we have worked on defining the subjects of two pictures. We've labored to find specific nouns to name them. We've studied the pictures, **culling** details so we can include accurate adjectives. Accurate adjectives help readers envision what we're seeing on the page.

In order to create a strong sentence, the next step is turning our subject into an actor. Creating actors requires verbs.

Specific, lively verbs propel good writing. How do you like that verb? *Propel* works well because it helps generate a picture of an object moving forward. And that's just what strong verbs do. They create action in your sentences. Strong verbs help your sentences get somewhere instead of stalling into vagueness.

Sometimes, though, nothing really happens in a sentence. The sentence might merely explain a state of being, or existence. *She is pretty. She was late. He was the winner.* These verbs—is, am, are, was, were, be, being, been—are all being verbs.

Sometimes we need this type of verb. But whenever we can employ a more descriptive verb, we should. Writing full of "being" verbs doesn't create vivid word images, so we should **eliminate** as many as we can.

T'S TAKE A LOOK AT OUR PICTURES AGAIN ▶

"The blonde toddler is looking at cupcakes" uses a being verb. Can you choose more descriptive verbs? How about:

▶ The little blonde-haired girl *sees* a plate of cupcakes. You could also use
▶ The little blonde-haired girl *stares* at a plate of cupcakes
▶ The little blonde-haired girl *gazes* at a plate of cupcakes

Can you think of any other possibilities?

Most students depend on sentences that use being verbs. This overdependence is natural (note that we just used a being verb!).

Some teachers respond to this overdependence by telling students to never use a being verb. This direction is unrealistic. Let students write with a being verb and then challenge them to revise the sentence with a stronger verb. Teach your student to recognize opportunities to improve their sentence with stronger verbs—verbs that give the audience a clear action.

"The artist is standing by a picture he painted" could use a stronger verb. The picture seems staged. Perhaps the photographer told the artist to stand next to the picture with his palate. If that's true, here's a good description:

▶ The artist *poses* next to a picture he painted.

Or we could say:

▶ The artist *pretends* to paint a picture.

◀ WHAT ABOUT THE ARTIST

You get the idea. You need to make every word—especially the verbs—in your sentences count. Otherwise, your sentences will lack action and be boring.

WORLD WISDOM

Kim Stegall, an Editor with *God's World News* magazines, always faces the challenge of telling big stories in small articles, without losing any of the interest. Her experience can help you learn to make every word count.

"Sometimes with a piece of writing I evaluate words individually. I ask whether each one pulls its own weight. Do some fail to convey precise meaning? Does a single word exist that could replace a string of them? Could any be cut entirely? Shorter isn't always better. But it often is. And since verbs are usually the workhorses of a sentence, they demand strict consideration. Verbs should tighten and clarify content, infuse color, progress plot, and imply tone. A lawyer I once worked for told me that he never used exclamation points. He said that if he found himself unable to achieve enough emphasis without them, he hadn't chosen the right verb."

— Kim Stegall

CWJ

◀ IN YOUR JOURNAL

PART A:
Pull out your picture again. What's happening in the picture? Choose two to three strong verbs (no being verbs) to describe the action and write them in your journal.

PART B:
What activities do you enjoy taking part in? Write six verbs that describe you—do you *run* track? Do you *read* great novels? Do you *love* animals?

USING ADVERBS TO ANSWER IMPORTANT QUESTIONS

With our subject and verb in place, we've got everything we need for a complete sentence:
▶ The toddler stares.
▶ The artist poses.

We've even added some adjectives to help set our subjects apart from the crowd—some details that help us recognize them:
▶ Blonde
▶ Goateed

But adjectives only describe nouns. And we haven't finished describing the picture. We still need more words to help readers create a mental image that matches the images we're looking at.

We need some adverbs. Adverbs describe or modify verbs, adjectives, and other adverbs. They answer important questions in a sentence. They tell where, when, and how actions take place. Adverbs also show degree (the *better* runner, the *worst* sandwich.)

Look back at the pictures. Can we add some adverbs that help describe *how*? (Hint: these adverbs often end in *–ly*.)

For instance, we could say:
▶ The blonde toddler gazes *longingly* at the cupcakes.
▶ The goateed artist poses *stiffly* in front of his painting.

Wow! We've come a long way. We can—and will—add some more words, but we'll bet you could already start forming pictures in your mind that match the ones on the page.

CWJ

IN YOUR JOURNAL ▶

PART A
What adverb can you add to your sentence that tells how, when, or where the action in your picture is taking place?

PART B
Look back at your verbs from last time. What adverbs could you use to better define HOW you do the things you do?
▶ I read *voraciously*.

If students find it difficult to think of adverbs, remind them that one way to make an adverb is to add *−ly* to an adjective. Go back to the adjectives they brainstormed in 1.2.2 and have them practice turning those adjectives into adverbs.

▶ I run *competitively*.
▶ I love dogs *more* than any other animal. (This is an adverb showing degree, or how much you love dogs.)

CAPSULE 5 1.2.5

SENTENCES CAN CREATE IMAGES

If you can learn to create images with words, you've mastered a skill that you'll need in all kinds of writing. Good writing helps readers see what you're talking about. Readers should be able to picture what you're describing in their minds.

Let's look back at our two pictures. Compare these two sentences about the first picture:
▶ A child sees some cupcakes.
▶ A small blonde-haired girl watches intently as an adult sprinkles toppings onto a plate of cupcakes.

Both accurately describe the picture. But one is clearly superior and more specific. By using adjectives (blonde), adverbs (intently), and strong verbs (sprinkles), a bland sentence can be transformed into a detailed, interesting one.

Compare these sentences about the second picture:
▶ A man stands by a painting.
▶ A middle-aged, goateed artist wearing a hat and holding a paintbrush poses next to a painting of a boat in the water.

Both meet the requirements for a sentence—they have a subject and a verb. But the first contains almost no information. Writing a sentence with no substance is like sending an envelope with no letter inside—it is a waste of postage.

If you learn to carefully choose your words and craft them into meaningful sentences, you've taken the first step toward becoming an excellent writer.

CWJ

PART A
Look back over the nouns, adjectives, verbs, and adverbs you came up with to describe your picture. Now put the best ones together into a sentence that creates a word-image of the picture you chose to describe. Write the sentence in your journal. Add additional words and phrases to fully detail what's going on in the picture as we did in the examples.

◀ IN YOUR JOURNAL

Now have a parent read the description; do not let her see the picture. After she has read the sentence, give your parent the magazine and have her look for the picture you described. Was she able to find it based on your description?

PART B

Now write a sentence about yourself as if you were describing someone in a newspaper article. Here's what mine might look like:

"The forty-two-year-old writer and mother of three enjoys relaxing with a good book when she's not busy running kids to and from school and extracurricular activities."

STYLE TIME

 In this lesson, we've tried to show you how to add details to make your sentences informative and interesting. But did you know that one of the most common mistakes writers make when they write sentences is not writing sentences at all?

Let us explain. A sentence must have a subject and a verb.

▶ Babies cry. (Subject) (Verb).
▶ Dogs bark. (Subject) (Verb).
▶ Birds fly. (Subject) (Verb).

I'm sure none of you would think this is a sentence:

▶ On the stove. It has a noun, "stove," but no verb.

But what about this one?

▶ Because I like to play tennis. It has a noun, "I," and a verb, "play." But is it a sentence? No.

Why not? It begins with *because*, which belongs to a group of words called subordinating conjunctions. Parts of sentences (clauses) that contain subordinating conjunctions have a subject and a verb. But they cannot stand alone.

If you sat down across from a friend at lunch and said, "Because I like to play tennis," he would wait to hear the rest of your sentence. It doesn't make sense by itself.

Later we'll learn more about parts and types of sentences and how to combine them. But for now, a good way to check your writing for this error, called a sentence fragment, is to read each sentence aloud. If you can't say it by itself and have it make sense in conversation, it's not a sentence. It's a sentence fragment.

This is the first "real" writing students are asked to produce. Furthermore, we ask that they "publish" their writing by sharing it with you.

This can be scary for some students because [1] they have to put everything together and [2] they have real consequences (you have to locate the image based on their description). Pay close attention to your student and be as supportive as possible when they approach this big step.

That's why

▶ I went roller-skating. Is a sentence . . . but
▶ After I went roller-skating. . . . is not.

Look back over the sentence you wrote about the image you chose. Does it have a subject and a verb? Now read it out loud. Does it make sense?

THE RIGHT WORD

 Below I've listed the five vocabulary words in context for this week. You should already have defined them in your journal as you found them in the reading.

▶ If you understand that simple illustration of the importance of **pertinent** details in writing, congratulations!
▶ Words like these used to describe or **modify** nouns are called adjectives.
▶ A **surfeit** of adjectives will create lots of detail. But some of that detail is unnecessary and distracting.
▶ We've studied the pictures, **culling** details so we can include accurate adjectives.
▶ Writing full of being verbs doesn't create vivid word images, so we should **eliminate** as many as we can.

Using your thesaurus, try to find the BEST word to replace the bold word in the sentence. Remember, you are looking for the BEST replacement. A thesaurus will give you a number of possible replacements, but you need to find the one word that captures perfectly what is happening in the sentence.

If you don't know all the words in the thesaurus, you may need to use your dictionary to look them up. That way you can choose the word that best fits the sentence.

After choosing your words, sit down with a parent or teacher and explain why your new word was the BEST word to replace the original one.

Write with WORLD

CAPSULE 1   1.3.1

STARTING TO THINK ABOUT PARAGRAPHS

Read this paragraph and follow the directions:

> I'm going to show you how to do energy transfer. Find two balls. One should be large and one should be small. Bounce them to see how high they bounce. Now bounce them again together. The small ball should bounce higher and the big one lower. That's because of energy transfer.

How did that exercise make you feel? If we tried to follow those directions, we would be a little frustrated.

Read this paragraph and try again:

> To see how energy is transferred from one object to another, you'll need two balls. One should be large, the other small. A basketball and a super ball (a small rubber ball) would work well. Take the two balls outside to your driveway or another hard surface. Drop the balls one at a time, noting how high each one bounces. Next, place the super ball on top of the basketball. Drop them while they are touching. They should still be touching when they hit the ground. The super ball should bounce higher this time. The basketball has transferred some of its energy to the super ball, so it should not bounce as high as before.

How did the ball experiment go this time? Was it better than last time?

In this lesson, you are going to read paragraphs. Some will be good paragraphs and some will not. We think you need to have the ability to **discern** a good paragraph from a weak paragraph before we ask you to begin writing your own.

We could just make a list, but we think you'll understand what makes a good paragraph and remember better if we show you some examples. That's why we started out with the example "energy transfer" paragraphs. They both include elements that a good paragraph should:

▶ topic sentence
▶ four to five supporting sentences
▶ all sentences unified around one topic

Yet one paragraph gets the information across better than the other one. Why? In this lesson, we are going to help you figure that out.

IN YOUR JOURNAL ▶

CWJ

Read back through both "energy transfer" paragraphs. Make a list of at least three differences you notice between the two paragraphs. Now answer this question:

What main reason explains why it is easier to follow the directions in the second paragraph?

THE RIGHT WORD:

 Remember to look for the words in bold each day. You should be looking the words up and writing down the most accurate definition—the one that best describes what the word means in **context**. (There's another one!)

CAPSULE 2   1.3.2

PARAGRAPHS HELP READERS UNDERSTAND YOUR POINT

 Imagine someone came up and dumped a jigsaw puzzle on the table in front of you but then wouldn't let you see the picture on the box. Without the picture, the puzzle would be very difficult to put together.

We hope this lesson will serve as a picture of what we're looking for in good paragraphs. We want to provide you with some examples—pictures or models—of good paragraphs. That way you'll have an idea of what you're trying to create once you begin writing your own paragraphs.

In the last capsule, what did you determine as the main reason explaining why the directions in the second "energy transfer" paragraph were easier to follow? The second one contains more specific, relevant details. The first one is rather vague. It simply tells you to "bounce the balls together," but it does not tell you how. The second one gives you a picture you can see in your mind: "place the super ball on top of the basketball.

Let your student note three differences. Many students may settle for a statement like these two: "the second paragraph is easier to follow" or "the first paragraph is difficult to understand." Do not let your student settle for these general answers.

If you see differences like these, ask the "Why" question: "Why is the second one easier to follow?" Try to get the student to talk about the differences. Chances are your student will speak more intelligently about the differences than they will write about them.

Drop them while they are touching." Specific details are the building blocks of a good paragraph.

As teachers of writing, we've seen lots of writing that does not include enough detail, and we think we know why. When you write a paragraph like the first example above and then read it back to yourself, it makes sense. If you've tried the experiment, you know how to do it, so your brain fills in the details that aren't on the paper.

Real writers know others will be reading what they write. So they constantly think of their readers. After each sentence, paragraph, or section, most read back over their work to see if it would make sense to others who read it.

WORLD WISDOM:

Surprise yourself. Sometimes we think our writing is good because we know what to expect. We wrote it, after all. If you want to get a more objective view of your work, leave your writing for a while. Get it out of your mind. Then come back later, "put on" the mindset of your intended audience, and read it fresh. You'll be surprised what you discover. Here is how Warren Smith, the Vice President of World News Group, takes it a step further.

"I often read what I have written OUT LOUD. I used to think I was weird for doing this, and I know that sometimes the people around me think I'm weird. In fact, one day I was concentrating so hard that I started reading out loud on an airplane. I'm sure the guy sitting next to me wished he could change seats, or even change planes. But I've talked to other writers and discovered that this practice is more common than I first thought. It's one of the best ways I've found to make sure that each sentence makes sense, that each word is in the right place."

— Warren Smith

CWJ

One good way to test how well your writing works is to read it out loud. Sometimes hearing what you've written helps you to see what you've left out.

◀ IN YOUR JOURNAL

Read the two paragraphs below aloud. Both contain specific details, but one is superior:

> The first time I performed in a play, I was so nervous. My costume was really cool. I got to wear a suit of armor that looked real and carry a sword. I just had one line, "Hark! Who goes there!" but my mouth felt so dry, and my lips felt huge. I was afraid when my turn came no sound would even come out. It did though, and it was great. My best friend was in the play so that was really fun too. I was nervous, but it all worked out in the end.

Don't let students skip the exercise of reading their writing—and other's writing—aloud. This is a vital strategy for writers and one that we will encourage throughout the various lessons. Reading aloud helps writers determine whether their writing is active and flows well. If writers stumble over their own words, they can expect that readers will too!

I'll never forget the first time I broke a bone. Snap! Searing pain ran up my leg, and I fell to the floor of the kitchen. We were packing to move. As I had run through the kitchen to the laundry room, my toe caught on a leg of the baby's high chair. I immediately felt a rush of heat on my face as a wave of nausea washed over me. I looked at my toe. It was beginning to swell. Quickly I lay back down on the floor and closed my eyes tightly. If I lay still enough maybe I could fight off the sick feeling. I had a strong suspicion I had just broken my toe.

Now answer these questions:

1. Which paragraph did you think was better? Give two reasons why you thought the paragraph you chose was better.

2. Did you see any details in either paragraph that were not relevant? If so, take your pencil and cross the irrelevant details out.

CAPSULE 3 1.3.3

SENTENCES WORK TOGETHER TO CREATE FOCUS IN A PARAGRAPH

Let's go back to our puzzle **analogy** for a moment. But this time, let's imagine you dump a 1000-piece jigsaw puzzle in front of someone. Not only do you hide the picture on the box, but you also include a few extra pieces that don't fit!

When you write a paragraph that does not have clear direction and includes unrelated details, it's like giving someone a puzzle to figure out. Paragraph number one in 1.3.2 about the writer's first drama experience could be a good paragraph. It starts by talking about the writer's feelings when he performed in his first play. But then the writer becomes sidetracked and begins talking about his costume, instead. He gets back on track for a moment and offers some good details—what he said in the play, how he felt physically (dry mouth, huge lips), and what he feared (that no sound would come out). He skips over the actual event itself—he does not include any specific information about his performance.

Why does the second paragraph work better? Unlike the first paragraph, which fails to include the drama performance, this paragraph actually tells how it feels to break a toe. And the paragraph is unified. All the sentences stay on the topic of the writer's broken toe.

A good general rule to follow when writing paragraphs is all sentences in the paragraph should focus on one topic. When you change the subject, it is time to start a new paragraph.

This activity also helps writers identify mistakes in punctuation and grammar that they might have skipped over in a silent reading. For instance, the natural pauses used in speaking can help writers identify where they need commas and what sentences may be run-ons.

If students are hesitant to read aloud at first, offer to read the passage aloud to them or encourage them to read it in private.

Before moving to the CWJ, you might want to look at effective paragraphs in books your students read. Point out how the sentences work together in these paragraphs. Students who grasp this lesson are more likely to have an easier time composing larger essays.

CWJ

◀ IN YOUR JOURNAL

Read these two versions of the same event:

I couldn't see the board very well. My teacher sent a note home and said I should get my eyes checked. The doctor said I was nearsighted. I tried to pass the eye test, but my eyes were too bad. I got glasses and I was amazed by how much better I could see! Before trees had looked kind of like big furry green cotton balls, but now I could see each leaf clearly. I also was better at sports. That happened when I was in the second grade. I cried when I found out I had to get glasses.

When I was in the second grade, my teacher sent a note home that said, "I think Allan may need glasses. He is squinting to see what I write on the board." The next day, my mom made an appointment with the eye doctor even though I protested that I did not need or want glasses. The day of the appointment arrived, and I was determined to somehow pass the eye test so that I didn't have to get glasses. But it was no use. My eyes were so bad, I could barely see the big "E" at the top of the chart! I started to cry. I was afraid I wouldn't be able to play sports anymore. The doctor assured me that this wasn't true, and he personally walked me over to the optical store next door and showed me several styles of glasses that were made just for sports. I picked out a regular pair and a pair of sports glasses. From that day forward, I haven't taken my glasses off except to sleep. I'm a much better baseball player now that I can see the ball coming!

We've already looked at two key "rules" of good paragraphs: They must 1) include relevant details and 2) be unified. Let's see if you can figure out another rule by examining the paragraphs above.

1. List the differences you notice between the two paragraphs.

2. Underline all the words and phrases in the second paragraph that relate to time.

3. What do the "time" words do for the paragraph? How do they help you as a reader?

CAPSULE 4

TRANSITIONS HELP ORGANIZE PARAGRAPHS

Did you figure out the third "rule"? Good paragraphs—and good writing in general—is organized. Not every paragraph has "time" words in it. But all well-organized paragraphs give readers some cues to help them see how the sentences relate to each other. These words or short phrases are called *transitions*. They help the reader see the logical connections between your ideas. Words and phrases like *first, second, finally, after that, the next day*, help guide the reader through your paragraph.

They can also help YOU as a writer. For instance, in the first paragraph, if the writer had tried to logically connect the paragraph about his glasses, he might have realized that the final two sentences—when he got his glasses and that he cried when he got them—were out of order. It's more logical to include that information earlier in the paragraph.

Often paragraphs can be organized by thinking about either stories or steps. In a narrative paragraph—where you are talking about something that happened to you or someone else—think of it as a story. A story has a beginning where the situation is explained, a middle where some sort of conflict occurs, and an ending where the matter is resolved or concluded.

Consider the second "glasses" paragraph:

Beginning: The writer tells when and how he found out his vision was bad.

Middle: The writer goes to his eye exam and tries to fake his way through it but fails. He is upset because he's afraid he won't be able to play sports. But the doctor explains that's not true and helps him find some sports glasses.

End: The writer realizes he really did need glasses, and in fact is a better athlete because of it.

When paragraphs are explaining a process, they are organized in steps. Look back at the paragraph from 1.3.1. We can easily list the steps:

1. Take the two balls outside to your driveway or another hard surface.
2. Drop the balls one at a time, noting how high each one bounces.
3. Next, place the super ball on top of the basketball.
4. Drop them while they are touching.

If you were building a house, you would want a good strong frame to hold it up. Organization is the frame of your paragraph. You need a sturdy structure to hang the details on. Otherwise you just have a big pile of information that your reader must try to make sense of.

CWJ

IN YOUR JOURNAL ▶

Think of a process you frequently engage in. Choose something simple (like brushing your teeth or making a scrambled egg). Make a list of the steps in order in your journal. Then test yourself by actually DOING the steps of the process. Did you leave anything out?

CAPSULE 5

1.3.5

EVALUATING PARAGRAPHS

In this lesson, we have examined three characteristics of good paragraphs. From now on, as you read paragraphs and other writing, these characteristics will serve as **criteria** to help you evaluate that writing. Is the writing well-organized? Does it contain enough relevant detail to be clear and interesting? Is it unified, or does it contain unrelated sentences?

Let's look at one final paragraph. Keep the criteria in mind as you read.

> I didn't think I liked cats until Ariel adopted us. I say she adopted us because she showed up on our back porch and wouldn't leave. Mom said not to feed her, but after a week or so of Ariel's constant presence, I began to feel sorry for her. Mom finally **relented** and allowed me to give her some food. Ariel challenged my belief that cats are boring pets. She would chase a ball if you threw it. Then she'd bring it back and drop it at your feet just like a dog playing fetch. Dogs are good pets too. She loved to be carried around. Mom grew to like her too. She even reluctantly allowed herself to be dressed up like a baby. That made her the perfect pet for a six- year-old girl. We got her a collar with our address on it and took her to the vet.

CWJ

Answer these questions about the paragraph in your journal:

1. What specific detail in the paragraph did you like? What would you have liked to have more information (details) about?

2. What problems in organization did you notice? How could you fix the problems?

3. Was the paragraph unified? What sentence or sentences didn't fit?

STYLE TIME

One key to writing good paragraphs is being specific. One place it's easy to become vague is when we use pronouns. As a reader it's confusing to read a paragraph that uses the word "it" or "he" or "she" and not be able to figure out its antecedent (the earlier word the pronoun refers to).

◄ IN YOUR JOURNAL

This is a terrific exercise to repeat over and over. Continue to have students evaluate paragraphs.

At first, students will learn to comprehend the strengths and weaknesses of paragraphs they read. Eventually, this skill will transfer to their own paragraphs: they will be able to [1] compose more logical paragraphs and [2] evaluate the weaknesses in their own paragraphing.

Take a look at this sentence:

The girl put the baby down for a nap, but she didn't sleep.

That's a vague pronoun reference. We can't be sure if "she" refers to the girl or the baby. Let's see if we can make the sentence better by being more specific.

Better: The girl put the baby down for a nap, but the baby didn't sleep.

Let's try a different sentence:

I grabbed hold of the door handle to put the key in, and it broke.

Again, the sentence is unclear. Which one broke, the key or the door handle? We can improve this sentence with greater specificity.

Better: I grabbed hold of the door handle to put the key in, and the handle broke.

How about one final example?

The fifth graders played the sixth graders in soccer. They couldn't believe it when they won.

Who won, the fifth graders or the sixth graders? The sentence does not share that information; the reader has to guess who won the soccer game. Specificity solves this problem.

Better: The fifth graders played the sixth graders in soccer. The fifth-graders couldn't believe it when they beat the sixth graders.

Now look back through the paragraph in Capsule 5. Do you see any vague pronoun references? Show how you would improve the sentences by rewriting them here.

THE RIGHT WORD

By today, you should have defined all the words for this lesson. Now it's time to look the words up in your thesaurus. Remember, your goal is to find the best word to replace the bold word in the sentence—the word with the most similar meaning. You may need to use your dictionary to help figure out what some of the synonyms mean.

▶ We think you need to have the ability to **discern** a good paragraph from a weak paragraph before we ask you to begin writing your own.

▶ You should be looking the words up and writing down the most accurate definition—the one that best describes what the word means in **context**.

▶ Let's go back to our puzzle **analogy** for a moment.

▶ From now on, as you read paragraphs and other writing, these characteristics will serve as **criteria** to help you evaluate that writing. (The singular of criteria is criterion.)

▶ Mom finally **relented** and allowed me to give her some food.

Write with WORLD

CAPSULE 1   1.4.1

WHAT IS AN ESSAY?

 How would you describe an essay? Perhaps teachers have taught you to write a five-paragraph essay—an introduction, three points, and a conclusion. Or maybe you have written essay answers on a test. Both are types of essays. But the definition of *essay* is much broader.

Famous essay writer and novelist Aldous Huxley once said, "[T]he essay is a literary device for saying almost everything about almost anything," and it's true. Essays have been written on every topic that you can imagine. They're usually short works. But this is in comparison to full-length books, so "short" could still mean 15 or 20 pages.

Essays serve a variety of purposes too. Students write essays in school to show their knowledge of a subject. Academics write essays to reveal new discoveries they've made in their field. Journalists write essays called editorials to offer their opinions on world events.

Are you getting the idea that *essay* is a very big category that encompasses many types of writing? Rather than try to come up with a perfect definition, let's make a list of a few characteristics found in most good essays:

▶ Effective essays offer a well-supported opinion or position that makes readers think
▶ Effective essays are organized
▶ Effective essays are written by authors who have a distinct "voice" or style (unique way of saying things)

In order to put together a well-written essay, you first need to be able to distinguish between a good essay and a so-so one. In this lesson, we're going to help you learn to see the difference.

While our list of three characteristics doesn't hit all the important features of an essay, it's a good starting point. If you can evaluate these three elements in an essay, you can make a determination about how strong or weak the essay is.

IN YOUR JOURNAL ▶

CWJ

Flip through copies of *God's World News* or *WORLD Magazine*. In *God's World News*, the Bible2Life sections are short opinion essays that don't merely tell the news. They often offer a Biblical perspective on the news stories. In *WORLD Magazine* on the content page, there's a section called "Voices" that lists page numbers for essays by *WORLD* writers.

Choose one essay and answer these questions:

1. What is the essay about?

2. What is the author's opinion or belief on the subject he or she is writing about?

3. What did you like about the essay?

Students may try to answer questions #1 and #2 with the same answer. Question #1 identifies the topic of the essay. Question #2 asks the student to identify the author's thought on the topic.

While both questions are important, question #2 really pushes the student to consider how essays reveal what an author believes. When the opportunity arises, help your student see the difference between the first two questions.

CAPSULE 2
1.4.2

READING AN ESSAY

You may have noticed that the title of this lesson is "Developing Critical Readers." If so, did you wonder why we wanted to make you critical? After all, *critical* means, "inclined to find fault or judge with severity."

Well, that's one meaning of the word. We are focusing on another meaning here: "involving skillful judgment as to truth and merit." So how do you develop skillful judgment?

If you've ever taken piano lessons, played soccer, or taken part in any other skill-based activity, you probably drilled basic skills over and over. The truth is, if you want to get good at anything, you have to practice. Even if you have natural talent, to become successful, you can't skip the practicing part.

We're going to spend the rest of this lesson demonstrating and practicing how to skillfully judge essays. You have to keep practicing in order to become skillful. Regular reading of all types of literature, including essays, is one of the very best ways to improve your reading and writing skills.

Today, we'll look at an essay by *WORLD* writer Janie B. Cheaney that appeared in the July 2, 2011 issue of *WORLD Magazine*. We've shortened it a little and simplified the language a bit.

Students need to understand the difference between these two definitions. We do not want students to become grumpy and nasty readers. Instead, we want them to analyze writing, recognize what works and what does not, and develop plans for improving that writing.

This is a more mature understanding of "critical," and it is one that often escapes more seasoned college writers. Evidence that this understanding of "critical" is lost can be found on "news" shows where critical debate declines to nothing more than screaming attacks at other ideas.

Becoming Readers

I remember the moment when I became a reader. I always liked to read, but that's not the same thing. What made a *reader* of me was a novel I received through a children's book club.

It was the story of a journey from Poland to Switzerland by four children in search of their parents after World War II. I had never experienced anything similar, so the story was a little hard to get into. But by 30 pages in, the story had hooked me. In Chapter 12, it changed me.

Two sisters arrive at an orphan camp in search of their brother Edek, captured two years earlier and sent to Germany. But it appears he's run away. They join a soup line. Someone trips and spills his food. The hungry children dive for it. Ruth, the oldest sister, tries to protect some of the little children. In the confusion, she catches hold of a hand. "For some reason or other she clung on to the hand, and when everyone about her had got up and her hand was free she had not let go. Then she looked to see whose hand it was, and it was Edek's" (Ian Serraillier, The Silver Sword). The best way I can describe how I felt at that moment is to say that the story itself reached out and grabbed my hand.

How mysterious is that? Words arranged in sentences, built into a story, made me bigger. It's a bit like creation itself: light spoken into being. Writing imitates creation by "speaking" ideas into being.

But reading can be creative as well. When readers become real readers, they interact with the book. They're in a conversation with it. It can change the way they look at things. It can make them more sympathetic. It can make them angry. It can help them develop ideas.

Not everybody is a reader in this sense. In fact, it can be argued that real readers are in the minority even in societies where almost everyone can read (C.S. Lewis, *An Experiment in Criticism*). Most people read for two reasons: entertainment and information. These are genuine needs. But they can be met other ways.

There's another reason to read—enlightenment. That means letting the ideas created by written language challenge or change us. Literature courses were originally created to develop enlightened readers.

Literature isn't often taught that way any more. Liberal college professors teach students what to look for in the text—things like race and class and how people are mistreated because of them. Instead of letting the text speak to them, students learn to tell the text what it says. That reduces the text's importance and flattens its meaning.

New technologies can also have a "flattening" effect. A book on an iPad is both more and less than a book. It's an app. The text is not the main thing. It shares importance with animations, photos, video and audio files.

That's fine for shorter forms. But it's probably not the best way to understand literature. By poking, swiping and touching, the reader is not just reading. He's also manipulating. He may be telling the text what he thinks, rather than letting it speak to him. This can be true, or especially true, of Bible apps. They're wonderful tools, but be careful. If you're too busy poking and swiping, the text may not be able to reach out and take your hand.

CWJ

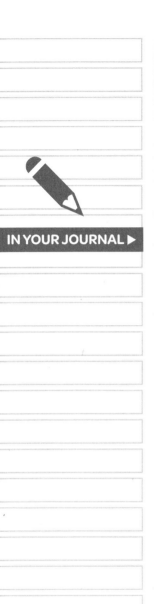

IN YOUR JOURNAL ▶

Answer the following questions about "Becoming Readers":

1. What is the essay about?

2. What is the author's opinion or belief on the subject he or she is writing about?

3. What did you like about the essay?

WORLD WISDOM

Janie B. Cheaney is a writer for *WORLD Magazine* whose essays regularly bring enlightenment to her readers.

"What does the word 'essay' bring to your mind? A volume of some dead author's thoughts collecting dust in a library? Something you have to read for school, and forget as soon as you've read it? Or worse, something you have to write for school, and try to stretch to 500 words? Scary as they may seem, essays are nothing to be afraid of. You've probably already read several that were interesting, or even fun.

I started writing essays (though I didn't always realize what they were) because I found that organizing my thoughts in a readable form helped me to understand what I really thought. Sometimes the process helped me realize that I needed to do some more thinking! Over time, essay-writing became the means by which I earn a significant amount of income. You may never make any money from it, but someday you may need to move a reader, or change a mind, or just determine what you really think about a subject. However you use them, knowing how to write clear and effective essays is a skill worth having."

— Janie B. Cheaney

Some students may not like this essay. After all, in the final lines, the essay critiques something many of them love: technology. If a student disagrees with Ms. Cheaney, congratulate him for having an opinion.

Remind him, however, that his disagreement should not hinder his ability to find something he likes. If his disagreement makes it impossible for him to like aspects of the essay, he is embracing the definition of "critical" that concentrates more on finding fault and severity.

READING WITH SKILLFUL JUDGMENT

Begin this capsule by rereading the essay, "Becoming Readers."

Did you find it to be a little more complex than writing you usually read? Did you have a difficult time putting your finger on the essay's exact meaning? If so, that's good.

You get better at running long distances by pushing yourself to run further. You get better at reading by choosing literature with more complex organization and vocabulary. If writing makes you think harder, it's strengthening your thinking skills.

Today, we will examine whether or not Mrs. Cheaney's essay contains the three elements most good essays include:

1. Does "Becoming Readers" offer an opinion or position that makes readers think?

We believe it does. If we reduced Mrs. Cheaney's opinion to a few sentences, it might look like this:
Literature courses were intended to develop enlightened readers, but today, they often create readers who tell the text what it says instead of listening to the text. If readers are not careful of how they use technology such as iPad apps, technology can have the same effect. It can prevent the text from speaking to readers and enlightening them.

Take time to investigate C.S. Lewis and understand why he was a well-known writer. He represents a good model of a writer, public intellectual, and Christian for students to admire and study.

If you look back at Capsule 1, you will notice that we didn't merely say that a good essay had to offer an opinion. It also needs to be well-supported. We believe Mrs. Cheaney offers good support for her opinions. She uses two types. First, in order to explain what an enlightened reader is, she uses the example of when she became an enlightened reader herself. Personal examples provide one form of evidence writers can use to support their opinion or position.

Moreover, understanding Lewis' history, explains the power of effective and thoughtful writing: Mrs. Cheaney knows Lewis' opinion and character so well that she can use it confidently in her writing. The clarity, grace, and thoughtfulness of Lewis' writing has allowed it to live past his death.

Second, in discussing what an enlightened reader is and how rare this reader is, she refers to C.S. Lewis, a well-known writer and literary critic. Referring to respected outside sources offers another means of supporting her opinion.

2. Is "Becoming Readers" organized?

Yes, Mrs. Cheaney organizes her essay in a way that draws readers in at the beginning, then builds toward a point at the end.

▶ First, she uses a personal example to show readers what she means by enlightenment.

▶ Then she uses the argument of another writer, C.S. Lewis, to support her position that enlightenment in readers is rare.

▶ She builds on her position by telling us that college courses rarely develop enlightened readers anymore. Instead, they're teaching students to tell the text what it says.

▶ Finally, she warns that new technologies contain the same danger: Readers can get distracted from the text and fail to hear what the text says to them.

3. Does "Becoming Readers" have a distinct voice or style?

Yes, it does. By beginning with a personal story, Mrs. Cheaney writes an essay that no one else could write exactly the same way. She also offers her opinion. We know something specific about the author and what she thinks by the end. This is part of what we mean when we say the essay has a distinct *voice*.

These aren't the only elements that make "Becoming Readers" a good essay. For instance, we also like Mrs. Cheaney's image of the book reaching out and taking the reader's hand. She repeats that image at the end, which gives the essay a feeling of completeness.

We could make a long list of all the elements that make this a good essay, but that might be overwhelming. For now, concentrate on the three things we illustrated in this capsule. The more essays you read, the more you will recognize other common characteristics of good essays.

CWJ

IN YOUR JOURNAL ▶

Today, we want you to take another look at the essay you read in Capsule 1. Using the essay "Becoming Readers" that we worked through today as a model, answer these three questions about the essay you chose:

1. Does the essay offer an opinion or position that makes readers think? Is it well-supported?

2. Using the example in today's capsule as a model, show how the essay is organized.

3. Give one example of how the essay shows the author's voice or style.

Students may have difficulty understanding voice. If so, teach "voice" as "personality." Writing needs to have personality. Pull up a common encyclopedia entry for writing that lacks personality: anyone could have written that entry.

Understanding voice will put personality into the student's writing. They will make every word important and capture the attention of their reader. More importantly, they will enter a conversation—or better yet, a relationship—with their reader.

I enjoy a particular writer who tells stories and uses humor. He works through short sentences that use interesting verbs and interesting phrases. Every now and then he moves away from his main point to tell a family story. This is his voice, and I enjoy it.

The Milkshake Test is a fun voice test for students. Ask your student what it would be like to share a milkshake and conversation with an author. Would it be interesting and full of stories? Would the student understand the words being used? Or, would the conversation be so tedious that the sweetness of the milkshake would sour? Would they want to leave the table as quickly as possible? If a student can answer these questions specifically and have fun with this exercise, they are learning "voice."

MORE PRACTICE

Read this essay:

Should Teens Have Cell Phones?

About 75 percent of American teens have cell phones according to the Pew Research Center (2010). More than half send 50 or more texts each day.

There are some good reasons for teens to have cell phones. If a teen gets into a dangerous situation, he or she could call a parent to come help him or her out. They can be used as alarm clocks. If a teen has a smart phone, he or she can use it to check the news.

But cell phones can also cause some problems for teens. Too much texting can be a distraction. Cell phones cost a lot of money. They can keep teens from talking to each other in the old-fashioned way.

It's also possible to make compromises. Teens can purchase prepaid phones so they don't text too much. Parents can access programs that let them view all their teen's texts. Parents can take phones away if teens abuse them.

So should teens have cell phones? That's something each family must decide for themselves.

Please note that the length of this essay does not make it an ineffective essay. Short essays can be excellent, and long essays can be ineffective. We need to evaluate this essay. If we test this essay against the three elements most good essays contain, how does it compare?

1. Does "Should Teens Have Cell Phones" offer an opinion or position that makes readers think?

The opinion is missing here. The writer gives reasons in favor of and against teens having cell phones, but she never tells readers what she thinks and why.

Similarly, the writer offers some reasons why cell phones can be good and bad for teens, but they are not supported in any way. She could offer personal examples or the opinion of experts, but she does not. She offers one statistic at the beginning, but she doesn't use it to support a position.

2. Is "Should Teens Have Cell Phones" organized?

Yes, the writer organizes her ideas this way:

▶ Introduces the topic by showing widespread use of phones by teens
▶ Lists some positives of teens having cell phones
▶ List some negatives of teens having cell phones
▶ Offers possible compromises between not having a cell phone at all and unlimited use
▶ Concludes by saying each family must decide for itself

3. Does "Should Teens Have Cell Phones" have a distinct voice or style?

No. This element is completely missing. By the end of the essay, readers have no sense of who the writer is or what she thinks about the topic. By offering personal examples of her own experience with teen cell phone use, the writer could add her voice to the essay.

As teachers of writing, we've read plenty of essays that aren't so different from this one. It doesn't require any thought on the part of the writer. It's really just a hodge-podge of general knowledge that almost anyone over the age of 10 who lives in America could write.

We are sure you could see a big difference between the two essays we've read so far. The differences won't always be so drastic, but we hope comparing these two essays will help you begin distinguishing between well-written and poorly written essays.

CWJ

IN YOUR JOURNAL ▶

If you were writing this essay, what position would you take? Do you think teens should have cell phones?

Write an example from personal experience (either a situation you've found yourself in or a situation you've observed) that supports your position. Your example should be a short paragraph—four to five sentences long at least.

STYLE TIME

● In this lesson, we won't introduce any new grammar issues. Instead, we'll review what we've learned in this unit.

1. Sentence fragments

Read back through the example paragraph you just wrote. Underline each subject once and each verb twice. Does each sentence have both? If not, you do not have a complete sentence.

Once you have made sure you have a subject and verb in each sentence, read each sentence aloud, stopping at the period. Make sure that each sentence is a complete thought: (Example: "I went roller-skating," is a complete thought. "After I went roller-skating" is not.) If you find yourself with this kind of fragment—the kind that begins with a subordinating conjunction—combine it with another sentence.

2. Vague pronoun reference

Circle all the pronouns in your example paragraph. Draw an arrow from the pronoun to its antecedent (the noun the pronoun refers back to). Now look at the sentence again. Is there another noun the pronoun could possibly refer to? (Example: The fifth graders played the sixth graders in soccer, and they couldn't believe it when they won.)

3. Its/it's

You've already circled all your pronouns. Do you have any *its* or *it's* circled? If so, read each aloud, substituting "it is" for *its* or *it's*. If "it is" doesn't make sense, *its* is the right choice. If "it is" does make sense, use *it's*.

CAPSULE 5 1.4.5

ESSAY WRITING REQUIRES PRACTICE

Today we want you to read another essay from *WORLD Magazine* by writer Andrée Seu. It appeared in the June 4, 2011, issue. We've shortened it a little and simplified the language a bit.

Living in the Middle

In 2003 I had a new roof put on, and the roofer was careless with the flashings. I don't know what flashings are, but experts told me that carelessness with the flashings caused the collapse, several years later, of my attic ceiling.

It started small. I make infrequent trips to the third floor. One day I spotted a slight bulge overhead that was not there before. I ignored it and over time a bulge became plaster and dust on the floor, and then a cascade.

There are good small beginnings too. I like to press zinnia seeds into the soil and day after day squint for the first sign of a crack in the ground that precedes the "birth" of a tiny crooked-necked head, so much like a human baby's beginnings.

But what I was thinking is that the slowness of things in nature—and in the supernatural—makes for a strange earthly experience. Things appear the opposite of their true condition for a while.

"Because the sentence against an evil deed is not executed speedily, the heart of children of man is fully set to do evil" (Ecclesiastes 8:11). When I have lived against God's law, I have often seemed to get away with it. The more time that went by, the more I believed I was getting away with it. But the uneventfulness proved only a gestation [growth] period.

There are people out there right now who think things are going well for them, when actually things are going quite badly for them. But they do not yet see it. The inner workings of their unrighteousness is not visible to the naked eye. They imagine they have finally hit on happy times, when they are in fact on the Titanic at about 6 p.m. on April 14, 1912.

On the other hand, there are people who think things are going quite badly for them, when actually things are going quite well. But they can't see it yet, either. These include people who have obeyed the Lord and incurred immediate unpleasantness for doing so. Perhaps their whole world seems to be caving in, and there is no human logic that can imagine a good outcome.

There is a man who walked in integrity when his marriage and church life and friendships and health suddenly all failed him, the way the rafters of a house will all fall one by one. It was like the series of messengers in Job, each bringing a new telegram of improbable catastrophes. I could imagine no scenario that would make it right again for that man.

Then like a magic that starts to slowly reverse a curse, I watched the hand of God reverse the fortunes of my friend. The law of God is a divine physics. Jesus broke free from His tomb by the third day because the forces of hell could not hold him down (Acts 2:24).

This is all to say: Cheer up if your world is crashing at the moment and you are abiding in Christ's will. Tomorrow or next year will look completely different. We see but middles. And if your past sins have made a mess of things, this present day's new obedience is the beginning of your movement toward a new place, though you may have to wait a while to see it. The eyes of faith are more reliable than the eyes of sight.

"Living in the Middle" is another good example of essay writing. You can find the three elements we're looking for in this lesson, but there's also much more. One example is Mrs. Seu's use of juxtaposition (setting two things side by side for comparison—for instance, catastrophic and good beginnings).

And that's why it's so important to your progress as a writer to keep reading. Even though you might not know the names of all the elements of good writing that you'll see, you'll begin to reflect these characteristics in your own writing.

Identifying the organizational structure of an essay can seem like a daunting task when taken as a whole. To help simply the process for students, have them read and write down a short—no longer than one sentence—summary of each paragraph in the essay.

Rather than trying to figure out the organization based on the entire essay, they can focus on the summaries they have created to see how the writer moves from one idea to another.

CWJ

Answer these questions in your journal:

1. Does "Living in the Middle" offer an opinion or position that makes readers think? Is it well-supported?

2. Following the model in Capsule 3 (1.4.3), show how "Living in the Middle" is organized.

3. Give one example of how "Living in the Middle" shows the author's voice or style.

THE RIGHT WORD

 In this lesson, we'll review all the words we've learned so far in this unit. Choose the BEST word for each sentence and fill in the blank.

1. She studied the newspaper articles, _____ details to add to her story.
a) boasting   b) implicit   c) culling

2. Hank is an _____ baseball fan; he never misses a Ranger's game.
a) avid   b) implicit   c) ubiquitous

3. Our city _____ more new residents than any other in the state of Indiana.
a) discerns   b) culls   c) boasts

4. You should include only _____ details in your story.
a) criteria   b) ubiquitous   c) pertinent

5. Words are best understood in _____.
a) surfeit   b) context   c) criteria

6. Fast food restaurants are _____; you can hardly go anywhere without passing one.
a) ubiquitous   b) surfeit   c) criteria

7. After begging, ordering, and bribing the child, the babysitter realized she was going to have to try a different _____ to get the child to bed.
a) analogy   b) context   c) tactic

8. The _____ message of almost all advertising is, "Your life will be better if you buy this product."
a) implicit   b) surfeit   c) modifying

9. Words that _____ adjectives are called adverbs.
a) eliminate   b) modify   c) discern

10. His mother finally _____ and allowed him to get a puppy.

a) boasted   b) culled   c) relented

11. At the party a _____ of potato chips and soda left all the children with stomach aches.

a) surfeit   b) tactic   c) criteria

12. The judges must _____ all but the final two contestants.

a) eliminate   b) surfeit   c) analogize

13. If you learn to _____ the elements of a good essay, you'll be on your way to writing one.

a) eliminate   b) analogize   b) discern

14. An _____ compares two things to help clarify one of them.

a) avid   b) analogy   c) eliminate

15. We must have clear _____ to accurately judge.

a) criteria   b) modification   c) pertinence

Write with WORLD

TEACHER GUIDE UNIT 2/ LESSON 1

DEVELOPING WRITERS: BUILDING BLOCKS AND BIOGRAPHY

THE PARAGRAPH

GENERAL OVERVIEW

In Unit 1, students learned to thoughtfully and critically compare sentences, paragraphs, and essays. Now that they possess the necessary skill to identify the characteristics of strong and weak writing, it is time to put that knowledge to work.

Accordingly, Unit 2 teaches students to apply this knowledge as they craft their own sentences and paragraphs. Here we avoid the popular "worksheet" method of teaching writing. According to this method, students are given a principle – such as using a comma and coordinating conjunction to combine sentences – and then asked to reproduce that principle by connecting dozens of pre-written sentences. The "worksheet" method fails in at least two regards: (1) it denies students the chance to create their own writing and (2) it suggests that writing takes place apart from context. Although we will provide many examples, we will not teach through pre-fabricated sentences that require little more than formulaic thinking to complete. We do offer principles to follow, but then we ask students to thoughtfully craft sentences and order those sentences into paragraphs in their own way.

Our goal is to help students understand that all the writing they do has purpose and meaning. Effective writers don't just know a lot of big words or compose flowery, unrelated sentences. They know how to link words together to create meaningful sentences. They know how to order those sentences to construct unified paragraphs. And they know how to organize paragraphs to explain an idea, tell a story, or make an argument.

To help students grow into effective writers, this unit focuses on teaching students how to use words to build sentences and sentences to build paragraphs that clearly and logically communicate their ideas. Doing so requires them to think and make choices, not just follow a formula. We don't want to tell students to always combine sentences. Instead, we want students to ask whether a short, simple sentence or a longer, compound sentence would be more effective in the context of what they are writing. We don't want to tell students to always start a new paragraph after five sentences. Instead, we want students to consider if a one-sentence paragraph might help engage their readers' attention or if a longer paragraph might be necessary to fully explain their point. Ultimately, we want students to see that writing is making meaning through words – and that they get to make choices about how they convey that meaning to their audience.

DETAILED OVERVIEW

2.1.1-5 (Unit 2, Lesson 1, Capsule 1-5): Lesson 1 begins with the qualities of a successful paragraph introduced in Unit 1 and offers some concrete ways for students to increase the effectiveness of their paragraphs. Students will practice writing engaging topic sentences, selecting details that support the main idea of a paragraph, and ordering sentences in a logical manner. We begin with the paragraph rather than the sentence to reinforce the idea that all the writing students do is contextual. When students write sentences, they should think about the purpose of the sentence within the larger context of the paragraph or essay they are composing.

2.2.1-5: In this lesson we return to the sentence as the fundamental building block of writing. In our experience, students are comfortable writing simple sentences, but may avoid creating more complex sentence constructions. Here we hope to demystify the process of linking sentences by breaking down the process for students through interesting examples. We also hope to show students that it's not just about writing longer sentences. Sometimes a particular way of linking sentences will better express their meaning. You will notice that the exercises in this lesson only ask students to compose two sentences, instead of the many examples required by the "worksheet" method. This is your opportunity to encourage students to thoroughly consider word choice and their intended meaning, perhaps coming up with several different options, before selecting the option they believe is the best. They can write two exceptional sentences, rather than twenty mediocre ones.

2.3.1-5: Lesson 3 introduces students to the concepts of focus and arrangement. In order to be successful, paragraphs must have a single focus and be ordered logically. Students are given practice with creating focus as they construct topic sentences that will prompt readers to ask a question. The rest of the lesson offers different methods—including chronology, location, and order of importance—that a student might select for organizing the remainder of a paragraph.

2.4.1-5: The final lesson of this unit shows students how the organizational skills they have been practicing at the sentence and paragraph level can be applied to longer pieces of writing. They find that if they can transition from sentence to sentence within a paragraph, they can also transition from paragraph to paragraph. Doing so is not just a matter of adding in a few transition phrases, but is dependent upon the writer understanding and signaling to his readers the precise connection between the ideas in each paragraph. We walk students through the crafting of one well-written, logically ordered paragraph which they then situate within the context of a piece of biographical writing. This subject matter – writing about someone else's life – provides a nice connection to the topic of Unit 3: Autobiography.

THREE WAYS TO HELP YOUR STUDENT WRITER IN UNIT 2

SPECIFICALLY ENCOURAGE

In Unit 1, we advised you to encourage specificity in student responses. It is just as crucial that you provide specific encouragement to student writers. As you read through the CWJ, cheer your student in her efforts. Rather than writing "good" or "nice job," aim for comments that attend to exactly what you liked about the work. For instance, "Your sense of humor really comes through in this sentence." When a student reads this comment, she knows that you are really reading her work. Such comments can also help her begin to identify her personal strengths as a writer.

Furthermore, positive comments such as this present you with the opportunity to offer constructive criticism in other areas. Instead of marking a passage as "dull" – a comment that might be perceived as discouraging – you can encourage a student by recommending, "What if you included some humor here?" Since the student already knows you view her humor as a positive quality of her writing, this response will be perceived as encouraging and will likely make the writer more excited to revise her work.

EMPHASIZE TAKING CHANCES OVER CORRECTNESS

Remember when we mentioned a red pen bleeding all over student papers as a deterrent to a student's enjoyment of writing? Well, teachers who focus too heavily on correctness will create students who never take chances because they are too worried about getting something wrong. In this unit, as well as those to follow, we want to emphasize taking chances more than we want to be sticklers for getting things right.

Correctness certainly has its place in writing, and we offer time in each unit for attending to these matters through revision and editing. But as you'll see, correctness is not primary. As students try on new skills, there must be room for failure without penalty. If a student attempts to use one of their new vocabulary words but does so incorrectly, applaud them for taking a risk rather than sticking with an easier word. This doesn't mean that you should always overlook blatant errors to make a student feel better. (If a student uses a word incorrectly, do let him know and help him find a word that better suits his purposes.) What it does mean is focusing your responses to student writing. When we are working on transitions between sentences, don't worry too much about if all the commas are in the right place. Rather, focus on how well the student is linking ideas.

If a student is freed from some of the restrictions of correctness, he may be more willing to experiment with new ideas and different styles of writing.

PROVIDE AN AUDIENCE FOR STUDENT WRITING

People write for an audience. It's just that simple. Newspaper columnists, novelists, literary scholars, bloggers, and scientists all write for someone else. You will likely be the primary audience for your students' writing. But the audience of a teacher, no matter how important, does not always provide a very realistic audience. Most people write for a variety of different readers, readers who do not know exactly what the writer has been learning or understand what the writer "meant" to say, even if she didn't really convey that particular meaning. In other words, most people write to an audience that is not a teacher.

Whenever possible, get students to read or send their writing to a different audience. This could mean e-mailing their writing to a grandparent, reading it to a sibling, or even blogging about it. Being able to receive and process responses from different people is a vital part of learning to be an effective writer. You may even want to include an "audience" component in each exercise requiring students to share their CWJ entry with at least one person other than you.

Ask students how they feel about sharing their writing with others. Perhaps they've never showed their writing to anyone but a teacher. If they are nervous about the audience reaction, they may want to start with someone they know will be kind in their response – a grandparent or good friend. As they become more confident in their writing, challenge them to share their writing with someone who might disagree with them. There's nothing like a skeptical reader to help writers fine-tune their message.

WHAT WRITERS WILL NEED FOR THIS LESSON:

▶ Your writer's journal
▶ Dictionary
▶ Thesaurus
▶ A favorite book or magazine
▶ A highlighter

CAPSULE 1

2.1.1

EFFECTIVE PARAGRAPHING

Take a quick look at your bedroom. How would you describe its appearance? Is it organized, with the bed neatly made, clothes put away, and everything in its proper place? Or are things a little unruly, with the bed covered in wrinkled laundry and the floor hidden beneath a layer of who knows what?

You probably have a messy room at least some of the time. In fact, that may be what is most comfortable for you. But when you invite friends over, you probably try to make your room a bit more orderly. (After all, your friends may prefer being able to walk around without tripping over piles of smelly socks.)

Sometimes writing can be messy too. It's okay to have "messy" writing when you are thinking of ideas. In fact, it's beneficial for writers to write down all their ideas at first without judging or ordering them. Then, writers work to organize their thoughts so that their readers won't get "tripped up." This is where the paragraph comes into play. Paragraphs help writers and readers stay on track.

Do you remember the three qualities of a successful paragraph we learned about in 1.3.1-5? Successful paragraphs . . .
1. are unified,
2. include relevant and interesting details, and
3. are well-organized.

In this lesson, we will be looking more closely at these qualities so that you can learn to identify and write effective paragraphs.

WORLD WISDOM

 Victoria Drake is an editor for *God's World News* magazines. Professional writers like Mrs. Drake work hard to communicate their ideas clearly to an audience in the form of the written word. After all, it's their job! Here's what Mrs. Drake has to say about the qualities of an effective paragraph.

"Rare is the opportunity when I write about—or even use—paragraphs in my job. You see, I write for God's World News' very youngest readers: Pre-K to second graders. They are still working on sentences! And sentences are important: When sentences work together, they have the potential for creating strong paragraphs.

Let me show you what I mean. I used to spend at least a week each summer at my grandmother's home. So I thought I'd write a paragraph telling you what sort of lady she was.

My dad's mom—Grandma Anderson—was a study in contrasts: crockery and china. Crockery—the earthy stuff. Tough, hard-working, plain, salt of the earth. China—delicate, lovely, refined. Her 'crockery' self rose early in the morning. She put on a plain, baggy housedress. She was all business. When I was really young, she cooked on a coal-burning range. She had to get up early to stoke the fire so she could cook breakfast. It was hearty: oatmeal, eggs and bacon, or pancakes. That fueled her for her morning. Dishes were done. Laundry was washed and hung out to dry. Rugs were pounded and furniture was dusted. The vegetable garden was weeded. 'Dinner,' the main meal of the day, was prepared. Again, dishes were washed. Then the kitchen floor was scrubbed. Now began her 'china' part of the day. She usually took a bath and put on a clean housedress. Then we would lie down together to take a nap. I was restless. She could 'power nap.' And after that, her 'china' self would emerge. She would sit at her vanity and out would come face powder, rouge, and lipstick—things my mother never used. I was fascinated! Grandma then put on a pretty dress, earrings, and a necklace. It was time for us to go to town. We would grocery shop, visit Woolworth's—a child's delight, or browse J.C. Penney's. Then it was the Uptown Café for a butterscotch sundae. And on we went home. Out would come the china teacups and the green tea. Time for afternoon 'coffee' with friends or neighbors. Her china self ended most days in gracious hospitality.

I think you can see that this paragraph is unified around the contrasting characteristics of crockery and china and how they depict qualities my grandmother displayed. I included details about her day to support those qualities. And I organized those details in chronological order because that's what my grandmother did six days each week. On Sunday, the Lord's Day, she was all china!"

—Victoria Drake

THE PROFESSOR'S OFFICE

On a scale of 1 to 10 how much thought do you give to paragraphing when you write? If you are like most people, you probably placed your rating around a -10. Getting your words down on paper seems much more important than inserting small indentations into your writing every few lines. But there's more to paragraphing than just pushing the tab button on the computer.

I once had a student who paid very little attention to paragraphs when he wrote. He would write for three typed pages without even one paragraph break. He was a bright student with a sophisticated vocabulary; he simply did not believe he needed to organize his thoughts into paragraphs. On the day we split up into

Make sure to point out how these two examples of student writers provide extremes. One writes with no use of paragraphs, while the other overuses paragraphs. We want students to [1] understand the concept of a paragraph and [2] use paragraphs wisely and logically.

small groups so the students could read and comment on each other's papers, he felt confident that his group members would **extol** his research and writing abilities. But when the time came for the group to discuss this young man's paper, all he received were blank stares. Finally one of his fellow students mustered up the courage to say, "I'm sorry. I just have no idea what your paper was about." Not one of his classmates was able to finish reading his paper!

Not all students avoid paragraphs like this young man. I had another student who was a gifted writer with exceptional ideas. However, she changed paragraphs so frequently that reading her writing was like riding in a bumper car. The paper was continually starting and stopping, starting and stopping. Just about the time the student introduced a provocative idea, she dropped it and moved on to something else. When I spoke with the student about her short, choppy paragraphs, she admitted that every time she stopped to think about what she wanted to write next she began a new paragraph. What a frustrating experience she created for her readers!

The lesson we learn from each of these writers is that it doesn't matter how important your ideas are if your reader can't follow them. The choice to start a paragraph should be deliberate and purposeful. Readers need paragraphs just as much as writers do.

CWJ

If your student has past writings, take a look at these to answer this first question about using paragraphs.. For a student who does not have past writings, consider looking at the materials the student reads and adjust the questions to evaluate the writer's paragraphing.

In your journal, jot down your thoughts on using paragraphs. First think about yourself as a writer. Do you use paragraphs when you write? Why or why not?

◄ IN YOUR JOURNAL

Now think about yourself as a reader. How do paragraphs help you as a reader?

Grab one of your favorite books or an article you've recently read in a magazine. Select a paragraph you found interesting and copy it into your journal.

Reread the paragraph. Try to identify a few of the things that make the paragraph interesting to you as a reader. (You may want to read the paragraph aloud and consider what aspects of the paragraph—words, sentences, ideas—stick out to you.)

What did you learn about paragraphs from our World Wisdom writer, Victoria Drake, that you may be able to apply to your own writing?

ACHIEVING UNITY IN A PARAGRAPH

Unity is the first characteristic of a successful paragraph. But how does a paragraph achieve unity?

To answer this question, let's think about what unifies members of a group. As a fan of a sports team, you are unified with the rest of that team's fans by the belief that your team is the best. As a citizen of the United States, you are unified with other American citizens by the belief that all people are entitled to "life, liberty, and the pursuit of happiness" (*Declaration of Independence*). As a Christian, you are unified with other followers of Christ by the belief that Jesus is "the way and the truth and the life" and "no one comes to the Father except through [him]" (John 14:6).

So, members of a group are unified by a central belief, or idea. We can think about paragraphs in a similar way. In order for a paragraph to be successful, its sentences must be unified by a central idea.

But how do writers clearly express that central idea to readers? In 2.1.2, we will focus on the topic sentence as the main tool writers use to establish the central, or controlling, idea of a paragraph and maintain its focus. The topic sentence is usually located near the beginning of the paragraph. Less often the topic sentence is located at the end of the paragraph. You just have to be on the lookout to find it.

Read this paragraph.

> It was a hot summer. Forget frying an egg on the sidewalk; I think even a chicken may have been in trouble. I sometimes imagined tripping over a crispy-fried bird in the street, which would have been a fortunate occurrence since it was too hot to turn on the oven anyway. Dogs panted, soda cans perspired, and babies whined under the sun's scorching rays. People melted like snowmen wherever they stood. By August, even the thermometers had gone on strike and refused to display the temperature. Like everything else in town, they had simply turned red.

After reading this paragraph, what would you select as the topic sentence? Think about which sentence best expresses the paragraph's controlling idea. Yes, the first sentence is the clear winner. Every other sentence in the paragraph offers specific details—such as dogs panting, soda cans perspiring, and people melting—to show that it was, indeed, a hot summer.

Have you ever experienced a hot summer? Was it anything like the one described in this paragraph? If you live in a very hot region like Texas or Arizona, you may identify with the extreme heat the writer describes. When I read this paragraph, it seems to me that the summer the writer describes was more than a hot summer; this was an unusually hot summer—a rare scorcher.

We've seen instructors teach the idea of "unity" through examples of teams. A baseball team has nine players on the field; each player performs a different role, but each role is essential to the team working well. It takes unity of purpose and action for the baseball team to play as a team.

Paragraphs are like teams. Every paragraph needs a topic sentence. The other sentences perform their own roles, but those roles fall in line with the purpose created by the topic sentence.

Throughout each lesson, we will ask students questions to help them engage with the material we are discussing. This technique will be most effective if students are encouraged to take a moment to stop and answer the question before reading on. Jotting down their answer in the margin or their CWJ are good options. Since these answers are not going to be evaluated, such opportunities encourage students to make guesses without fear of getting it wrong.

As you talk through this lesson with your student, take a moment and discuss other possible topic sentences to replace, "It was a hot summer." By practicing this exercise verbally, you will help your student to begin thinking creatively before he begins writing. Especially for a student who discusses with ease but freezes up when given a pencil, this type of verbal practice can help ease the writing process.

This is a key lesson. Students must learn to compose specific topic sentences that create purpose or direction for a paragraph. If students learn this lesson, they will have increased their odds for learning how to compose strong, logical paragraphs.

Surprisingly, many students never learn this lesson or they overlook it.

This leads us to the problem: While the topic sentence is accurate, it isn't as interesting or revealing as the humorous details in the rest of the paragraph. This makes me wonder if the topic sentence could be more effective.

You see, writers spend a lot of time composing topic sentences that will keep readers interested from paragraph to paragraph. Let's brainstorm some new topic sentences that communicate the same idea that the summer was hot, but do it in a more interesting way.

Original Topic Sentence:
It was a hot summer.

Improved Topic Sentences:
1. Use descriptive words like adjectives and adverbs

It was an oppressively hot summer.

The word "oppressively" is an adverb that describes the summer heat. When I read this word, I understand that the summer was so hot that people could barely go outside.

2. Employ a simile (comparison using like or as) or metaphor (comparison that says one thing is another thing)

That summer our town felt like a pot of water about to boil.
That summer our town was a sauna.

The simile "like a pot of water about to boil" creates a picture for me. I would never put my hand into a pot of water that was that hot; it would hurt! Because of the simile, I understand how uncomfortable this summer must have been for the writer. The metaphor "our town was a sauna" creates a similar image. I can only sit in a sauna for a short time—30 minutes at most. After that time, I get really sweaty, uncomfortable, and thirsty. Again, the writer shows me how he felt during this summer.

3. Make the claim more specific

I remember that summer as the hottest three months of my life.

This specific claim tells me in a straightforward, plainspoken manner that this summer was the hottest the writer ever experienced. I get the writer's point without confusion.

See how easily the topic sentence was tweaked to be just slightly more intriguing. With one of these sentences at the beginning of the paragraph, the reader is more likely to understand the central idea of the paragraph and read on.

IN YOUR JOURNAL ▶

CWJ

Now it's your turn. Read this passage:

Setting up the nineteenth-century circus was difficult work. Before dawn, people waited for the circus train to roll into town so they could witness the creation of a portable city. Then, hundreds of circus laborers piled off the train to raise the "big top" and dozens of other tents that housed the **menagerie** and sideshow acts. Elephants even helped with the back-breaking work. Surprisingly, the grueling set-up was complete before breakfast! Finally, after a long day of performances, workers packed everything up in time for the train to crawl out of town late that night. In a few hours the train would reach its next stop, and the traveling city would rise again.

1. Find and write down the topic sentence.

2. Try rewriting the topic sentence to make it more intriguing to readers using each of the techniques from the sample exercise. You should have three new topic sentences when you are done.

3. Pick your favorite topic sentence. Why do you like this one the best?

THE RIGHT WORD

 Remember to pay attention to the words in bold and define them in your journal. If you come across other unfamiliar words, be sure to look them up too.

CAPSULE 3   2.1.3

CREATING THE TOPIC SENTENCE

 The smell of buttery popcorn permeates the air. As the lights dim, you settle into your chair in anticipation of watching "When Robot Writers Attack!" You have waited months for this movie, and it is about to start. But wait, what's this? It's not your movie at all, but a two-minute preview for a different movie titled "Crocodile Tears." Your momentary frustration soon subsides as you are drawn into the trailer's message. You find yourself laughing to the point of tears. Suddenly, you are wishing you could watch "Crocodile Tears"— right now! By the time the trailer is over you are convinced that you HAVE to see this movie. When you see the date for the movie's release, you can't help but sigh in frustration—you'll have to wait five months. That's just not soon enough!

If you've already begun a discussion of the capsule's topic sentence, you can ease into this CWJ. Read the paragraph together, then talk through possible topic sentences before your student begins writing. Especially for a reluctant writer, beginning with discussion is helpful.

Take a moment to discuss movie trailers. What elements make a good one? Which of these elements could be carried over to make a good topic sentence? (suspense, humor, interesting details, leaving the reader wanting more, etc.)

If you've had an experience like this, the movie's trailer did its job well. Trailers are meant to create excitement and anticipation about a movie. Trailers give viewers an idea of what they can expect.

But what happens when the movie doesn't deliver? We've probably all experienced the disappointment of a movie not living up to its trailer. Based on the two-minute trailer, "Crocodile Tears" looked like the most hilarious movie ever filmed. However, when you sat in the theater for a full 180 minutes, there was nothing at all funny about "Crocodile Tears." Perhaps it wasn't a bad movie, but it was so far from what you expected based on the trailer, you couldn't help but feel dissatisfied.

A paragraph's topic sentence functions a lot like a movie trailer. Like a trailer, a topic sentence should (1) create reader interest and (2) tell readers what to expect. Then it is up to the paragraph to fulfill that expectation. Writers carefully select details that will develop and explain the controlling idea expressed in the topic sentence. If the topic sentence says to a reader, "Just wait, this is what you are about to see," the paragraph should say, "Here it is."

As we learned in 1.3.2, successful paragraphs should include specific, relevant details. But how do you, as a writer, know what details to include? Put simply, the details you choose should fulfill the expectations created by the topic sentence. Let's see how well the details in this character description paragraph follow the path set out by the topic sentence.

> Though she had lived all of her fifty-seven years in Rapid Falls, Ms. Crenshaw was a **reticent** woman whom no one really knew. On her baking day, the sweet scent of bubbling fruit wafted through open windows and doors. When she ventured out of her small house on Bank Street, she wore a brown overcoat and brown shoes with a small hat atop a crown of graying hair. She had pale green eyes the color of the sea; they were her one beautiful feature.

First, we need to determine what expectations are created by the topic sentence. The first sentence suggests that the paragraph will tell us about a quiet woman who is unknown by others in her hometown. As we read on, there are several specific details about Ms. Crenshaw: she likes to bake pies, she wears boring brown clothing, and she has lovely green eyes. But, as descriptive as these details are, do they tell us specifically about her reserved personality? Do they explain why no one in her hometown knows Ms. Crenshaw? No, not really. The paragraph doesn't accomplish what it sets out to achieve. The topic sentence suggests the paragraph will tell one story, but the paragraph tells a different one.

Here is a revised version of the paragraph that more closely follows the path set out by the topic sentence.

> Though she had lived all of her fifty-seven years in Rapid Falls, Ms. Crenshaw was a reticent woman whom no one really knew. Her baking day teased the neighbors who smelled the sweet scent of bubbling fruit wafting through open windows and doors knowing they would never sample a slice. When she ventured out of her small house on Bank Street, an occasion that took place without fail every second Tuesday, she wore a brown overcoat and brown shoes with a small hat atop a crown of graying hair. Her clothes seemed designed to make her invisible to

others, and they did their job well. No one ever noticed her anymore. She had pale green eyes the color of the sea, but since they were continually glued to the pavement, her one beautiful feature remained unknown.

How does this paragraph improve upon the previous one? Well, the most notable difference is that the details are explained and connected to the topic sentence. For instance, in this paragraph Ms. Crenshaw still bakes pies, but we have the additional information that she never shares them with neighbors. We find that she leaves her house very rarely, and her clothing was meant to make her invisible to others. Finally, the mention of her eye color, which seemed totally out of place in the first paragraph, shows that no one knows her well enough to appreciate her most beautiful feature.

When you select and explain details in a way that supports your topic sentence, as the second paragraph does, you create a more satisfying experience for readers.

CWJ

IN YOUR JOURNAL ▶

For this journal entry, you will work on your own character description.

1. Select the subject of your description. You may pick someone you know well or invent someone.

2. Make a list of descriptive details about this person. You may want to include:
▶ Physical characteristics (eyes, hair, age, facial expressions)
▶ Occupation and hobbies
▶ Disposition (grumpy, sociable)
▶ Typical way of dressing
▶ Quotes or typical sayings
▶ Description of home or hometown

3. Write a topic sentence that communicates a specific idea about this person.

4. Go back through your list and highlight three to four details that you think can best help you explain or support your topic sentence.

5. Make a new list with the three to four details you selected. Rewrite them so that they provide specific support for the point you have made in your topic sentence.

THE PROFESSOR'S OFFICE

There's no exact rule for how long paragraphs should be. There are times when long paragraphs are appropriate, for instance in research writing. However, paragraphs that are longer than one typed page probably need to be broken up for the sake of readers. There are also some

Question #4 challenges students to think about idea development: they are learning how to build ideas around a topic sentence. At the same time, they are learning to organize those ideas. Right now, that organization is limited to listing. Soon, they will build the organization through logical transitions.

The challenge is to avoid over-simplistic and legalistic rules for idea development and organization. Sometimes teachers tell students a good paragraph has four supporting points. What's important in that rule is the idea of supporting points: every paragraph has supporting points. However, many students latch onto the number four. As a result, they become paralyzed as writers when they cannot find four points or discover seven points.

Teaching concepts and how to use those concepts is essential to developing thoughtful writers capable of making meaning in any context. Quantitative rules like the one mentioned above sometimes cause more damage in the life of a writer.

types of writing where short paragraphs—even as short as one sentence—are appropriate. This is particularly true in journalistic styles like newspaper writing. As a writer, you have to match your paragraph length to the expectations of the genre in which you are writing.

For most of the writing we will be doing, paragraphs should be around four to seven sentences. This is just a general guideline, NOT a rule. The only real rule for paragraph length is that a paragraph should be as long as it needs to be to get the job done. The more you write, the more natural paragraphing will become for you. Until then, you may want to practice starting a new paragraph:
▶ *when there is a change in time or place*
▶ *when there is a new speaker (dialogue)*
▶ *when you begin discussing a new idea*
▶ *for dramatic effect*
▶ *to introduce a contrasting point*

CAPSULE 4

2.1.4

SENTENCES MUST "TALK" TO EACH OTHER IN PARAGRAPHS

 Have you ever listened to a baby talk? Did you understand it? Probably not. Baby talk is usually made up of unintelligible babblings that sound like nonsense to everyone else. That's because babies are experimenting with sounds and language. They don't understand how to use words in a way that makes sense to others.

But this is precisely the job of writers: to use words in a way that makes sense to others. When we write, we don't want to **ramble** aimlessly. We want to order words and sentences in a logical manner so that readers can follow along without having to work too hard. If writing is too difficult to follow, readers may misunderstand the message—or just give up!

This is why in order for a paragraph to be successful it must be well-organized. In 1.3.4 we learned some strategies for creating organization within paragraphs. For example, transition words help readers understand the connections between sentences and ideas. And organizing a paragraph as a chronological story or a series of steps provides a solid foundation for the rest of the details.

Part of creating a well-organized paragraph is making sure that all the sentences "talk" to one another. Each sentence in a paragraph should be a response to the one before it and lead into the one after it.

Let's read the following paragraph for more clues about creating well-ordered paragraphs.

For his schoolmates, home was the place they returned to after a semester of world history and lacrosse, but *for Samuel home was the place he returned to* when he opened the pages of a favorite book. *Home was* a makeshift raft on the Mississippi River. *Home was* a frigid dogsled in the Klondike during the gold rush. *Home was* a balmy Indian jungle where wolves raised boys. *Home was* not found among *walls and windows and stairs*, but *leather and paper and ink*. For as long as he could remember, home had traveled with him wherever he went.

As you read the paragraph, you probably noticed certain words and phrases being repeated. The italicized words all represent a form of repetition known as parallel structure. You create parallel structures in your writing when you use similar patterns of words or grammatical structures to express ideas of equal importance. Parallel structures can be found within sentences or among two or more consecutive sentences. This may sound complicated, but it's actually pretty simple once you get the hang of it. And it's very effective.

Using parallel structures is an effective organizational technique for a few reasons. First, it helps readers understand the connection between ideas. For example, in the first sentence the writer uses a parallel structure to show how Samuel's concept of home is different from his schoolmates' since it is not connected to a physical place like a house. The use of similar, or parallel, phrasing in both parts of the sentence provides a connection between two different concepts of home.

In addition, the use of parallel structures in writing helps emphasize an important point. In the second through fourth sentences the writer is trying to explain how books are a home for Samuel. The writer incorporates **allusions** to three well-known books: "a makeshift raft on the Mississippi River" refers to Mark Twain's *Huckleberry Finn*, "a frigid dogsled in the Klondike during the gold rush" refers to Jack London's *White Fang*, and "a balmy Indian jungle where wolves raised boys" refers to Rudyard Kipling's *The Jungle Book*. By using the parallel structure of "Home was" at the beginning of each sentence, the writer shows that each book is as important as the other. Home is not found in a specific setting of a specific book, but in whatever setting Samuel encounters when he escapes into a writer's imagination.

Finally, incorporating parallel structures adds rhythm and balance to writing, enhancing its flow. The fifth sentence is a good example of this. Here the writer balances three nouns (walls, windows, stairs) that make up a typical home with three nouns (leather, paper, ink) that make up Samuel's idea of home—a book. Even the unusual repetition of the conjunction "and" adds emphasis and a stronger sense of balance to the sentence.

CWJ

IN YOUR JOURNAL ▶

For your journal entry today, let's practice writing a paragraph with parallel structures.

1. First, think of an idea or concept that interests you. Try picking something general such as school, music, sports, writing, cooking, traveling, art, or home. You will use this concept as the topic of your paragraph, just as home was the topic of the sample paragraph.

Because parallel structures add rhythm to writing, they also make it sound more pleasing to the ear. This is one reason speech writers often utilize parallel construction. Repeating important words and phrases keeps people's attention and makes it easier for listeners to remember what they have heard.

For excellent examples of this technique, have students read excerpts from Abraham Lincoln's "House Divided" speech (1858) or Martin Luther King's "I Have a Dream" speech (1963).

Though parallelism isn't a particularly difficult concept, it is often ignored by writing curricula. We've chosen to include this concept early in *Write with WORLD* because understanding and utilizing parallel structures can make a great deal of difference in your student's style. If your student begins to grasp the concept early on that the way words sound together matters, he is more likely to see the value of choosing them carefully—and, we hope—will come to love the way a well-written sentence sounds. We want students to learn to craft sentences, and parallelism is an important tool.

2. Now spend some time brainstorming about this concept.

List five to six words, images, or details that come into your mind when you think about the word you have chosen. For instance, if I chose "writing" as my word, I might list:

▶ creative task
▶ pencil scribbling down ideas
▶ giving life to characters

3. List five to six images or details that might come into other people's minds when they think about your chosen word. For this I might list:

▶ boring chore
▶ red pen slicing through words
▶ grammar rules

4. Using the sample paragraph as a model, create your own paragraph using parallel structures. Refer to your brainstorming list to help you fill in the sentences. (I used a thesaurus to improve some of the words I came up with as I was brainstorming.)

For example, if I were going to create a paragraph about writing, it might begin like this:

> *For my friends writing is* a tiresome chore, but *for me writing is* a creative enterprise. Writing is giving life to the characters that populate my mind. *Writing is…*

After you've finished your paragraph, read it aloud. Do you like the way it sounds? Explain why or why not.

CAPSULE 5

2.1.5

PARALLEL SENTENCES

STYLE TIME

i Parallel structures help writers create well-organized, coherent paragraphs. Parallel structures also help writers create clear, well-ordered sentences by avoiding confusing grammatical shifts. In order to create parallel structures in your sentences, simply make sure that when you begin a pattern in a sentence, you follow it through to the end. Consistency is the key. Here are some examples of how to fix non-parallel sentences:

Non-parallel:

My aunt enjoys knitting scarves, baking cakes, and roller coasters.

> knitting scarves = gerund (-ing) phrase
>
> baking cakes = gerund (-ing) phrase
>
> roller coasters = noun

Parallel:

> My aunt enjoys knitting scarves, baking cakes, and riding roller coasters.

Non-parallel:

A gymnast needs coordination, strength, and to balance well.

> coordination = noun
>
> strength = noun
>
> to balance well = infinitive phrase (to + verb)

Parallel:

A gymnast needs coordination, strength, and balance.

Non-parallel:

Michael threw a baseball and the vase was broken.

> Michael threw = active voice
>
> the vase was broken = passive voice

Parallel:

Michael threw a baseball and broke the vase.

Non-parallel:

It is true that giving is better than to receive.

> giving = gerund
>
> to receive = infinitive phrase

Parallel:

It is true that to give is better than to receive.

It is true that giving is better than receiving.

You don't have to know the names of the parts of speech to do this. Creating parallel structures is easy if you just focus on keeping your patterns consistent through the entire sentence, particularly when you use coordinating conjunctions such as "and" or "or."

But striving for parallelism in your sentences is not just about correctness. It's also a matter of style. As we learned in the last capsule, when used in the right way, parallel structures promote the flow within and among your sentences. When parallel structures are out of balance, the effect can be jarring, and just plain confusing, for readers. The sentence

I love scaling mountains and the sunrise

suggests that the writer likes to climb two things: mountains and the sunrise. But when the sentence is parallel, the writer's actual meaning is clear:

I love scaling mountains and watching the sunrise.

CWJ

REVISE: Look through the following passage and find sentences that have an asterisk at the end. These sentences have flawed parallel structures. Rewrite them in order to make them parallel.

You may believe in the old adage that dogs are man's best friend, but from my perspective, the opposite is actually closer to the truth. Where would dogs live if people didn't provide them shelter? What would dogs eat if people didn't shop the dog food aisle every other Saturday? What would dogs do for fun if people didn't entertain them with squeaky toys and slimy tennis balls? Without people, dogs wouldn't be wearing sweaters on chilly days or have names like Fido and Lady.* In the friendship between dogs and people, it seems to me that dogs get the most out of the deal.

Last summer I did a small experiment to test my hypothesis and spent two weeks cataloguing all the ways I took care of my dog. Every day I lavished attention on him by petting him, feeding him, and I played with him too.* As often as I was reminded to, I filled his water bowl to stop him from whining and cleaned up the "stuff" he left for me in the backyard. More than once, I took him on a walk and he was given a bath.* Given the evidence I collected, at the end of the two weeks, I was pretty sure I was my dog's best friend.

I understand there is a very strong counter opinion that people are the ones who benefit the most from having dogs as pets. This argument suggests that dogs are loyal companions who guard our homes from dangerous individuals (like mail carriers). Dogs also cut down on the time we spend vacuuming by disposing of food dropped or purposefully discarded under the table at mealtimes. And no one can deny that dogs provide their owners with exciting stories to share. Remember the time your cherished pet devoured an entire bowl of Halloween candy so you could rush to the doggie emergency room at 4:00 a.m. to get his stomach pumped?

Have students read each sentence aloud once or twice to help them hear the faulty parallelism. Though there are correct and incorrect ways to rewrite these sentences, there is more than one correct answer.

To help students understand this, have them rewrite one of the sentences in a couple of different ways. Then, have students pick which sentence they prefer and explain why. The goal is to understand that grammar is as much about stylistic choices as it is about correctness.

Possible corrections:
"dogs wouldn't **wear** sweaters/have names"
"petting him, feeding him, and **playing** with him"
"and **grins** at you"

◀ IN YOUR JOURNAL

It's starting to sink in, isn't it?

Dog isn't man's best friend, but honestly, it doesn't really matter. You will still love him when he chews off the corner of the coffee table. You will still love him when you waste fifteen minutes picking white dog hair off the black shirt you just put on. And you will still love him when he takes off after a squirrel, runs five blocks before slowing down, and is grinning at you because that was the best part of his day.* I know because I still love my dog. After all, I'm his best friend, and that's what best friends are supposed to do.

THE RIGHT WORD

By today, you should have defined all the words for this lesson. Now it's time to look the words up in your thesaurus. Remember, your goal is to find the best word to replace the bold word in the sentence—the word with the most similar meaning. You may need to use your dictionary to help figure out what some of the synonyms mean.

▶ On the day we split up into small groups so the students could read and comment on each other's papers, he felt confident that his group members would **extol** his research and writing abilities.
▶ Then, hundreds of circus laborers piled off the train to raise the "big top" and dozens of other tents that housed the **menagerie** and sideshow acts.
▶ Though she had lived all of her fifty-seven years in Rapid Falls, Ms. Crenshaw was a **reticent** woman whom no one really knew.
▶ When we write, we don't want to **ramble** aimlessly.
▶ The writer incorporates **allusions** to three well-known books, Mark Twain's *Huckleberry Finn*, Jack London's *White Fang*, and Rudyard Kipling's *The Jungle Book*.

Write with WORLD

DEVELOPING WRITERS: BUILDING BLOCKS AND BIOGRAPHY

COMPOSING AND LINKING SENTENCES

CAPSULE 1

2.2.1

STARTING TO THINK ABOUT SENTENCES

 Have you ever attended the symphony? It can be a breathtaking experience. Even if you have never had a piano lesson, the swelling of the orchestra at the end of a movement is likely to produce chills.

If you do play a musical instrument, you can appreciate the intricacy of the compositions performed by a symphony on a different level. As you listen, you hear notes joining together to form chords and chords to form phrases. Your experience as a musician helps you identify melody, harmony, tone, rhythm, and texture within the music.

Both people who play instruments and those who don't may be able to enjoy great music when they hear it. But those who play an instrument can tell you more accurately why the music is great.

It's the same with writing. Anyone may be able to pick up a well-written book and enjoy it. But people who are trained writers can identify why the writing is exceptional. That's because they have technical knowledge of the craft of writing; they understand how words, phrases, and clauses work together to form sentences and sentences to form paragraphs.

And that's our goal here: to help you learn the craft of writing so you can identify what constitutes great writing—and so you can create great writing yourself.

You'll be glad to know, we do not think knowledge about writing should be based on learning lots of **abstract** terms and rules. Though we will introduce you to the terminology of writing, it is not our aim for you to memorize it. Instead, we want you understand how words work together. And it all starts with the sentence.

Do you recall the two basic components of a sentence? You've got it: A subject and a verb. If you have these two components, you can write a basic sentence like this one.

A lizard recites Shakespeare.

While this is our goal, we do not expect every student to be excited by the overall content of the following capsules. Students may see these lessons as "grammar," and most students do not jump for joy when they think about grammar. If your student regularly exclaims, "I love the semicolon!," . . . congrats!

This is a *simple sentence*. It may be a bit odd, but it has a subject (lizard) and a verb (recites) and expresses a complete thought.

In 1.2.2. and 1.2.3, we learned how to make sentences more interesting by adding descriptive words like adjectives and adverbs. We could add an adjective (long-winded) and an adverb (poetically) to this sentence to paint a more detailed picture for our readers.

A long-winded lizard recites Shakespeare poetically.

Similar to adding adverbs and adjectives, incorporating phrases is another strategy that helps make sentences specific and colorful. A *phrase* is a group of words without both a subject and a verb. All the words in a phrase function as a single unit. Bottom line: a phrase gives you extra information about the subject or the verb of the sentence.

For instance, we could add a phrase to the original sentence to tell readers where the lizard does his recitation.

Perched on the roof, a lizard recites Shakespeare.

Notice that there is a verb (perched) in this phrase but no subject. Because it doesn't tell us who or what is perched on the roof, this group of words is a phrase.

We could also add a phrase that tells readers about the lizard's appearance.

Perched on the roof, a lizard in a three-piece suit recites Shakespeare.

Notice there is a noun (suit) in this phrase but no verb. The suit isn't performing an action. So, this group of words is also a phrase.

We could even add a phrase that tells what the conditions are during this performance.

Perched on the roof during a blizzard, a lizard in a three-piece suit recites Shakespeare.

Are you starting to form a picture in your mind? The original sentence, "A lizard recites Shakespeare," may have been difficult to envision. But, with the addition of these phrases, you can't help but imagine a well-dressed lizard reciting Shakespeare in a snowstorm.

Writers use phrases to add interest and information to a basic sentence. Phrases can be found at the beginning, in the middle, or at the end of a sentence. It's usually best to place the phrase closest to the part of the sentence it is offering information about.

Let's look at another example.

We believe these lessons are essential to students developing a sense of style that is clear, graceful, and eloquent. Students need to enjoy these lessons, so do everything you can as a teacher to make sentence work exciting.

Let students compose sentences that are funny. They will be more likely to experiment with these types of sentences, and this experimentation is key to their learning sentence variety and much-needed mechanics.

After midnight on New Year's Eve, near the water's edge, I spied two dozen monkeys, wearing bathing suits and carrying accordions, catapult onto a freighter bound for Antarctica in order to deliver twelve-thousand popsicles.

You may have to catch your breath after reading that one! I'm sure you have figured out the point of this example. When you write you must exercise selectivity. Include phrases that add to your sentence, but be careful not to detract from your ideas with **extraneous** information.

This time, instead of building our sentence with phrases, we are going to remove phrases to make the sentence informative, rather than stuffed with information. There's a difference.

Ask yourself, what is the essential information the reader needs to know? What information will help paint a picture for readers without overwhelming them? For instance, do we need to know the monkeys are wearing swimsuits and carrying accordions, and they will be delivering popsicles? Probably not. What other phrases would you remove?

There are several ways to rewrite this sentence, but I would revise it this way:

> On New Year's Eve, I spied two dozen monkeys catapult onto a freighter bound for Antarctica.

Now that you've examined some simple sentences that incorporate phrases, do you think you can write your own? We think you can.

CWJ

PART A
Here is a simple sentence: The lion tamer stumbled. (subject) (verb)

Add one to two phrases to this sentence. Highlight the phrase(s). To come up with your phrase(s), you may want to consider how, when, or where the lion tamer stumbled.

PART B
Refer back to the character description you brainstormed in 2.1.3. Read through the details and topic sentence you wrote about your chosen subject.

Write a simple sentence about your character. You can incorporate adjectives or adverbs, but don't include a phrase yet.

Now add one to two phrases to that sentence. Highlight the phrase(s). Remember, a phrase is a group of words that offers additional information about the subject or the verb of the sentence.

◀ IN YOUR JOURNAL

In several of the CWJ prompts, we give students examples of how we might complete the task they have been given. Whenever possible, do these exercises alongside your students. Instead of telling them to run six laps, run with them!

If I were doing this exercise, my sentence might look like this:

My grandfather crafted custom cowboy boots out of rough cowhide. (subject) (verb) (adjective)

CAPSULE 2 2.2.2

COMPOSING COMPOUND SENTENCES

Remember our simple sentence from the last capsule?

On New Year's Eve, I spied two dozen monkeys catapult onto a freighter headed for Antarctica.

Let's turn this simple sentence into a compound sentence. A *compound sentence* is just two or more simple sentences joined by a comma and a coordinating conjunction or a semi-colon.

In order to do this, we need to write another simple sentence that is related to our original sentence. Then, we need to link them. How does this sentence sound?

I hurled myself aboard as well.

Now we just have to decide how to join the two sentences. A *coordinating conjunction* is a linking word that connects ideas of equal importance. Each coordinating conjunction expresses a different relationship. Which conjunction best expresses the connection between our sentences?

Coordinating Conjunctions	Function
for	means *because*
and	offers additional information
nor	tells what something is not
but	offers a contrast
or	offers a choice
yet	offers a stronger contrast than but
so	means *as a result, therefore*

Well, let's try some that look promising. "And" is the most frequently used conjunction so it will probably work.

On New Year's Eve, I spied two dozen monkeys catapult onto a freighter bound for Antarctica, and I hurled myself aboard as well.

Students will often forget they need a comma with the coordinating conjunction. This is a major mistake that often results in a run-on sentence. Two mnemonic devices writers use to remember the comma with a coordinating conjunction are FANBOYS or BAFNOSY (from the first letter of each coordinating conjunction). If your students understand that a comma + a bafnosy (fanboys) can join two sentences, they will compose compound sentences successfully.

In the same vein as the previous teacher comment, note that students who forget the coordinating conjunction also have a major problem on their hands. A comma cannot join two sentences. We call this problem a comma splice. It takes a comma + a fanboys (bafnosy)

That works, but let's see if there are any that offer a more specific connection.

> On New Year's Eve, I spied two dozen monkeys catapult onto a freighter bound for Antarctica, so I hurled myself aboard as well.

Which conjunction – "and" or "so" – works better here? Did you pick "so"? We did too. "So" is a better choice because it shows that the subject of the sentence ("I") jumped aboard *as a result of* seeing the monkeys do so first.

Now you can make a compound sentence, but can you identify if a sentence is compound? Take a look at this one. Is it simple or compound?

> "Happy families are all alike; every unhappy family is unhappy in its own way."

Ask yourself: how many simple sentences, or complete thoughts, are in the sentence?

> Happy families are all alike.
> Every unhappy family is unhappy in its own way.

There are two. That makes this opening line from Leo Tolstoy's *Anna Karenina* a compound sentence. Here, the two simple sentences are joined by a semi-colon instead of a comma and a conjunction. Semi-colons also bond two sentences together.

But how do you know when to use a semi-colon and when to use a comma and coordinating conjunction? Most writers use semi-colons sparingly, reserving them for times when the ideas are very closely related. Conjunctions tell readers the relationship between ideas; semi-colons require readers to figure it out on their own.

Here is one last example. Is this sentence simple or compound?

> "My father was a St. Bernard, my mother was a collie, but I am a Presbyterian."

This humorous opening line from Mark Twain's *A Dog's Tale* is a compound sentence. Remember, to be compound, a sentence must join *at least* two simple sentences. This sentence joins three.

> My father was a St. Bernard.
> My mother was a collie.
> I am a Presbyterian.

Simple sentences can be very effective. Skilled writers use *both* simple and compound sentences to make their writing vibrant and varied, rather than **homogeneous**. But that's not all. By linking sentences, writers tell readers more about the relationship between their ideas.

You'll notice that we have incorporated sentences from well-known books in this capsule. That's because we want to encourage students to begin looking at all the writing they encounter – not just what is included in their textbooks – with an eye to its form and function. As they do so, they will begin reading texts as writers.

As students interact with other written texts – novels, magazines, blogs – challenge them to search for the different types of sentences we are studying in this unit. They may even want to keep a running list of effective simple, compound, complex, and compound-complex sentences they come across in their CWJ. The more familiar they become with identifying these sentence constructions in other people's writing, the more likely they are to begin confidently writing their own.

Read Twain's original sentence. Now read it as three separate sentences. Which one do you prefer? We prefer the original sentence. It tells us that the narrator wants to stress the fact that his identity as a Presbyterian is what distinguishes him from his parents. When the sentences are separate, this relationship is unclear, especially since dog breeds and denominations don't seem related.

So there you have it. If you can write a simple sentence, you can write a compound sentence. All you have to do is link two (or more) simple sentences using (1) a comma and coordinating conjunction or (2) a semi-colon.

CWJ

IN YOUR JOURNAL ▶

Let's continue our work from the last capsule.

PART A

1. Copy your sentence about the lion tamer here.

2. Now write another simple sentence about the lion tamer. (To generate ideas, you may want to consider what could have happened as a result of his stumble.)

3. Link your original sentence with your new sentence using either (1) a comma and a conjunction or (2) a semi-colon.

PART B

1. Copy the sentence you wrote about your character here.

2. Now write another simple sentence about your character. To generate ideas, you may want to look back over the details you brainstormed in 2.1.3.

3. Create a compound sentence by linking your original sentence with your new sentence. Use either (1) a comma and a conjunction or (2) a semi-colon.

If we were doing this exercise, our sentence might look like this:

> My grandfather crafted custom cowboy boots out of rough cowhide, and every pair he created was a masterpiece.

CAPSULE 3

2.2.3

CRAFTING COMPLEX SENTENCES

By now we have introduced you to two kinds of sentences: simple and compound. You'll remember that simple sentences have a subject and a verb and express a complete thought. Compound sentences consist of two simple sentences joined together.

Did you notice anything wrong with that last sentence? Read it again out loud. When you get to the end of the sentence, do you feel like it stops too soon? It feels like we need more information.

Do you remember what it is called when a sentence fails to express a complete thought? Yes, it is a fragment. And there's a specific name for this kind of fragment: a dependent clause.

A dependent clause has both a subject and a verb but doesn't express a complete thought. It is called dependent because it cannot stand on its own; it needs additional information to hold it up.

Here is an example of a dependent clause. Notice it has a subject (I) and a verb (strolled), but it isn't a complete thought.

> While I strolled along the boardwalk

The first word of a dependent clause is called a *subordinating conjunction*. While there are only seven coordinating conjunctions, there are lots of subordinating conjunctions.

Common Subordinating Conjunctions		
after	if	though
although	if only	till
as	in order that	unless
as if	now that	until
as long as	once	when
as though	rather than	whenever
because	since	where
before	so that	whereas
even if	than	wherever
even though	that	while

We can't leave the clause as it is. So, to make this dependent clause into a complete sentence, we need to link it with a complete sentence, also called an independent clause. An independent clause has both a subject and a verb and expresses a complete thought. Let's see how this dependent clause fits with our sentence about catapulting monkeys.

> While I strolled along the boardwalk on New Year's Eve, I spied two dozen monkeys catapult onto a freighter bound for Antarctica.

The sentence we just created is known as a complex sentence. A *complex sentence* consists of a dependent clause and an independent clause joined by a subordinating conjunction.

Okay, that was a mouthful! But you get the idea, right? A group of words that can't stand alone (dependent clause) needs to be joined to a group of words that can (independent clause). What glues the two parts together is a connecting word. As you can see from the example, complex sentences are not necessarily complicated. (Hey, there's another one!)

The best part is, when you add a dependent clause to your sentence, you get a better sentence, one that helps your reader see the precise relationship between your ideas.

Take this sentence, for instance:

> Kate always ordered a peanut butter and pepperoni sandwich with an avocado milkshake unless her friends protested.

First, what is the dependent clause in this sentence? To find the dependent clause be on the lookout for subordinating conjunctions. "Unless her friends protested" is the right pick. Now, consider how the dependent clause in this sentence helps clarify its meaning. If this were written as two simple sentences, it would look like this.

> Kate always ordered a peanut butter and pepperoni sandwich with an avocado milkshake. Her friends protested.

How well does the second version of the sentence communicate the intended meaning? Not that well. In the first version, we could tell that Kate ordered her strange food combinations as long as her friends didn't complain. (I don't really blame them, do you?) When the connector "unless" is absent, the sentence's exact meaning is **ambiguous**. As readers, we don't have any idea what or why her friends are protesting.

Did you also notice the placement of the subordinating conjunction "unless"? It is found in the middle of the sentence rather than at the beginning. Subordinating conjunctions can be found at the beginning or the middle of a sentence. This is because the dependent clause can come before or after an independent clause. As a writer, you get to choose.

Just remember to put a comma between the dependent and independent clauses if the dependent clause comes first. Otherwise, you don't need a comma.
Are you ready to give complex sentences a try?

If your student is stuck, flip back to the chart of Common Subordinating Conjunctions. Go down the list together, taking turns creating dependent clauses that he could use with his sentence.

CWJ

PART A

1. Copy the simple sentence you wrote about the lion tamer in 2.2.1 here.

2. Now create a dependent clause to add to your sentence. Remember that to make a dependent clause you simply write a sentence and then place a subordinating conjunction like "because," "while," or "when" at the beginning. (To generate ideas, consider who or what could have caused the lion tamer to stumble.)

3. Create a complex sentence by linking your simple sentence with your dependent clause. You may want to try the dependent clause before and after the simple sentence to see what sounds best.

PART B

1. Copy the simple sentence you wrote about your character in Capsule 2.2.1 here.

2. Now create a dependent clause to add to your sentence.

3. Create a complex sentence by linking your simple sentence with your dependent clause.

If I were doing this exercise, my sentence might look like this:

> As long as he could keep a steady hand, my grandfather crafted custom cowboy boots out of rough cowhide.

STYLE TIME

 In this lesson, you have learned how to correctly join sentences. However, when writers don't follow these guidelines for linking sentences, they are in danger of writing run-on sentences. A *run-on sentence* is created when two sentences are joined without any words and/or punctuation to connect them.

How would you fix this run-on sentence?

> The farmer glimpsed storm clouds on the horizon he waited expectantly for the downpour.

You could separate it into two sentences.
> The farmer glimpsed storm clouds on the horizon. He waited expectantly for the downpour.

You could add a comma and a coordinating conjunction.

> The farmer glimpsed storm clouds on the horizon, so he waited expectantly for the downpour.

You could also add a subordinating conjunction to the beginning of the sentence and a comma at the end of the dependent clause.

After the farmer glimpsed storm clouds on the horizon, he waited expectantly for the downpour.

By now you have probably figured out the key to correcting run-on sentences. Turn them into one of the three kinds of sentences we have studied – simple, compound, or complex.

Any of these choices are correct, but they all express slightly different meanings and have a different "feel" to them. As a writer, you choose the construction that best suits your personal voice and purpose.

Look back at each of the sentences you wrote in the first three capsules. If the sentence expresses more than one complete thought, check to make sure it is joined correctly. If it's not, take a moment to fix it.

CAPSULE 4   2.2.4

CONSTRUCTING COMPOUND-COMPLEX SENTENCES

At this point, you may be thinking, "I've learned so much technical jargon my head is about to explode!"

It probably seems like we've introduced you to a lot of complicated terms in this lesson—and we have—but the terminology is just to help us talk about sentences. When you write, you don't have to think about whether what you are writing is a complex sentence or a coordinating conjunction.

Instead, we want you to be able to think like this. "Hmmm…what I wrote doesn't sound like a complete thought. I should join it with another sentence to make it complete." In technical terms you just said, "This dependent clause needs to be joined with an independent clause." It's the same idea—and it will work—with or without the terminology.

So, are you ready for another term? We are just linking what you learned in 2.2.2 with what you learned in 2.2.3. That leads us to the compound-complex sentence.

A *compound-complex sentence* consists of two or more independent clauses and one or more dependent clauses. In other words, it is at least two complete thoughts joined with at least one incomplete thought. Don't worry, even if it sounds confusing, this is an easy one.

Consider how we can take our sentence about Antarctica-bound monkeys and make it into a compound-complex sentence. So far we have:

The idea of a compound-complex sentence may seem daunting to students simply because of its name. Reinforce how easy it is to construct these sentences by having students brainstorm a dozen or so simple sentences about anything at all. They don't need to be related – and the more humorous, the better.

Make half of the simple sentences into dependent clauses by adding subordinating conjunctions to the beginning. Have students join the simple sentences and dependent clauses in as many different combinations as they can. Even if the resulting sentences are nonsensical, if they are linked in the ways we discussed throughout the lesson, they will work.

On New Year's Eve, I spied two dozen monkeys catapult onto a freighter bound for Antarctica. (simple sentence/independent clause)

I hurled myself aboard as well. (simple sentence/independent clause)

While I strolled along the boardwalk (dependent clause)

Here we have all the components necessary for a compound-complex sentence. We just have to put them together.

> While I strolled along the boardwalk on New Year's Eve, I spied two dozen monkeys catapult onto a freighter bound for Antarctica, so I hurled myself aboard as well.

When you build a sentence in this way, it is easy to see how the different parts work together to clearly communicate your ideas.

Once you understand the principle of joining dependent and independent clauses, you can link a number of them together. The following sentence incorporates several dependent and independent clauses. Can you identify them all? (Remember that dependent clauses begin with a subordinating conjunction. Refer to the chart in 2.2.3 if you need to.)

> Whereas my sister's more sophisticated palate prefers French cuisine, grilled cheese ranked as my favorite food until I turned twelve, and I discovered sushi.

Dependent Clauses
▶ *Whereas* my sister's more sophisticated palate prefers French cuisine
▶ *Until* I turned twelve

Independent Clauses
▶ Grilled cheese ranked as my favorite food
▶ And I discovered sushi

Nice work. You're getting the hang of it.

Remember the musician who could better appreciate the symphony because he understood how notes, chords, and musical phrases combine to make great music? Well, now you can better appreciate the written word because you understand how words, phrases, and clauses combine to make great writing.

WORLD WISDOM

If you asked a writer where all great writing begins, he might tell you that it starts, not with a word or even a good idea, but with an artfully crafted sentence. You see, writers love words, but words don't accomplish anything on their own. To have meaning beyond their dictionary definition, words need to be skillfully joined together by a writer's pen. Read what Mickey McLean, the Web Executive Editor for WORLDmag.com, thinks about writing vibrant sentences.

"A reporter for WORLD Magazine or WORLDmag.com may write as many as 3,000 words in a major news story. But if the words in the story's first few sentences (called a "lede") are boring or are difficult to read, most people won't read the rest of the article—except maybe the writer's mother! And if no one except Mom reads all 3,000 words, we've wasted a lot of paper and ink or bandwidth. That's why it's important for WORLD reporters and editors to know how to write interesting and informative sentences that paint pictures in the minds of our readers, making them want to go to the trouble of reading every last word.

So how do you, young WORLD reporter, write sentences that are interesting and informative and will make your readers want to read more? Well, you're learning how to do that in these lessons on how to build more complex sentences, adding descriptive clauses to help grab your readers and make them feel like they were right there with you when you reported the story.

Keep working on your writing so that one day you will write sentences that your mother and WORLD readers will love."

—Mickey McLean

CWJ

IN YOUR JOURNAL ▶

PART A

1. Copy the complex sentence you wrote about the lion tamer in 2.2.3 here.

2. Create a compound-complex sentence by linking this complex sentence with the simple sentence you wrote in 2.2.2.

PART B

1. Copy the complex sentence you wrote about your subject in 2.2.3 here.

2. Create a compound-complex sentence by linking this complex sentence with the simple sentence you wrote in 2.2.2.

If I were doing this exercise, my sentence might look like this:

> As long as he could keep a steady hand, my grandfather crafted custom cowboy boots out of rough cowhide, and every pair he created was a masterpiece.

3. Compare the original simple sentences you wrote in 2.2.1 with the compound-complex sentences you have here. Discuss the transformation of your sentences with your parent or teacher. Talk about why you made the choices you did—in wording, use of conjunctions, punctuation, and ideas.

PART C
What do you think makes a good "lede" sentence, like Mickey McLean described?
Look back through the contents of your CWJ. Highlight the favorite sentence you have written so far. In your opinion, what makes it a good sentence?

CAPSULE 5   2.2.5

MORE THOUGHTS ON SENTENCES
THE PROFESSOR'S OFFICE

I often ask students to think about the first time they tried a challenging physical activity like snowboarding, water skiing, skateboarding, or even bike riding. Then I ask them to identify what they remember most about that experience. You may not be surprised to hear that nearly every person has the same answer. They all remember falling down – A LOT!

But you've probably also heard the saying "If you're not falling down, you're not learning." You see, it's commonly understood that when you challenge yourself to learn a new sport, you will make a lot of mistakes.

When beginning writers push themselves to try a new skill, they usually make a lot of mistakes too. But sometimes these mistakes discourage writers instead of encouraging them that they are indeed learning. So, instead of trying a new technique, they stick with what they know they can do.

What do you think would happen if we, as Christians, didn't pursue spiritual growth? We would miss out on a deeper knowledge of who God is. Though the process of growing is sometimes uncomfortable, it is more than worth it in the end. We know from Philippians 1:6 that God will continue the good work he began in us our entire lives! He never wants us to stop growing.

As writers, we can continually grow as well. It can be uncomfortable trying out new skills, but it is rewarding in the end. That's why I encourage students to stop worrying about making mistakes and start writing.

One area where it's easy to "play it safe" is sentence construction. Almost anyone can write a simple sentence, but other kinds of sentences require connecting words and specific punctuation. Simple sentences can be well-written, interesting, and powerful. But when writers stick exclusively with simple sentences, their writing may sound choppy. And, as we have seen, the relationship between their ideas may not be as clear as it could be.

This paragraph from a student's paper should give you an idea of what I mean:

> I am a pickle fanatic. Maybe connoisseur is a more appropriate description. My obsession with pickles is unmistakable. My mom cracks open my door. "Dill pickle omelet, please," I holler. I devour a lunch of pickle and mayonnaise sandwiches. Sometimes I eat two or three. Dip anything in pickle juice. You have created a **delectable** snack. Pickle juice is a perfect complement. Did I mention that fried pickles are amazing? You may not share my enthusiasm for pickles. You might be surprised by how many people do.

There is nothing glaringly wrong with this paragraph. All of the sentences are complete, and it is focused. However, it sounds choppy and a bit disconnected.

This student has definitely played it safe. Every sentence is a simple sentence. If she varied the kinds of sentences she wrote, not only would the paragraph flow better, but the connections between her ideas would be more obvious to her readers. Just by linking several of the sentences and making slight changes in wording, the revised paragraph sounds much better.

> You could say I am a pickle fanatic, but maybe connoisseur is a more appropriate description. My obsession with pickles is unmistakable every morning when my mom cracks open my door, and I holler, "Dill pickle omelet, please!" I devour a lunch of pickle and mayonnaise sandwiches; sometimes I eat two or three in one sitting. Dip anything in pickle juice, and you have created a delectable snack because pickle juice is a perfect complement to every food. Did I mention that fried pickles are amazing? Even though you may not share my enthusiasm for pickles, you might be surprised by how many people do.

Being a good writer involves taking risks. You may get it wrong the first, second, and third times, but eventually you will master the skill.

I remember I could barely stand up the first day I skied, but the next day I could balance, and the third day I could ski a beginners' run without falling on my face every two feet! If I had never pushed past the discomfort of the first day, I would have been sipping hot chocolate in the lodge instead of experiencing the exhilaration of speeding down a mountain on fresh powder.

Writing a well-crafted sentence can be an exhilarating experience too. You'll see.

With your student, compare the two "pickle" paragraphs. What changes did the writer make that improve the second paragraph? Underline or circle the conjunctions she added. Read the two aloud. Can your student hear the difference between the "choppy" paragraph and the one that includes a variety of sentence structures?

Reinforce this lesson by looking at a book by your student's favorite author. Does the author use phrases? Coordinating conjunctions? Subordinating conjunctions? Now take the paragraph and rewrite it using all simple sentences. Is it just as good? Or does it lose meaning and style?

Small exercises like these where students break down and build up sentences can help them understand the inner workings of sentences and paragraphs in a way worksheets never can. Instead of looking for right/wrong answers, they become word architects who know how to put words together to build effective sentences.

CWJ

PART A

1. Go back through the revised sample paragraph in *The Professor's Office* and highlight the changes the writer made. Note what kind of sentence—compound, complex, or compound-complex—the writer created by revising.

2. How and where did the writer incorporate phrases to add interest and information to the paragraph?

PART B

Here is another sample paragraph that uses simple sentences.

1. Rewrite this paragraph, linking sentences to create compound, complex, and/or compound-complex sentences. Incorporate phrases where appropriate to offer additional information to readers. (Don't feel like you have to change all the sentences. Sometimes a simple sentence works great.)

> What had happened to the scrolls remained a mystery. The burden of recovering them rested on Abel's fourteen-year-old shoulders. His great-great-grandfather had hidden the scrolls. Now the tribe needed them. A century had passed. Knowledge of the scrolls' whereabouts had long been forgotten. Some doubted their existence. A tattered note held a single clue. No one living could decipher its meaning. Abel Alexander's determination was unwavering. He had to restore his family's legacy. It was a matter of honor.

2. Highlight the changes you make. Note what kind of sentences you created by revising.

3. Explain to your parent or teacher why you linked the sentences the way you did and why you chose to add specific phrases. If you left any simple sentences, explain that choice too.

It's important to remember that there are many ways to do this exercise. Very few people will do it the exact same way. Let go of the pressure to "get it right" and be creative!

THE RIGHT WORD

By now you should have defined all of the vocabulary words for this lesson. Now it's time to use your thesaurus to find the best replacement for the word in bold. Make sure you check out the definition of the synonym you choose to make sure it is the best choice. Here are the words in context.

▶ You'll be glad to know, we do not think knowledge about writing should be based on learning lots of **abstract** terms and rules.

▶ Include phrases that add to your sentence, but be careful not to detract from your ideas with **extraneous** information.

Students are rarely asked to explain the stylistic choices they make. Question #3 challenges students to explain why they made the changes they made, why they joined sentences, and why they left certain sentences alone. This can be difficult, so you need to be patient.

As they explain their choices, challenge them with other options and make them consider other choices. As a student learns to regard other choices and argue for the ones they made, they are learning ownership, a responsibility for thinking about the style of their writing.

▶ Skilled writers use both simple and compound sentences to make their writing vibrant and varied, rather than **homogeneous**.

▶ Without the connector "unless," the sentence's exact meaning is **ambiguous**.

▶ Dip anything in pickle juice, and you have created a **delectable** snack because pickle juice is a perfect complement to every food.

Write with WORLD

CAPSULE 1

2.3.1

TOPIC SENTENCES SPARK QUESTIONS

 Do you remember our sentence from the last lesson about an impromptu New Year's Eve trip?

> While I strolled along the boardwalk on New Year's Eve, I spied two dozen monkeys catapult onto a freighter bound for Antarctica, so I hurled myself aboard as well.

Pretend this is the last sentence of a paragraph. A new paragraph is about to begin. What would you expect to happen next? The next paragraph will likely provide clues about what happens once the writer arrives on board.

Now take a look at a possible topic sentence for the next paragraph.

> After alighting on the vessel and surveying my surroundings, I quickly realized that I had made a huge mistake.

In 2.1.2, we studied topic sentences and learned that they have two main jobs: (1) to grab the reader's interest and (2) to introduce the central, or controlling, idea of the paragraph.

Essentially, a topic sentence sets the stage for the rest of the paragraph by creating a question in the reader's mind. Did a question pop into your mind after you read this topic sentence? Perhaps you thought, "Why is it a huge mistake?" A paragraph with proper focus will go on to answer this question.

Whenever you write a topic sentence, it's a good idea to identify what question it will spark for your readers. If you then strive to answer that question in your paragraph, you are well on your way to writing a successful paragraph. But, if you realize this is not the question you want to answer, it's a good time to revise your topic sentence.

What questions do the following topic sentences raise in your mind?

> The leap landed me atop the freighter, offering me a bird's eye view of the strangest sight I have ever seen.

When you read this sentence, you probably wondered, "What was this strange sight?" The paragraph to follow should offer a description of what the writer saw when he arrived on board.

> Though it may sound dangerous to the unskilled, jumping represented the safest and most expedient option for getting aboard.

This sentence may have made you question, "Why was jumping the best option for getting aboard?" Now you need to see proof that jumping was a safe and practical option, especially since the opposite seems true.

The three sample topic sentences we have looked at so far are thought-provoking and clearly written. They establish a specific focus for the paragraph by creating a question in the reader's mind.

We have already discussed adding interest to **lackluster** topic sentences. But what about topic sentences with the opposite problem?

> Even though it cost me dearly, I'm still glad I jumped off that platform, plunging full throttle into the air, defying gravity for a solid five seconds, soaring over shark-infested waters, and finally landing on the deck where a task force of CIA-trained monkeys held a large bunch of ripe bananas and orders to apprehend me.

Wow! That sentence was very lively, incorporating a lot of specific details about the danger of the jump, as well as what awaited the writer on the other side. In fact, it was a little too detailed. The topic sentence should be the most general sentence within a paragraph. It's the job of the supporting sentences—the other sentences in the paragraph—to fill in the details. The following might be a better topic sentence.

> Even though it cost me dearly, I'm still glad I jumped off that platform.

After reading this sentence readers will wonder, "Why is he glad he jumped if it cost him dearly?" Next the writer can provide supporting sentences with colorful details to help answer this question. (This is probably where the shark-infested waters and monkey task force enter the story.)

So there you have it. A topic sentence establishes the focus of the paragraph by prompting readers to ask a question. The job of every other sentence in the paragraph is to help answer that question.

We promised this lesson was coming in 2.1.2. Students must understand the power of the topic sentence. They must master the topic sentence to compose essays that are logical and intriguing.

Mr. Pitt's World Wisdom is a great endorsement of the importance of crafting lively, interesting sentences that keep readers turning the pages. Use this WW as an opening for discussion with your student. Would the sentences Mr. Pitts chose keep her reading? Why or why not? What is one thing she likes about the second sentence? Have her underline all the verbs in the second sentence. What does she notice about these verbs?

WORLD WISDOM

Here *WORLD Magazine* writer Edward Lee Pitts shares with us one of his favorite sentences, and his view on how a well-written sentence focuses the paragraph and drives your reader forward.

" 'Whether I shall turn out to be the hero of my own life, or whether that station will be held by anybody else, these pages must show.' *This opening line from Charles Dickens'* David Copperfield *is one of my favorite sentences. Why? It makes me want to keep reading. All a writer desires as he builds his story, sentence brick by sentence brick, is that captivated readers will keep turning the pages. How can anyone read this sentence without wondering if Copperfield will become the hero?*

I believe the best sentences are the ones yet to be written. Maybe you will be the one to write them! The amazing thing about words is that the combinations are endless. You'd think that with all the writers throughout history that we'd have run out of new sentences by now. But there are still plenty of completely fresh sentences for you to write.

When crafting that next great sentence remember to choose words that show the reader what you are describing. For example, in the Pulitzer Prize winning Western classic The Travels of Jaimie McPheeters, *author Robert Lewis Taylor opens the story with the 14-year-old Jaimie and his friends throwing rocks at a store sign. Read how the shop owner reacts:* 'So toward the end of the afternoon he pranced out with a double-barreled shotgun loaded with pepper and blistered Herbert Swann's seat as he zigzagged to safety through the high grass.'

Clearly, this man is not happy. But Taylor didn't merely tell readers that the shop owner was mad. Instead he showed the reader using memorable details and action like a double-barreled shotgun, blistered, zigzagged and- yes- Herbert Swann's seat.

Books should have more color than black ink and white pages: Words are like different colors on a painter's palette that allow you, the writer, to describe persons and places and events in a way that readers get a clear picture at the end of every sentence. As you paint with words just remember that with each sentence you are trying to get someone to keep reading your story."

—Edward Lee Pitts

CWJ

Pretend each of these sentences is the last sentence in a paragraph. Select three of these sentences and write a topic sentence for the paragraph that is about to begin.

► The sound of the screen door slamming assured me she was gone.
► At that moment, as he grinned like a Cheshire cat, I was certain my little brother existed simply

◄ IN YOUR JOURNAL

to irritate me.

▶ Though the storm intensified and waves crashed upon them without respite, their hope revived when they spotted a distant strip of land.

▶ Palms sweating and heart racing, Anna peeled back the curtain, took one step onto the stage, and realized there was no turning back.

▶ As I lifted the spoon to my lips, I wondered if anyone in the history of the world has actually loved lima beans.

▶ Like everyone else, you're probably thinking that it's a little strange for a thirteen-year-old kid to live alone in the desert.

Read the three topic sentences you have composed. Write down the question your topic sentence will prompt readers to ask. If you have a hard time identifying the question, try revising your topic sentence.

If I chose the first sentence, my topic sentence for the next paragraph might be:

I couldn't believe it, but I had just lost my best friend over a deck of cards and a half-eaten package of gummy bears.

Reader Question:
Why did you lose your best friend because of these items?

CAPSULE 2   2.3.2

ARRANGING IDEAS

Once writers have established the focus of a paragraph through a clearly written topic sentence, they have the task of filling that paragraph with supporting details. As you'll recall from 2.1.3, the details a writer chooses must be relevant. In other words, they need to fulfill the expectations set by the topic sentence.

After selecting those details, it's time to arrange them. Arrangement refers to the way information is organized within a piece of writing. Different kinds of writing call for different methods of arrangement. In this lesson, we are going to introduce you to three basic methods for arranging your ideas: (1) chronology, (2) location, and (3) order of importance.

But before we get into specifics, let's talk about why it's important to make purposeful choices when you arrange your ideas.

THE PROFESSOR'S OFFICE

Sometimes arranging ideas in writing seems like a foreign concept. Students commonly enjoy generating ideas and even freewriting about those ideas, but when it is time to put those ideas into a logical order, they freeze up.

*Perhaps this is because arranging ideas means assigning value to them, selecting some and discarding others, and somehow making what's left fit together in a pleasing way. And maybe the biggest **quandary** is the fact that there are so many different ways to arrange writing. There is no "best" way, although some methods, you will find, are certainly better than others.*

To help students get over their initial dread of arrangement, I begin class by having them empty the contents of their pockets, backpack, or purse. I ask them to take a few minutes to consider the items they find. If a stranger looked through the pile, what would it reveal about the owner of the items? In other words, what focus is there among the items?

At this point, students formulate a basic topic sentence based on what this collection of items reveals about them. Here is one student's topic sentence:

> *The contents of my backpack reveal that I am obsessed with technology.*

Pretty basic, right? Now it's time to be selective. Students then choose the three or four items that best support their topic sentence. Once they have selected these items, they write a short paragraph to present to the class. The only stipulation is that they must have a purposeful arrangement for their items. In other words, the I'm-talking-about-this-item-because-it's-the-first-one-I-picked-up arrangement is not going to cut it.

Here is the rest of this student's paragraph:

> *The first item you'll find in my backpack is a mechanical pencil. I don't bother with regular pencils because they don't do anything except write. I like things that have functions. That's why you'll also find a cell phone on me at all times. Of course I like to be able to call people, but I mostly use my phone for text messaging, playing games, and checking my e-mail. My last item is my personal computer. In some ways it is a bigger version of my phone, but it can do much more. I use it for taking notes in class, video chatting with friends and family, and editing digital images for my major in photojournalism.*

After students read their paragraphs aloud, their classmates try to guess what type of arrangement pattern the student used. What would you guess was this student's strategy for arranging ideas?

▶ *Smallest to largest item?*
▶ *Item with the fewest functions to item with the most functions?*

The Professor's Office CWJ—If you're working with a larger class, the backpack game can be done together. Have one volunteer share the contents of his or her backpack. After the student unloads her backpack, you can work as a group on deciding what the backpack's focus or "topic sentence" should be. Next, discuss the possible organizations you might use to tell how the items in the backpack reveal that focus. You don't even need to actually have students write the paragraph—though they can if you choose. The point of the exercise is for students to see in a concrete way how paragraphs are organized around one focus and arranged using some sort of logical pattern.

▶ *Least expensive to most expensive item?*
▶ *Least important to most important item?*

Once the class has offered a few guesses, the students reveal the arrangement they followed and explain why they chose that particular pattern. This student's specific method of arrangement was from the item with the fewest functions to the item with the most functions.

Students are often surprised to find that the class can identify an organizational strategy just by listening to a few brief sentences about their items. They see that when writers are purposeful in their choices, their audience takes note.

Students are also surprised to find that by creating a focus statement and pattern of arrangement, they are able to make logical sense out of a few random items. If you can do that with what's in your pockets, just think of what you can do with your ideas!

CWJ

IN YOUR JOURNAL ▶

Why don't you give the professor's activity a try? Empty your pockets, purse, backpack, or the contents of your desk drawer. Survey the contents. If a stranger looked through the pile, what would it reveal about the owner of the items—you?

1. Write a topic sentence that tells what people could learn about you by looking at these items.

2. Select three to four of the items that best support your topic sentence.

3. Write a basic paragraph that explains each of your chosen items. Make sure you select a purposeful arrangement for the items. (Don't worry about your wording or sentence construction. This paragraph can be very rough.)

4. Read the paragraph aloud to a parent or teacher. If you can have a larger audience, that's even better. After you read, ask your audience to guess what kind of arrangement pattern you used.

5. Now tell them if they guessed right. Explain how you chose your particular pattern of arrangement. If you did the exercise again, would you pick a different method of arrangement?

Here we've asked students to write a full paragraph, but we tell them to focus on arrangement, rather than wording or sentence construction. They should be putting most of their effort into considering how to organize their thoughts. So, it's okay if they end up with sloppy or fragmented sentences. Students don't need to attend to all the elements of effective writing at once.

If you want to address sloppy sentence work, do so after writers have completed this CWJ exercise.

ARRANGING IDEAS CHRONOLOGICALLY

 Now that we've introduced the concept of arrangement, it's time to learn some specific methods of arrangement.

Why don't we start with our developing storyline from 2.3.1? What big mistake did the writer make when he jumped aboard the freighter? The topic sentence has done its job of hooking us, but now it's got to deliver on its promises.

Here, once again, is our first topic sentence.

> After I alighted on the vessel and surveyed my surroundings, I quickly realized that I had made a huge mistake.

And here is our question: What is the huge mistake?

Read through the paragraph to see if it answers our question.

> After I alighted on the vessel and surveyed my surroundings, I quickly realized I had made a huge mistake. As soon as the brisk night air pricked my face, sending shivers from head to toe, my coatless body alerted my brain to the problem. Before I could **chastise** myself for being forgetful, I began fumbling my way through the energetic crowd of parka-clad monkeys, knocking a few about and muttering speedy apologies. Just then, the ship's massive engines started to groan, and the deck swayed unsteadily beneath me, assuring me that there was not a moment to spare. The ship was moving, but I needed to move faster. By the time I lunged onto the starboard side of the freighter, darkness had swallowed all signs of land. I was headed to the South Pole, while my luggage, including my brand new down parka, waited patiently for me on the dock.

So, does the paragraph answer our question by revealing the big mistake? Yes, it shows that the writer jumped on board, but in his excitement, he forgot to bring his luggage—including his coat—along. Forgetting your coat on a journey to Antarctica does seem like a pretty big mistake.

Now reread the paragraph, paying attention to how the information is arranged. Again, arrangement refers to the way a writer chooses to organize details within a paragraph.

As you read the paragraph, did you recognize that it is a story? Because this paragraph tells a story, it is arranged in chronological (time) order. In other words, the events are related in the order in which they happened.

Before you even begin this lesson, you might have your student list off what he did yesterday. Tell him, start at the beginning with what time you got up. Most will naturally give this information in chronological order. You might also read a simple chronologically ordered story together, noting that this is the primary pattern used in most fictional and autobiographical literature. These activities can serve as a concrete introduction to this topic. We tend to think chronologically. By bringing to the student's attention 1) how common this pattern is and 2) that he already knows how to order events chronologically, you can demystify this organizational pattern for your student.

This paragraph could actually be listed as a series of steps that followed one another. Let's jot down each step in the narrative:

1. Cold night air reminds the writer that he doesn't have his coat.
2. He begins pushing through the crowd.
3. The ship shows signs of movement.
4. He needs to move faster.
5. He makes it to the side of the ship, but land is already out of reach.
6. He realizes that he is going to the South Pole without his luggage.

Stories, or narratives, should contain strong, active verbs to keep the action moving along and keep it interesting. What verbs propelled the action in this narrative? I liked the verbs *alighted, pricked, swayed*, and *lunged*.

Narratives also use transition words to show how one event moves to the next. Can you identify any transition words in this paragraph? Remember to look for words that relate to time. We found several transition words that helped lead us through the events: *after, as soon as, before, just then, by the time*.

While transition words are often used to move readers forward in a narrative, they can also be used to signal a flashback by taking readers backwards in the storyline. For example:

▶ *Last year, I played flag football…*
▶ *Before my family moved here…*
▶ *When I was in the third grade…*
▶ *Yesterday, as I was doing homework…*

A flashback interrupts the chronological development of a story to show a scene that happened at an earlier time. Flashbacks offer information about the past to help readers understand the present story. For instance, a character's choice to abruptly quit her job in the city and move to a rural town may be explained through a flashback to the happiest time in this character's life: spending summers on her grandmother's farm. And remember, flashbacks are stories too, so they should also be arranged chronologically.

Here's a flashback that offers more information about how our writer found himself on a boat to Antarctica without his bags:

Just minutes before, I had parted from my parents with high hopes for the year ahead. Since I'm not one to make a show, I was thankful they consented to saying our goodbyes early instead of waiting for the boat's departure. After my mother reminded me for the hundredth time to stay warm, and my father drilled me on the methods for treating frostbite, they reluctantly drove away and left me behind. It thrilled me to think that I would soon be on my way to Antarctica thanks to a pilot program that paired students with trained primates for a year-long excursion on the continent of ice. However, my reverie was soon interrupted by the sight of several apes making a mad dash for the ship. Terrified that I might miss the boat, I leapt without thinking, absentmindedly leaving my luggage behind. Now, ten minutes later, I stood on the ship, stared into the darkness, and tried to recall what my father had said about frostbite after all.

Writing a flashback sequence is pretty simple. You just have to remember two things. First, you have to make sure your readers know that they are entering a flashback. In this paragraph, what phrase signals that the flashback is beginning? Yes, the introductory phrase, "Just minutes before," signals to readers that the story is moving backwards.

The second important point to remember is that you must usher your readers back into the present time of the story. With the phrase, "Now, ten minutes later," this writer signals to readers that the flashback is complete. Easy enough.

CWJ

PART A
Select one of the topic sentences you composed in 2.3.1. You are going to brainstorm a story to go along with this topic sentence.

1. Reread the question this topic sentence should spark for readers. Remember that your job is to answer this question.

2. List four to five events or circumstances that could follow this topic sentence.

3. Arrange the details you wrote in chronological order.

3.. What transition words could you add in to help connect the events?

4 Read through your topic sentence and details in order. Have you sufficiently answered the reader's question?

PART B
Let's add a flashback to the story we began in PART A.

1. Consider what part of the story you want to fill in for readers. You may want to jot down a few different ideas in your journal.

2. Write a sentence that moves readers backward into your flashback. Remember to utilize time transition words that signal to readers they are no longer in the current story.

3. List three to four details that help fill in the backstory. Make sure to arrange them chronologically.

◀ IN YOUR JOURNAL

4. Write a sentence that signals to readers that you are returning to the original storyline.

CAPSULE 4

ARRANGING IDEAS SPATIALLY

In the last capsule, we focused on one specific pattern of arrangement: chronology. This type of arrangement is likely the most natural for you—and you are probably pretty good at it. After all, humans were created to be storytellers. We are made in God's image (Genesis 1:27), and God is the greatest storyteller of all. He is writing a specific story through each one of us, and He has given us the ability and the creativity to tell our own stories as well.

In fact, we tell stories every day. When your family is gathered around the dinner table, do you spend time relaying stories about the day's events? If your family is anything like ours, everyone is talking at the same time, eager to share his or her own version of what happened that day.

Every time you tell or write a story, you arrange the information as a sequence. One action follows another until you conclude the story. However, in the midst of storytelling, writers (and speakers) sometimes take a break from the chronological development of the story to engage in description.

When writers need to set the scene or introduce characters, they try to create a visual picture in readers' minds. To help readers form this picture, it is helpful to arrange descriptions spatially. In other words, writers describe by moving from top to bottom, left to right, foreground to background, or **periphery** to center.

Consider this passage from Willa Cather's novel, *My Antonia*. Here, a ten-year-old boy who has lost both his parents and traveled across the country to live with his grandparents in Nebraska, meets his grandfather's hired hand.

> I looked up with interest at the new face in the lantern-light. He might have stepped out of the pages of Jesse James. He wore a sombrero hat, with a wide leather band and a bright buckle, and the ends of his moustache were twisted up stiffly, like little horns. He looked lively and ferocious, I thought, as if he had a history. A long scar ran across one cheek and drew the corner of his mouth up in a sinister curl. The top of his left ear was gone, and his skin was brown as an Indian's. Surely this was the face of a desperado. As he walked about the platform in his high-heeled boots, looking for our trunks, I saw that he was a rather slight man, quick and wiry, and light on his feet.

How does Cather organize the details in her description? Look at where she begins the description and where she ends it. In the first sentence, readers are introduced to a "new face," and the last sentence ends with a comment about the man's feet. We would say this passage follows a top-to-bottom pattern of arrangement.

Notice that the writer did not describe everything about the man from "top to bottom." Instead, she exercised selectivity, concentrating on those features—such as his twisted moustache, long scar, and damaged ear—that made him seem like a suspicious character from *The Life of Jesse James*.

Now read this setting description, paying close attention once again to the writer's arrangement.

> Though the gas station restroom wasn't exactly the most inviting place Maggie could imagine, it was a quiet place to think. The walls of the small, squarish room shone oddly beneath the humming fluorescent light in the ceiling. Perhaps they had been white once, but now they resembled oily cheese. To her left, a small, cracked mirror reflected the overall dreariness, adding to it a slight haze. Around the edges of the room, a few clumps of wet toilet paper stuck to the cold concrete floor. So stark were her surroundings, Maggie might have imagined herself in a hospital room, but several cockroaches, in various states of surrender, seemed to prove otherwise. In the middle of the far wall, set slightly to one side, the toilet basin emitted an unpleasant odor, but it provided the only available seat for contemplation. So Maggie locked the door, planted her hands firmly on her knees, and sat down on the toilet to think.

What type of spatial arrangement does this writer employ? This one may be a bit trickier than the last one. Here the writer begins by describing the walls and ceiling and ends "in the middle" with the toilet. This description is ordered from the periphery to the center.

And this arrangement is purposeful. The first sentence establishes the focus of the paragraph: *"Though the gas station restroom wasn't exactly the most inviting place Maggie could imagine, it was a quiet place to think."* The description then moves from the outer walls of the room slowly to the center. We are shown how uninviting the restroom is before we are introduced to what it does offer. In the center of the scene is the toilet, a place for Maggie to sit and think.

Can you find any transition words or phrases in this writer's paragraph that relate to location? Sure you can. Sentence openers like to her left, around the edges, and in the middle help readers orient themselves within the "picture" and construct a more accurate mental image.

CWJ

PART A

You've probably heard before that the best descriptions engage a reader's five senses: sight, smell, taste, touch, and hearing. How well does the description of the gas station restroom appeal to your senses?

▶ IN YOUR JOURNAL

Look back through the paragraph for details that engage each of the five senses. List each of the senses in your journal. As you come across details that engage a particular sense, jot them down. If there are any senses that are not represented by a descriptive detail, make up your own.

PART B

Often writers must describe something that exists only in their minds. For practice, however, we will start with something a bit more concrete.

1. Locate a photograph that appeals to you. You can use a photograph of your own, or you could look in other sources, such as *Top Story* or *WORLD Magazine*. Even a piece of art in your home would work. Just make sure that it: (1) shows one person or one location and (2) is realistic looking.

2. After studying the picture for a few minutes, write down your dominant impression of the scene or person. For example, in the first sample paragraph, the boy's impression of the hired hand is, "He might have stepped out of the pages of Jesse James."

3. Now think through some possible patterns of spatial arrangement. If you were describing this picture to someone, would you move from one side to the other, from the center outward, from the background to the foreground? Make a note of why you chose this arrangement.

4. Once you've decided on your spatial arrangement, begin listing details in that order. Be sure to include details that appeal to as many of the five senses as you can. And be selective! Remember that you want to include only those details that help support the impression you decided upon in the first question.

STYLE TIME

 In this lesson, you've learned that it's a good idea to include transition words and phrases to help lead readers from sentence to sentence. Most of these introductory phrases and clauses should be followed by a comma.

For example, take a look at a sentence from the sample paragraph in this capsule. Notice the comma after the introductory phrase.

> Around the edges of the room, a few clumps of wet toilet paper stuck to the cold concrete floor.

In order to figure out if a phrase or clause is introductory, simply locate the subject and verb of the sentence. Anything before the subject and verb is usually an introduction.

> After she went to the dentist, Hattie consumed an entire package of caramels. (subject) (verb)

If the introduction is short, you may choose to omit the comma. However, using a comma after an introductory element is always okay. Both of these sentences are correct.

It's important to remind students that details are subjective. For example, the hired man's "long scar" seemed to prove he was a crooked character to the narrator of *My Antonia*; however, the same feature can be interpreted in a number of different ways. It could suggest this man has endured a life of hardship. It could have marked him as a war hero. It could be a physical deformity that made him self-conscious.

When we write, we get to make meaning out of the details, and no two writers will do so in the same way. To illustrate this point, have students trade images and write a description of their partner's image as well. Compare descriptions to see what different choices each writer made in (1) their dominant impression of the image, (2) pattern of arrangement, and (3) selection of descriptive detail.

▶ In January I learned to sky dive.

▶ In January, I learned to sky dive.

Be careful, though, because failing to use a comma could lead to confusion.

Before eating my hamster dances.

If you don't want to sound as if you are eating your hamster, try this instead.

Before eating, my hamster dances.

REVISE: Take a few minutes to look through the writing you have done in your journal for this lesson. Do any of your sentences include introductory phrases or clauses? Check to make sure the introductory elements are followed by a comma.

CAPSULE 5   2.3.5

ARRANGING IDEAS TO ARGUE

 Let's reconvene at the dinner table, shall we? Imagine that after a day of school, work, and practices, your family is reconnecting over bowls of steaming soup and grilled cheese sandwiches. Once the initial eating frenzy dies down, the stories begin.

And it isn't long before your story turns into a whole family discussion. First, you describe, in too much detail for your mother, a squashed squirrel you saw on 5th Street. Then your father asks why you were on 5th Street in the first place and launches into a **rant** about the importance of always taking the most efficient route. Suddenly, the rest of the table is discussing the best routes to and from the library – at various times of the day, in various modes of transportation, and during various weather contingencies.

Humans aren't just natural storytellers; we are analytical thinkers. When your family members discuss the best route home, they are engaging in analysis mixed with a bit of friendly argumentation.

When we write, we also analyze and argue. And this type of writing calls for a third pattern of arrangement: order of importance. Writers arrange their reasons from least to most important or most to least important depending on purpose and audience.

Check out this argument paragraph about banana peels. Do you think the details are arranged in order of least to most important or vice versa?

The banana peel has a reputation for being valuable only to practical jokers, but this fruit exterior is actually quite useful. For one, I'm sure most people would agree that banana peels are useful to bananas. Riding around in a backpack for half the day could cause some serious damage to this soft fruit if it didn't have its skin. You wouldn't want to eat that mushy mess come lunchtime. But banana peels are not only useful to the fruit itself. They also make an excellent polish. When you finish eating a banana, grab your boots and a fork because the inside of a peel can shine everything from shoes to silverware. Moreover, ripe banana skins are a time-tested home remedy for several ailments. Since peels have cooling properties similar to aloe, you can lay the inside of the peel on sunburns, scrapes, or poison ivy for instant relief. Likewise, the skins of this delicious fruit have been known to dislodge splinters and remove warts. The next time you think of tossing that banana peel—in the trash or in someone's path—I hope you'll consider using it instead.

To help us answer our question, let's first identify the specific argument this writer is making. A writer's argument should be established in his topic sentence. Find the topic sentence, and you have found the argument.

Topic sentence:
    The banana peel has a reputation for being valuable only to practical jokers, but this fruit exterior is actually quite useful.

What question does this sentence make you ask? After reading the sentence, I want to know, "How are banana peels useful?" The supporting sentences should answer this question for readers.

So, what three reasons does the writer give us to prove that banana skins are useful?

▶ Banana peels are useful because they protect bananas.
▶ Banana peels are useful as polish.
▶ Banana peels are useful as a home remedy for several ailments.

If you had to rank these reasons in order, what would you rate as the most important and what would you rate as the least?

You might rank the use of bananas as a home remedy as the most important reason because it would be the most surprising and the most convincing to readers. Who would have thought you could get rid of a wart with a banana peel? The use of banana peels to protect bananas seems the least important because it is the most obvious.

So this writer chose to arrange his reasons in order from the least to the most important. This is perhaps the most common arrangement because it is usually advisable to end your paragraph with your strongest point.

Why might you utilize the opposite arrangement, moving from your most important reason to your least? If you want to make an immediate impact on readers, grab them with your best reason first, instead of leading up to it.

For instance, what if you wanted to write a paragraph about the negative effects of homework? You would begin by brainstorming some of those effects.

▶ Students must work for several more hours after spending all day at school.
▶ Families don't get to spend as much time together in the evenings.
▶ Teachers have to grade homework, giving them extra work as well.
▶ Studies show that homework doesn't improve test scores for students younger than high school age.
▶ Homework puts stress on students at a young age.
▶ Homework is not enjoyable for students.

Now it's time to select which reasons you want to use in your paragraph and arrange them in order of importance. Imagine you are writing to an audience of parents. Which reasons would you choose?

Here's one writer's version of this paragraph arranged from the most important reason to the least.

> Of course students would prefer not to do homework, but I think it's time for more parents to say "No" to homework as well. Perhaps the most significant reason parents should reject homework is that it keeps families from spending time together. Once students finish afterschool activities such as sports practices, music lessons, and church functions, they often spend the last few hours of the evening in their rooms completing homework. They go to bed late, wake up exhausted, and still haven't gotten time to reconnect with their loved ones. Furthermore, requiring students to do homework is like asking a full-time employee to work overtime. After completing a seven hour workday, should students be asked to put in two or three more hours of work? That seems like a bit much to ask of a seventh grader. Added to all this, homework is simply not fun. If students enjoyed homework, it might make sense to require it, even with its other drawbacks. However, given its negative effects, it seems reasonable that parents take a stand with their kids and against homework.

We are sure you figured out this paragraph's argument quickly. It suggests that parents reject homework and offers these reasons:

▶ Homework reduces time spent together as a family.
▶ Homework is the equivalent of working overtime.
▶ Homework isn't enjoyable.

Can you see why the writer chose to arrange her ideas beginning with the most important and moving to the least? If she had started with the idea that homework isn't fun, the audience of parents would probably have stopped reading. According to most parents, if something is good for you, it need not be fun (for instance, eating brussels sprouts or cleaning your room). By first showing that homework has negative effects on students and families, the writer turns the idea that homework isn't enjoyable into a point parents will want to consider.

Finally, you will notice that the writers of both sample paragraphs utilize transition words to help order their argument. Can you identify some of these transitions?

Here are a few transition words that are particularly useful in paragraphs that analyze and argue.

Transition Words	Use
for example, for instance, in fact	to introduce examples
in addition, also, furthermore, a second	to offer an additional point
similarly, on the other hand, likewise	to compare or contrast ideas
however, yet, moreover, so, nevertheless	to connect ideas
therefore, for this reason, as a result	to show effects

CWJ

IN YOUR JOURNAL ▶

Brainstorm an argument *in favor of* one of the following items: flies, soda, allergy shots, making your bed, dessert before dinner

1. First list as many reasons as you can think of that are *in favor of* your chosen item.

2. Identify your audience. Whom do you want to convince? (siblings, parents, dentists, the family dog, etc.)

3. Select three to four reasons that you think will be most convincing to that particular audience.

4. Rank those reasons in order of importance.

5. Decide on an arrangement pattern for your paragraph. Would you order your reasons from most to least important or vice versa? Explain why you chose this order.

Now brainstorm an argument *against* one of the following items: mouthwash, cupcakes, TV or video games, exercise, pillows.

1. First list as many reasons as you can think of that are *against* your chosen item.

2. Complete questions two to five from the previous exercise.

Transition words are very helpful in developing an effective sense of style. Make sure that students develop a full arsenal of transition words, for some of them will find their favorites and depend on them too much. A student of ours once wrote a two-page paper in which *therefore* appeared nine times. Finding a favorite transition word is natural, but the overuse of the transition in a paper makes for uncomfortable and illogical reading.

THE RIGHT WORD

 It's that time again. You've defined all of the vocabulary words in this lesson. Grab your thesaurus and look up each of these words. Select the best replacement for the word in bold.

▶ We have already discussed adding interest to **lackluster** topic sentences.

▶ And maybe the biggest **quandary** is the fact that there are so many different ways to arrange writing.

▶ Before I could **chastise** myself for being forgetful, I began fumbling my way through the energetic crowd of parka-clad monkeys, knocking a few about and muttering speedy apologies.

▶ In other words, writers describe by moving from top to bottom, left to right, foreground to background, or **periphery** to center.

▶ Then your father asks why you were on 5th Street in the first place and launches into a **rant** about the importance of always taking the most efficient route.

Write with WORLD

DEVELOPING WRITERS: BUILDING BLOCKS AND BIOGRAPHY

LINKING PARAGRAPHS: TRANSITIONS AND LOGIC

WHAT WRITERS WILL NEED FOR THIS LESSON:

▶ Your writer's journal
▶ Dictionary
▶ Glue stick or tape
▶ A highlighter

CAPSULE 1

2.4.1

ORGANIZING THE MIDDLE OF AN ESSAY

 Dr. Rayshelle Dietrich remembers traveling with her family in the following paragraph:

> When I was growing up, my father kept a large road map in our station wagon. While he drove us on an adventure, I'd carefully unfold the map until it became nearly as big as I was. Then I would study the roads and highways crisscrossing the state like a huge spider's web. I loved tracing our route with my dad's ballpoint pen, indicating our starting and ending points with two small blue dots. It thrilled me to be able to see where we were headed.

Planning a written document is akin to planning a driving route. Before writers begin to draft, they usually take time to develop a logical organizational strategy for their text. They identify where they are beginning, where they want to end up, and how they are going to get there. So, it is helpful to think about organizing a text into these three parts: a beginning, a middle, and an end. As they plan, writers ask themselves questions such as:

▶ How am I going to begin my text and introduce my main point?
▶ How am I going to develop and explain my main point in the middle?
▶ How am I going to wrap-up my main point in the conclusion?

In this capsule, we are going to discuss how to organize the middle of the text.

Honestly, there are numerous ways to do so. It's important to choose a strategy based on the information you are presenting to readers. Do you recall the patterns for paragraph arrangement we introduced in Lesson 3 of this unit? Chronological, spatial, and order of importance arrangements can be applied to larger texts as well.

That gives you three possible organizational strategies. Can you think of any others? For example, how might you logically organize:

▶ An examination of the controversy: Is mayonnaise or mustard better? (Remember an examination

won't offer your own opinion on the controversy, but rather examines the various sides of the issue.)
▶ An argument for or against scrambling eggs

What did you come up with? Here are some possibilities:

▶ Tell what people have to say in favor of mayonnaise and what people have to say in favor of mustard.
▶ Then tell what people have to say against mayonnaise and what people have to say against mustard.
▶ State my opinion that scrambling eggs is a great idea. Offer three reasons why people don't like to scramble eggs. Refute each reason by explaining why scrambling eggs is actually a good idea. (I could list these reasons in order of importance too!)

Do you see the logic behind each of these arrangements?

Maybe you are wondering, "Why should I go to the trouble to think about the logic behind my organization? Wouldn't it be easier if you just gave me a list that told me how to organize different types of writing?"

We *could* offer you a list of patterns for arranging many of the different types of writing you will encounter, and it would be helpful to an extent. But we believe that formulas don't ultimately lead to effective writing. Though we will offer you tips and ideas about organization, we think it is *more* helpful for you to learn how to think about organization logically. That way, you won't get stuck when you can't remember the "right" formula. Instead, you will confidently create your own. And that's what the best writers do.

WORLD WISDOM

 There is a reason people often refer to the art of arrangement. The most effective arrangements of ideas are not formulaic. Writers often develop their own style of arrangement that makes them identifiable to readers. Here's what Howard Brinkman, the Publisher of *God's World News*, has to say about the art of arrangement.

"Blah! Think how boring it would be to read a book, a magazine article, or even an email from a friend if we all wrote according to the same formulas. That's why a book or movie reviewer might criticize the author by saying his writing was 'formulaic.'

When I first began writing, I fell into a kind of formulaic approach even though I thought it was original. I wrote freely, and from my perspective. Whatever seemed the most important to me, that's what came first. The tone of the piece became however I felt like saying it. The vocabulary I used was what sounded good to me. It was stream of consciousness captured on paper, then tidied up a bit.

As I wrote more and more, and for different reasons and different kinds of readers, I realized that 'my style' was not the most effective – for almost any kind of writing! I learned to approach each piece as a unique problem to solve. Who is my audience? What do they need or want to know? What is important to them? How do they think, and how do they use language? Is a logical or an emotional approach more appealing to them?

Many students – and teachers – prefer to rely on formulas for writing because they make us comfortable. We want to be told the "right" way to write! Similar to a recipe, a formula can be useful for getting writers started. However, no one has become a master chef through a strict adherence to someone else's recipe, and we won't become masterful writers through a strict adherence to someone else's formulas for arrangement.

Discuss with students their feelings about formulaic writing. What formulas for writing have they been taught in the past? Have students identify the ways in which formulas are helpful, particularly to beginning writers, as well as the drawbacks of sticking to a few set formats for constructing texts.

In this WW, Mr. Brinkman brings up the concept of audience. His questions in the third paragraph are good ones to begin considering. If you have time, discuss them, helping your student become aware that WHOM we're writing for shapes what we say and how we say it. These would be good questions to jot down in the CWJ for future reference.

The are multiple ways to approach this CWJ. Most students will use words in their brainstorming. How they use those words will differ. Some students will work through lists, while other students will develop those lists into outlines. More visual students will create circles and patterns that link words. We are fine with any of these methods (and others that are not mentioned here).

In short, how I arranged the elements of my writing depended on the audience and the purpose of the piece. Sorting through that arrangement became my favorite part of a writing project (although I still enjoy the wordplay)!

Transport yourself into the minds of other people – your readers. See like they see. Try to think as they do. When you approach your writing in this logical way, certain facts become obviously important, whether you think they are or not. The order in which you arrange the elements of the story have a clear hierarchy. The tone you should use makes sense (which is why it is often a good idea to imagine yourself as your audience, then read your work aloud to yourself to see if it 'sounds' right).

When you arrange your writing according to your purpose and your audience, you'll find it becomes easier to outline your approach because it prevents 'you' from getting in your own way! And you'll discover something else exciting. You don't have just one 'voice' or one 'style' when you write. You have many. No 'Blah!' there. And each one is just the one you need to express an idea, a belief, an investigation, a report... so many things that go beyond expressing just 'yourself.'"

—Howard Brinkman

CWJ

◀ IN YOUR JOURNAL

With any writing task, there are multiple ways to organize your ideas logically. We helped you think of a few in this capsule. Now let's see if you can come up with some on your own.

In your journal, brainstorm a logical organizational strategy for each of these prompts.

▶ A biography of the family pet
▶ A review of C. S. Lewis's book *The Lion, The Witch, and the Wardrobe* (or the movie)
▶ A comparison of homemade hamburgers and fast food/restaurant hamburgers

Share your organizational strategies with your parents and teachers. Get their opinion about whether each strategy seems logical to them.

What tips for arranging ideas can you borrow from Howard Brinkman? Do you usually rely on "formulas" to organize your writing? Why or why not?

THE RIGHT WORD

In this lesson, you won't be introduced to any new vocabulary words. However, there is still a chance you might encounter words that are unfamiliar to you. Or you might come across words that are used differently than you would expect. If you do, jot that word in your journal and look up its definition. Adding new words to your writing arsenal is never a bad idea. ("Arsenal" might be a good one to start with.)

MAKING ORGANIZATIONAL CHOICES

By now you have learned to take simple sentences and build them into more complex sentences. And you have learned how to link sentences and arrange them into well-ordered, unified paragraphs. In the last capsule, we discussed why multi-paragraph texts need to be logically arranged.

What do you think of the arrangement of this passage?

> Noah needed this job. His father had borrowed money to send him to college. Now it was time for him to pay his father back.
>
> There were little ones who could not yet read. There were teenagers not much younger than himself. To make matters worse, he had almost no materials to work with—no maps, no blackboard, no chalk. There were few books.
>
> But Noah didn't like teaching school. His true love was words.
>
> The young schoolmaster stood at the front of a one-room schoolhouse. The room was overcrowded with children. He was expected to teach them all.

Is anyone else saying "Huh?" right now? Honestly, this passage doesn't make much sense. Can you guess why it is confusing? Exactly. It is unorganized.

See if you can remedy the situation. Return to the passage and try reordering the paragraphs by writing a "1" next to the paragraph you think should come first and so on until you have numbered all four of the paragraphs.

After you're done, look at how the writer chose to organize this passage. (No peeking!)

1   The young schoolmaster stood at the front of a one-room schoolhouse. The room was overcrowded with children. He was expected to teach them all.

2   There were little ones who could not yet read. There were teenagers not much younger than himself. To make matters worse, he had almost no materials to work with—no maps, no blackboard, no chalk. There were few books.

3   Noah needed this job. His father had borrowed money to send him to college. Now it was time for him to pay his father back.

4   But Noah didn't like teaching school. His true love was words.

How do your organizational choices compare to the writer's? We would guess they are pretty close. Do you know why? It's because the writer's arrangement of paragraphs is logical. Logical organization is simply what seems reasonable and understandable to the average person.

Looking at each of the paragraphs, we can identify a logical development of ideas.

> **Paragraph 1** — Introduces the schoolmaster who must teach a lot of children in a one-room schoolhouse
>
> **Paragraph 2** — Offers specifics about the children and the conditions at the schoolhouse
>
> **Paragraph 3** — Explains why the schoolmaster has chosen to work under these difficult circumstances
>
> **Paragraph 4** — Uncovers the schoolmaster's feelings about his occupation

These paragraphs together serve as the introduction to a biography of Noah Webster. Herein the writer provides a short anecdote, or incident, from Noah's life to introduce the man and lead us to the main point.

Read back through the well-organized passage and see if you can find the main point. Highlight the sentence(s) you identify. Here's a hint: The main point of a multi-paragraph text—like the controlling idea of a single paragraph—should be a relatively general idea, rather than a specific detail.

Which sentence(s) did you choose? We selected the sentence, "His true love was words." Could you have identified this as the main point in the unorganized passage at the beginning of this capsule? Probably not.

Even though both passages include the same sentence, the second introduction develops in a logical progression, moving from an example of something Noah did not love—teaching school—to something he did love: words.

Hopefully, you are getting a sense of why writers need to think about and plan the arrangement of their paragraphs. In the following capsule, we will look more closely at techniques for ordering paragraphs and helping readers move effortlessly from one paragraph to the next.

IN YOUR JOURNAL ▶

CWJ

Read this introduction to a biography of the missionary David Livingstone.

1   As he was being shaken, one of David's African friends, Mebalwe, shot at the lion and missed. The beast had enough life left in him to attack Mebalwe before falling down dead. David's bullets had finally taken effect.

2   David could see that his first shots had hit the lion in the bushes just a few yards away. As he rammed the bullets down the barrel of his gun, he heard the shouts of the natives in his hunting party. He looked up just in time to see the lion springing toward him!

3   Boom! The sound of a rifle echoed across the African landscape. Thirty-year-old missionary David Livingstone quickly began reloading. He and several native Africans were on a hunt, trying to kill a lion that was stealing their village's livestock.

4   David Livingstone and Mebalwe survived, but David's arm was never the same. The bones in his shoulder were in splinters. He had eleven tooth wounds on his upper arm.

5   The lion attack was just one of many challenges David faced as he followed the vocation God had called him to: penetrating the unexplored heart of Africa. He would spend most of the next 30 years doing just that.

6   "He caught my shoulder as he sprang," David later reported. "We both came to the ground below together. Growling horribly close to my ear, he shook me as a terrier does a rat."

Try reorganizing the paragraphs to represent a logical progression. Number the paragraphs as we did earlier in this capsule. (Once you number the paragraphs, read them aloud in that order. Hearing the words may help you decide if the order *sounds* right. Try a couple of arrangements before picking the best one.)

1. Summarize the ideas/information presented in each paragraph and write it down as we did with the passage about Noah Webster. Remember to list the paragraphs in the new order you decided upon. (Paragraph 1, Paragraph 2, and so on)

2. What sentence(s) would you identify as expressing the main point of this biography? Briefly explain how the reorganized introduction leads readers to this main point.

3. What cues from the writer helped you organize the passage?

4. Look back at our work with the sample passage in this capsule if you need help with the exercise.

Visual learners may want to copy the paragraphs, cut them out, and try piecing them together differently. When they decide on the best order, they can glue the paragraphs in their CWJ in that order.

Or, if they have access to a computer, students may want to type up the paragraphs and use the "cut" and "paste" features to rearrange paragraphs.

LINKING PARAGRAPHS WITH TRANSITIONS

Once you've determined an overall organizational strategy for your text, it's time to start drafting. You have the "big picture"—the road map—of how you are going to get from beginning to end. Now you have to lead your readers along the path you've created.

In 2.3.3, we learned how to organize information within paragraphs. Now we have to link those paragraphs so readers can move effortlessly from the beginning to the end of your text.

Let's continue reading the biography of Noah Webster. We'll start where we left off. Pay attention to how the writer organizes the passage and how she moves from paragraph to paragraph.

5 Born in 1758 in West Hartford, Connecticut, Noah Webster grew up on a farm. Few young men at the time went to college. But Noah was smart, and he loved to learn. So his father mortgaged the farm to allow him to attend Yale.

6 While Noah was in college, America was fighting the war for independence from England. Noah passionately believed in the need for America to be an independent nation. He joined the militia, though he never fought in the Revolutionary War.

7 Noah tried being a lawyer, but he didn't have any clients. He tried other things too, but kept ending up back in the classroom. That seemed the only way he could make money.

8 At the same time, he was active in the new nation's politics. He often wrote about the need for the United States to have a strong national government. And its people needed to view themselves as Americans—no longer as British subjects!

9 One day, Noah hit on an idea to help improve American education—and create better citizens. He would write a new spelling book to teach children to read. It would replace the British version most schools used. While children learned to read and write, they'd also learn about America—things like geography and important dates.

10 Noah's book—which was always covered in blue paper—took off like wildfire. Soon it was being used all over the new nation. In fact, it stayed popular for more than 100 years—teaching young children to read.

11 Noah's blue-backed speller sold millions of copies and made the publishers rich. But throughout his life, Noah himself always struggled to support his family. And his family was large. He married Rebecca Greenleaf in 1789 and over the next 19 years, she gave birth to eight children.

A student might comment on the shortness of these paragraphs. For example, paragraph #13 is a sentence! Clearly that cannot be correct.

These selections were composed for younger audiences who do not possess the knowledge of paragraphing *Write with WORLD* students possess. If a student questions the paragraphing, ask them to think about how they might write for small kids.

This lesson can be extended to a broader lesson on audience. Your audience determines the shape of your writing: the words you will use, how many sentences make up your paragraphs, and the overall length of your essay. This lesson is very obvious when you compare a book written for a young child, a beginning reader, and a novel composed for middle schoolers.

12   In 1800, Noah announced his intent to begin what would become his most significant achievement: a dictionary of the American language. Almost no one thought it was a good idea.

13   There were already plenty of dictionaries in English. Why write another?

14   But Noah didn't listen. He began his dictionary anyway. He thought it might take five years. He was wrong. It took twenty-five. There were several reasons for that.

15   For one thing, many distractions slowed him down. He served in the Connecticut legislature. He revised his spelling book. He helped his wife with the children.

16   For another thing, once he got started, he realized he had more to learn. To trace the origins of all the words, he had to teach himself languages. Along with the ones he already knew, he studied 20 in all.

What conclusion did you come to about the organization of this piece? I would guess you figured out that this biography, like most biographical accounts, is organized chronologically. Readers are led in sequence from Noah Webster's birth to his work writing an American dictionary.

The overall organization is based on chronology, but how does the writer move us seamlessly from one paragraph to the next? Transitions!

These helpful tools identify the connections between separate paragraphs. (There's one right there.) They also help readers see how all the paragraphs in a text work together to build towards the main point. Here are a few ways to transition between paragraphs, along with examples from the account of Noah Webster.

Use connectors (such as *however, consequently, moreover, in contrast, similarly, in fact, then, for example, in addition*) to show how the ideas you are about to discuss relate to the ideas in the last paragraph.

> **Example from Paragraph 16:**
> For another thing, once he got started, he realized he had more to learn.
>
> **Explanation:** The phrase "for another thing" shows this paragraph will offer a reason in addition to the one given in the previous paragraph.

End a paragraph with a sentence that leads forward to the next paragraph.

> **Example from Paragraph 14:**
> There were several reasons for that.

We've discussed how transitions between sentences can improve logic and style. Here transitions in and between paragraphs influences logic and arrangement—they help ideas stick together or have coherence. In other words, the gap between ideas is bridged smoothly.

Explanation: This sentence tells readers to continue on to the next paragraph where they will find out why it took Noah 25 years to complete the dictionary.

Begin a paragraph with a sentence that links back to the previous paragraph.

Example from Paragraph 6:
While Noah was in college, America was fighting the war for independence from England.

Explanation: The beginning of this sentence links back to the statement in the previous paragraph that Noah attended Yale.

Repeat key words or phrases (or variations of those words) to enhance a feeling of continuity.

Example from Paragraph 10:
Noah's book—which was always covered in blue paper—took off like wildfire.

Example from Paragraph 11:
Noah's blue-backed speller sold millions of copies and made the publishers rich.

Explanation: Each of these sentences link back to the "new spelling book" mentioned in paragraph 9, but use slightly different variations to keep from sounding too repetitious.

What other paragraphs in the passage effectively utilize these transitional techniques?

Are there any paragraphs that have weak or missing transitions?

The third paragraph could benefit from a stronger transition. Do you see a connection between Noah Webster joining the militia at the end of paragraph six and his working as a lawyer at the beginning of paragraph seven? Let's see if a stronger transition helps clarify things.

6   While Noah was in college, America was fighting the war for independence from England. Noah passionately believed in the need for America to be an independent nation. He joined the militia, though he never fought in the Revolutionary War.

7   **As the war raged on in the colonies, Noah graduated from college and looked for ways to earn a living.** He tried being a lawyer, but he didn't have any clients. He tried other things too, but kept ending up back in the classroom. That seemed the only way he could make money.

The new transition, in bold, links back to the information about the war in the previous paragraph.

IN YOUR JOURNAL ▶

CWJ

Time to continue on with the David Livingstone biography we began reading in Capsule 2.4.2. (The introductory paragraphs are included so you can see if you ordered the passage the same way the writer did.)

1   Boom! The sound of a rifle echoed across the African landscape. Thirty-year-old missionary David Livingstone quickly began reloading. He and several native Africans were on a hunt, trying to kill a lion that was stealing their village's livestock.

2   David could see that his first shots had hit the lion in the bushes just a few yards away. As he rammed the bullets down the barrel of his gun, he heard the shouts of the natives in his hunting party. He looked up just in time to see the lion springing toward him!

3   "He caught my shoulder as he sprang," David later reported. "We both came to the ground below together. Growling horribly close to my ear, he shook me as a terrier does a rat."

4   As he was being shaken, one of David's African friends, Mebalwe, shot at the lion and missed. The beast had enough life left in him to attack Mebalwe before falling down dead. David's bullets had finally taken effect.

5   David Livingstone and Mebalwe survived, but David's arm was never the same. The bones in his shoulder were in splinters. He had eleven tooth wounds on his upper arm.

6   The lion attack was just one of many challenges David faced as he followed the vocation God had called him to: penetrating the unexplored heart of Africa. He would spend most of the next 30 years doing just that.

7   By the time he was ten years old, David Livingstone was working in a cloth factory in Scotland. Fourteen hours a day, six days a week, he was constantly moving, tying threads together when they broke. But he kept a book open on the machine so he could study while he worked.

8   Each night, he attended the factory's school for another two hours. Often, when he got home, he would read until after midnight.

9   For the rest of his life, he was thankful for this early training in hard work. It prepared him for the privations he would face as a missionary.

10   When he wasn't working, David and his brothers loved nothing more than exploring nature. His interest in science led him to read everything he could find on the subject. By the time he

was in his early 20s, he had decided to become a doctor. He was greatly moved on hearing a missionary speak at his local church.

11 What if I could go and preach? As a doctor, I could help alleviate suffering too, he thought. With the blessing of his godly parents, he began working his way through college to become a medical missionary.

12 Eventually, with help from the London Missionary Society, he was on his way to Africa.

13 When David Livingstone sailed for Africa in 1840, maps of the country had huge blank spots. Much of Africa's interior had never been seen by a white man. Most missionaries lived on the country's edges, ministering to just a small fraction of Africa's inhabitants.

14 Disease, violence, and rough terrain made traveling across the middle of Africa extremely difficult. But from the beginning, David was committed to opening up Central Africa.

Do you recall the four methods for transitioning that we introduced in this capsule?

Read back through the passage, looking for examples of each type of transition. When you find an example of a particular transition, write down:

1. The transition

2. How this transition helps link the two paragraphs together

As with past exercises, challenge your student writer to explain as specifically as possible. If they give a general answer, ask "why" that is the case.

Find a paragraph that could benefit from a stronger transition.

1. Identify the type of transition you will use.

2. Rewrite the current transition sentence OR add in a transition sentence.

3. Explain how your new transition strengthens the connection between the paragraphs.

THE LOGIC BEHIND YOUR ORGANIZATION

THE PROFESSOR'S OFFICE

Organization often causes writers great difficulty.

Sometimes writers who are skilled wordsmiths depend so heavily on their words and fancy phrasing that they overlook the logic that is needed to link ideas. I once worked with a student who had great skill in crafting beautiful sentences; his verbs were always active and interesting, his subjects were specific, and his use of adverbs was impressive. His wording was like an empty song that lulled readers to sleep: they would hear beautiful music but miss that the words didn't work together to develop ideas.

Other times, students can produce writing that is nothing more than an organizational plan. A few years ago I taught a student who seemed to believe that every paper had three main points and could be no longer than five paragraphs. Every paper he wrote had this structure. If an argument had four points, the student would cram the four points into three paragraphs instead of developing the four points in four smart paragraphs. In this case, the student was unable to develop a paper around developed ideas—they were tied to a format.

You should aspire to be neither one of these writers. Fancy words alone do not make a paper great. Logical organization alone does not make a paper smart. Instead, you should want to be a smart, logical writer who uses words intelligently and organizes papers to reflect your thinking and to clarify your ideas for readers.

In this unit, we have introduced you to the building blocks you need in order to construct effective texts. In the final two capsules, you will use the skills you have acquired to compose a well-written, well-organized paragraph and situate it logically between two other paragraphs.

Don't worry. We will walk you through it.

First, let's finish our biography of Noah Webster. Picking up where we left off…

17 Then in 1808, Noah came to know Christ. All his life, he had tried to be good. He had professed belief in God—but he just wasn't certain that he believed all the doctrines of the Bible.

18 Then as he worked on his dictionary that year, he found himself distracted for weeks by the drawing of the Holy Spirit. He couldn't concentrate on his work.

19 One day, as he himself explains, "A sudden impulse upon my mind arrested me, and subdued my will. I instantly fell on my knees and confessed my sins to God, implored his pardon, and made my vows to him that from that time I would live in entire obedience to his commands."

20 Noah's new-found faith changed the course of his dictionary. He was determined that his magnum opus would glorify God.

21 He moved his family to Amherst, Massachusetts, where it was cheaper to live. He packed his office walls with sand to block out all noise. There he worked standing in the center of his custom-made desk—circular so that he could lay out around him dictionaries in many languages. That way he could "chase" the meaning of each word back to its original language.

22 In 1824, Noah sailed to Europe to complete his research. In 1825, in a boarding house in Cambridge, England, he finished the dictionary. Three years later, American Dictionary of the English Language was published. Everyone agreed that the two-volume dictionary—which included over 70,000 words—was the best in the world.

23 And on almost every page, Noah's faith shined forth: "Love, n. The love of God is the first duty of man. . . ." "Christian, n. A real disciple of Christ; one who believes in the truth of the Christian religion, and studies to follow the example, and obey the precepts, of Christ . . . ."

24 By now, Noah Webster was an old man. Many people who had laughed at his idea were no longer living. A new generation of Christians converted during the Second Great Awakening loved the Webster's dictionary nearly as much as they loved their Bibles.

Take a look at these details about Noah Webster's life that were not included in the biography.

▶ Noah's spelling book was also referred to as "Old Blue Back."
▶ Dictionary included 12,000 words that had never been included in any dictionary of the English language.
▶ In the dictionary, Noah changed the spelling of several words to make the English language more uniform:
  "musick" became "music"
  "honour" became "honor"
  "plough" became "plow."
▶ Noah believed girls should study the same subjects as boys in school, not just needlework and dance.
▶ The dictionary provided rules of pronunciation to help standardize American speech.
▶ At one point, there were more blue-backed spellers sold in the United States than Bibles.
▶ Noah's dictionary included distinctively American words such as skunk, hickory, and chowder.
▶ Noah earned a master's degree by writing a dissertation on how to improve public education.

Given these details, can we construct a unified, logical paragraph?

In order to do so, we must first select the details that are most closely related and leave out the others. Once we get rid of the unrelated details, here's what we have to work with.

▶ The dictionary included 12,000 words that had never been included in any dictionary of the English language.
▶ In the dictionary, Noah changed the spelling of several words to make the English language more uniform:
    -musick became music
    -honour became honor
    -plough became plow.
▶ The dictionary provided rules of pronunciation to help standardize American speech.
▶ Noah Webster's dictionary included distinctively American words such as skunk, hickory, and chowder.

What focus is there among these details? They all offer us specific information about Webster's *American Dictionary of the English Language*.

Now let's put the details in sentence form and arrange them into a paragraph. Here are two different paragraph options.

— 1 —

About 12,000 of the 70,000 words in Noah's *American Dictionary* had never been included in any other dictionary of the English language. Noah included rules of pronunciation to help standardize American speech. He changed the spelling of several words to make them simpler. He spelled *music* without a "k" at the end, *plow* without its original "ough" ending, and *honor* without a "u." Some words in the dictionary, like *skunk, hickory,* and *chowder,* were distinctively American.

— 2 —

Noah's dictionary proved to be a uniquely American publication. True to its name, the dictionary included many words that were specific to American English, including *skunk, hickory,* and *chowder.* In fact, there were 12,000 words in the dictionary that had never been included in any other dictionary of the English language. Through pronunciation rules, Noah tried to standardize American speech; with new spellings he attempted to simplify American writing. Perhaps most importantly, several of his spellings caught on and are in use today. For example, he changed *musick* to *music, plough* to *plow,* and *honour* to *honor.*

Which of the paragraphs do you prefer? We prefer the second paragraph. The first sentence is more general and establishes a central focus for the paragraph. There are also transition words that highlight the connections between different details. While it's hard to identify an organizational logic for the first paragraph, the second has a logical progression from what we considered the least important to the most important detail.

Now that we have a good paragraph, let's consider where it would fit best within the biography. Look back over the paragraphs included in this capsule and see where you think it should go.

It seems to make the most sense to place this paragraph between paragraph 22, which discusses the publication of the dictionary, and paragraph 23, which talks specifically about the dictionary's spiritual components.

> In 1824, Noah sailed to Europe to complete his research. In 1825, in a boarding house in Cambridge, England, he finished the dictionary. Three years later, *American Dictionary of the English Language* was published. Everyone agreed that the two-volume dictionary—which included over 70,000 words—was the best in the world.
>
> Noah's dictionary proved to be a uniquely American publication. True to its name, the dictionary included many words that were specific to American English, including skunk, hickory, and chowder. In fact, there were 12,000 words in the dictionary that had never been included in any other dictionary of the English language. Through pronunciation rules, Noah tried to standardize American speech; with new spellings he attempted to simplify American writing. Perhaps most importantly, several of his spellings caught on and are in use today. For example, he changed *musick* to *music*, *plough* to *plow*, and *honour* to *honor*.
>
> And on almost every page, Noah's faith shined forth: "Love, n. The love of God is the first duty of man. . . ." "Christian, n. A real disciple of Christ; one who believes in the truth of the Christian religion, and studies to follow the example, and obey the precepts, of Christ . . . ."

At this point we have just wedged the paragraph in the middle. Now we need to link the paragraphs together so that they flow easily from one into the other. By utilizing some of the tactics from Capsule 2.4.3, we can create seamless transitions.

> In 1824, Noah sailed to Europe to complete his research. In 1825, in a boarding house in Cambridge, England, he finished the dictionary. Three years later, American Dictionary of the English Language was published. Everyone agreed that the two-volume dictionary—which included over 70,000 words—was the best in the world. **Americans certainly thought so.**
>
> **After all**, Noah's dictionary represented a uniquely American publication. True to its name, the dictionary incorporated many words that were specific to American English, including skunk, hickory, and chowder. In fact, there were 12,000 words in the dictionary that had never been included in any other dictionary of the English language. Through pronunciation rules,

Noah tried to standardize American speech; with new spellings he attempted to simplify American writing. Perhaps, most importantly, several of his spellings caught on and are in use today. For example, he changed the spelling of *musick* to *music*, *plough* to *plow*, and *honour* to *honor*.

Even as the dictionary revealed his passion for orthography, it also revealed his passion for God. And on almost every page, Noah's faith shined forth: "Love, n. The love of God is the first duty of man. . . ." "Christian, n. A real disciple of Christ; one who believes in the truth of the Christian religion, and studies to follow the example, and obey the precepts, of Christ . . . ."

Now the paragraphs fit together well. Several transitional techniques are employed here.

▶ Ending a paragraph with a sentence that leads forward to the next paragraph (*Americans certainly thought so.*)
▶ Using transitional phrases (*After all, Even as*)
▶ Repeating important words or their synonyms (*orthography* is another word for *spelling*)
▶ Beginning a paragraph with a sentence that links back to the previous paragraph (E*ven as the dictionary revealed his passion for orthography...*)

It's not necessary to use every technique to transition effectively, but this should give you an idea of how easy it is to incorporate these techniques into your writing.

Can you guess what we're going to say next? Yes, it's your turn...

IN YOUR JOURNAL ▶

CWJ

Here are some details about Dr. Livingstone's life that were not included in the biography. Read through the list and select the ones that are the most closely related.
▶ David and his wife, Mary, had six children.
▶ He received honorary degrees from Cambridge, Oxford, and Glasgow universities.
▶ London Missionary Society asked him to resign after his interests shifted to exploration.
▶ He had his wife (often pregnant) and small children accompany him on his expeditions.
▶ During expeditions in 1850-51, his six-week-old daughter died of malaria and two of his children almost died of thirst.
▶ His one regret expressed late in life was not spending enough time with his children.
▶ He wrote a book *Missionary Travels and Researches in South Africa* (1857) that became a best-seller.
▶ His wife died of malaria in 1862 after following David back to Africa to join him on yet another expedition.
▶ He originally wanted to be a missionary to China.

1. Once you have chosen the details that go together, write them down in your journal.

We've included some additional details about David Livingstone's life so that you won't need to do any extra research. However, if you feel your student is ready, you might let him gather some of his own information from the library or through Internet searches. It's a good opportunity to do so: The scope of the project is small (a single paragraph). Additionally, some students enjoy looking things up themselves. Adding a research component may engage this type of student and make him more invested in his writing.

2. Construct a topic sentence that reflects what all the details have in common.

3. Look at these details and consider how you might want to organize them logically. Now turn the details into sentences and arrange them in paragraph form.

4. Add in transitions where they are needed to help connect your ideas within the paragraph.

5. Read through the conclusion of the Livingstone passage included in this capsule. Where do you think your paragraph would fit best?

6. Using the transitional, or linking, techniques we learned about in 2.4.3, link the paragraph you have written with the paragraphs before and after it. (Remember you may need to add sentences or transition words to the end of the paragraph that comes before or the beginning of the paragraph that comes after.) Write all three of the paragraphs in your journal.

Here is the rest of David Livingstone's biography.

15 He was disturbed to find that slaves were the country's most profitable export. He believed that if he could open a trade route to Central Africa, the sale of other valuable resources such as ivory, wood, and gold would replace the trade in human beings.

16 And he believed that as Christians came to Africa to trade, Christianity and civilization would come too.

17 As David crossed the country looking for a good spot to set up a mission, the strange tropical diseases and harsh conditions meant he was often sick and hungry. His life was often in danger. But he continued on—preaching to the natives everywhere he stopped.

18 He treated their illnesses and injuries. And as he explored, he sent detailed information of his findings back to England. To his surprise, he became famous as an explorer.

19 Dr. Livingstone once said, "Without Christ, not one step. With him, anywhere!"

20 As this missionary-explorer traced paths across Africa—going places white men had never gone before—he filled in many blank spots on Africa's map. And his exposure of the slave trade helped to end it. Once he had helped to map Central Africa, other missionaries came to serve.

21 When he died at age 60, Dr. David Livingstone was still exploring Africa. Though physically worn down and sick, he never gave up on the task God had set him to.

22 He died while kneeling in prayer beside his bed on the continent he had come to love as his own.

CAPSULE 5 2.4.5

LET GO, RETHINK AND REVISE

WORLD WISDOM

 No matter how careful and deliberate you are as you write, it is almost certain that your work will profit from some thoughtful revision. This is where you must learn to release the grip you have on your ideas, word choices and sentence structure – hold them loosely – because even the good ones may have to be discarded in favor of making the whole piece better. *God's World News* editor Rebecca Cochrane has learned to apply this lesson whether she is writing a book, news article, or personal essay.

"When I start a new writing assignment, I first brainstorm everything I have learned about the subject. I type as quickly as my fingers can go—what I know, what I think about what I know, what I wish I knew. This first exercise isn't even a 'rough draft.' It's an expedient way to dump out everything that is interesting or important about the subject.

Next I organize all that information. This is the time to consider who will be reading the work. I cut away anything that isn't relevant to my readers. I think carefully about the order in which the remaining information should be presented. What is the purpose of this assignment? How will I interest readers from the start?

A teaching essay's thesis—or main idea—shows up early in the writing. A blog entry might start out describing a memory or experience that readers will share. A news story opens with the most current facts. A children's book may begin with an action scene or some intriguing dialogue. In each case, supporting information follows the leading 'hook.'

Charlotte's Web author E. B. White taught that good writing gets 'to the point' quickly. The revision process should remove every word that isn't necessary to the assignment's purpose. Often it means letting go of descriptions I enjoyed writing. But Ecclesiastes 5:7 warns, 'Many words are meaningless.' There is wisdom in using words economically.

Sometimes it's hard to tell what needs to come out. Reading the draft aloud can help. And if time allows, a good rule is to 'shelve it and sleep on it.' Put your writing away overnight. If it still reads well to you the next day, you may have reached the final version."

—Rebecca Cochrane

In this last capsule, we are going to focus on revision. We like to talk about revising as rethinking. If you talk to any professional writer she will probably tell you that no matter how good her writing is, there is always room for improvement.

Even if you really like what you have written, it is a valuable exercise to take a break from your writing—usually a day or two—before returning to it. With a little distance, you may see things you didn't see before or have new ideas.

Revision represents an important part of a writer's process. Revision—seeing again—requires the writer to look at the essay with a critical and thoughtful viewpoint. Some students may not be able to do this. For students having difficulty, challenge them to find five items they would like to change. Encourage them to focus on the topics we've taught: topic sentences, paragraphs, and specific grammar lessons.

CWJ

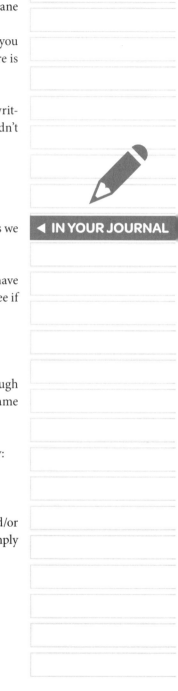

◄ IN YOUR JOURNAL

As you read back through the paragraph you wrote in 2.4.4, be on the lookout for the grammar issues we highlighted in 1.1.5—its/it's confusion, fragments, and vague pronoun references.

But pay particular attention to the grammar issues we have focused on in this unit. Since you only have one paragraph to revise, take a sentence-by-sentence approach. Read a single sentence, checking to see if it has any of these issues, and correct the issues, before moving to the next.

Here they are again:

Parallel Structure: Check to make sure that when you begin a pattern in a sentence, you follow it through to the end. Look for sentences that include lists of items and check that each item in the series is the same part of speech.

Here's an example of correct parallel structure from our paragraph about Noah Webster's dictionary:

For example, he changed the spelling of musick to music, plough to plow, and honour to honor.

Run-on Sentences: A run-on sentence consists of two sentences joined without connecting words and/or proper punctuation. If you find two independent clauses that are not properly connected, you can simply add a period and make them separate sentences.

What we would suggest, though, is linking them to create a compound or complex sentence. Remember that you make a compound sentence by adding a comma and coordinating conjunction (*and, but, so, for, yet, nor, or*) between the two sentences. You can create a complex sentence by adding a subordinating conjunction to the beginning of one of the sentences, turning it into a dependent clause.

If you don't find any run-on sentences, that is great! Now check to see if all of your sentences are simple. If they are, try linking some to make compound or complex sentences. Doing so will keep your paragraph from sounding choppy.

Comma after Introductory Word, Phrase, or Clause: To figure out if your sentence has an introductory element, locate the subject and verb of the sentence. Anything before the subject and verb is considered introductory. Insert a comma at the end of the introductory element, and you are done.

THE RIGHT WORD

You've learned 15 new vocabulary words throughout this unit. Now is the time for a review. Can you determine which vocabulary word is the BEST fit for each sentence?

abstract	extraneous	periphery
allusions	extol	quandary
ambiguous	homogeneous	ramble
chastise	lackluster	rant
delectable	menagerie	reticent

1. Joel's parents found it easy to _____ his athletic ability, but were unable to praise his horrendous singing.

2. Writers usually try to offer concrete examples to help readers understand _____ ideas such as love, success, and morality.

3. I do not consider spinach _____, nor do I find it remotely tolerable.

4. The professor's _____ lecture had everyone on the verge of falling asleep.

5. The professor's _____ criticizing his students for nodding off in class woke everyone up.

6. Noah's collection of animals on the ark is perhaps the most famous _____ ever created.

7. I don't mean to _____ you, but burping during a meal is terribly impolite.

8. Many novels contain _____ to Greek and Roman mythology.

9. By requiring public school students to wear uniforms, educators hope to downplay economic differences among students, thus making students more _____.

10. Selecting a college poses a _____ for many high school seniors.

11. Ryan thinks his mother includes too many _____ details in her storytelling.

12. When I am nervous, I tend to _____ on and on about trivial matters until someone stops me.

13. Authors may leave the ending of a book _____ to allow readers to draw their own conclusions.

14. While outgoing people enjoy being the center of attention, _____ people may prefer to remain on the _____.

Write with WORLD

TEACHER GUIDE UNIT 3 / LESSON 1

WRITING AUTOBIOGRAPHY

REPORTING FACTS

GENERAL OVERVIEW

In this unit, students will take on their first full-scale writing task. You may be surprised to find that most of the unit focuses on the lead-up to writing. Three of the four lessons prepare students to write by engaging them in prewriting exercises.

We could rush students through writing an "autobiography" of sorts in a single lesson. In most cases, students would list off a series of events that happened to them. Such an autobiographical story wouldn't require them to think much. Nor would it teach them skills that will make them better writers.

As students write an autobiographical story in this unit, we will be teaching them to think like real writers. Prewriting exercises are designed to help students cull through their experiences and thoughtfully consider which ones have the qualities that make a good story—a single incident with a beginning, middle, and end.

Other exercises help students to see that a listing of facts alone isn't a true autobiography. That's one part of the story, but what they thought, felt, and said during the incident are just as important. We provide a variety of questions and smaller writing assignments that help students reflect on the incident.

Perhaps most crucial, we ask students to look at photographs of their younger selves.
The use of pictures is vital to what we're teaching in this unit for two reasons. First, examining images continues to build on what we've done so far in this curriculum. In each unit, we've emphasized the importance of creating pictures in readers' minds. If readers can't visualize what you are talking about, you're not communicating with them. By once again providing students with real images to write about, we're reinforcing the importance of using specific details to create images in readers' minds. We're also giving students something visual to focus on. Rather than relying on fuzzy memories, photographs from their past will provide pristine details they can carry straight into their writing.

Second, we're demonstrating to them that writing isn't something you dash off in a few moments without adequate preparation. Digging up old pictures and looking at them is a form of research. In this case, students are using historical documents (photographs) to research their own lives.

If your student is a reluctant writer, this unit can serve as a real turning point. One reason is the subject is the student himself—he's the expert on the topic. That should provide some confidence. Another is that rather than quickly putting students through the paces of a writing exercise, we're requiring them to spend time thinking and mentally reliving their experience.

By taking more time and requiring more thought, students' investment in their story will increase. We also break the process down into manageable parts. By the time students have finished with the assignment, they should have a piece they take pride in.

Furthermore, in this unit students will begin to develop skills that will transfer to all types of writing—research skills, organizational skills, and critical thinking. This is a key unit in your student's development, so be sure to take each assignment seriously no matter how trivial it might seem.

DETAILED OVERVIEW

3.1.1-5: In this lesson, we begin by having students focus on the facts of their lives—things other people might know about them from observation. We have them describe their family members. We help them recognize and define the communities they are part of. All of these smaller brainstorming and invention exercises lead up to the unit's main purpose: developing a list of incidents the student may choose to write about for the auto-biographical essay. The student will create this list in 3.1.4. The student will refer back to this list multiple times in Units 3 and 4, so spend time helping your student brainstorm plenty of options.

3.2.1-5: This lesson challenges students to move beyond mere listing of events. The CWJ assignments require students to reflect on themselves. As students work through the capsules, they move from describing their personalities in general to reflecting on their emotions in specific situations. By mid-lesson, they're examining photographs of themselves from the past and answering questions about them. A main purpose of this lesson is for students to begin to see themselves as characters with specific features and personalities. In essence, we're asking them to do two very different things—1) see themselves from a distance and describe their external selves in specific detail and 2) share their innermost thoughts and feelings. When they can do both, they'll have laid the groundwork for revealing themselves as strong, distinct characters in their own narratives.

3.3.1-5: Students will focus on two potential autobiographical incidents in this lesson. We begin by having them test the stories for narrative strength using questions. Is the story really a story? Is there a purpose or reason for telling this story? Helping your student find his purpose before writing is key. He needs to know where he's heading with the story in order to organize it well. Knowing his purpose will help him choose relevant details rather than random ones. In capsule 3 you'll find a tool to help students make images central to their story—storyboarding. Here, students will imagine their story in "snapshots." They'll draw pictures for each scene in the story. Storyboarding will help your student organize her story, as well. Seeing the story in image form will help her realize what's missing. Later, when she begins to draft, storyboard cards will allow her to test potential organizational patterns for telling her story. A series of questions also helps elicit details students will use when they begin writing in the next lesson.

3.4.1-5: Students have been preparing to write about an autobiographical incident for the last three lessons. Here, they will put it all together and write their stories. On storyboard cards and in their CWJs, students have already developed an organization and collected many details they will be able to use as they write. We've broken the task into manageable pieces. Students will write the beginning of their story in one capsule, the body or middle in another, and the conclusion in a third. In capsule 4, you'll offer comments to help students with the revision process. An important feature of this lesson is the model autobiography. Seeing a concrete example gives both you and your student an idea of what an autobiographical incident might look like.

THREE WAYS TO HELP YOUR STUDENT WRITER IN UNIT 3

FOSTER OWNERSHIP

In Unit 3, students take on their first substantial writing assignment. We've chosen to begin by having them write about themselves. One reason is, from the very beginning, we want them to own their writing. With themselves—and their thoughts and feelings—as the topic, they cannot rely on you to tell them what to say.

At first, this may feel strange and uncomfortable for students. For many, their previous writing experience has prepared them to follow a form with little attention to content. In some writing curricula, how something is said is more important than students' ideas. If this has been their experience, reluctant writers may want you to tell them what to say.

If your student is silent and frustrated, it's tempting to pick up the pencil and start writing for him. But don't do it. Leave the pencil in his hand. Unless the exercise specifies that you're supposed to do it together, have him start on his own and check back a few minutes later. If his page is blank, don't start listing ideas for him. Use questions to help elicit ideas:

Parent: What's your favorite vacation that you've ever taken?

Student: Ummm. I don't know.

Parent: Well, let's think back through the vacations we've taken in the past few years. We went to Disney last year—that was a big one. The year before we went camping in Colorado . . . Didn't you take a bad fall when we were hiking?

Student: Yeah, I sprained my ankle and had to get an x-ray.

Parent: That's a good one—why don't you put it on your list? (Continue to help prompt the student until he has a few ideas to choose from.)

Similarly, you should help lead your student toward topics you think will make good narratives. By the time you narrow to the final two in Lesson 3, both should be workable topics. Even though you may think one is better than the other, let your student make the final choice. Talk through the pros and cons with her. Give her your opinion. But let the student have the final say.

In these small ways, you begin to demonstrate to the student that his opinions matter and that he has a voice. He needs to believe that he has something worthwhile to say if you want him to be excited about writing. By encouraging him to own his writing, you're building his confidence. You're paving the way for him to feel comfortable sharing his opinions in his writing—to develop a style and voice that are distinctly his own.

PROVIDE SPECIFIC FEEDBACK

Capsule 3.4.4. asks you to read your student's essay and comment on it—in a variety of colors. Using different colors to indicate strengths and areas that need improvement will help your student wade through the comments and make sense of them. The colors allow a student to first look through and see areas where she's doing well (marked in red and orange), then work on one issue at a time as she revises for clarity (blue) and added detail (green). The colors can be helpful to you, as well. As we've noted before, trying to fix everything at once can be overwhelming and defeating for students. When you pick up each pencil, you're looking for a specific strength or weakness in the paper. If you limit yourself to issues we've chosen to focus on in this unit, you'll be giving your student manageable tasks to accomplish as he revises.

You're encouraging your student to be specific, and you need to model that same specificity in your comments. Rather than placing a question mark in the margin when you are confused, write out a question: "I'm confused about the timeline. You say you broke your leg, but then two sentences later you are playing basketball. Is this much later? Or before you broke your leg?"

Even on the issues we're targeting in this unit, don't overdo the comments. It's better to have the student revise one paragraph well than to feel like he's being asked to redo every sentence. You need to strike the balance between pushing your student to grow as a writer but not overwhelming him.

Take the opportunity to conference with your student when you give the paper back. Start with the positives. Read aloud the parts you liked or thought were particularly strong. Then go through and explain each of your comments to the student, giving her time to ask questions as well.

Your student has put a great deal of time into this paper. When you take the time to thoughtfully comment on and discuss her writing, it shows her that you are taking her writing seriously.

FACILITATE REVISION

If your student isn't drafting on the computer, it would be an excellent idea to have him begin doing so in this unit. If he's not a proficient typist, it might be a good idea to let him practice as he goes, writing his CWJ entries on the computer.

There are a host of good reasons for encouraging computer drafting—not least of which is that you will be better able to read and comment on your student's writing if it is easy to read. Our main reason, though, is that the computer can be a tool to help your student become a better writer. If she handwrites an essay, she is going to balk when it comes time to revise and she has to squeeze her changes into the essay you've already marked up and then rewrite the whole thing. It's a huge job.

However, if she has drafted on a computer, she already has the bulk of the physical writing done. Changes are quick and easy to make. She can move things around. If revising is easy—even fun—she will be more inclined to make changes. And being willing and able to revise is essential to good writing.

CAPSULE 1

3.1.1

JUST THE FACTS, PLEASE

Lesson 1 of Unit 3 covers brainstorming. These lessons will provide beginning materials for the essay students will produce at the end of this unit.

Students can experience difficulties in brainstorming answers to questions. Encourage them to use details in their answers and to not settle for simple responses (I like third grade).

More importantly, as students brainstorm, stories or ideas may rise to the surface. Encourage your students to record these ideas in their CWJ; they may stumble upon their final topic before finishing the brainstorming exercises.

If someone who did not know you well observed your life, what facts could they learn about you? Imagine you have an across-the-street neighbor whom you barely know. What kinds of things might he be able to figure out from watching you come and go? Do you play basketball in the driveway every day? Do you ride your bike often? Do you have a dog? Do you go to church every Sunday?

These facts make up one piece of who you are. Though the cold, hard facts about your life tell only a little about you as a whole person, getting them down on paper is the first step to autobiographical writing. By the end of this unit, you will have written a short autobiographical essay—a paper that tells a story from your life. That may sound **daunting**, but relax. We're going to break the writing down into lots of little steps. And you're already the world's most highly-qualified expert on the topic at hand—you!

The first step is easy—in today's CWJ you will list ONLY facts someone could learn about you without ever having a conversation with you. Think of this as the "on paper" you. What does that mean? If you were filling out a job application, you would answer many of these same questions. When you read back over your answers, it tells something about you, but it doesn't really capture who you are. That's the "on paper" you. Later on we'll **delve** more deeply into your character. For now though, let's begin with the facts.

CWJ

Answer the following questions about yourself:

1. What is your name? Do you go by that name or do you have a nickname?
2. What is your birth date? How old are you?
3. What grade are you in? Are you homeschooled? If not, what school do you attend?
4. Describe how you look. Are you short or tall? What color hair and eyes do you have? Do you have glasses? Contacts? Braces?
5. Most days, I wear _____. (How do you dress when you have the choice?)

◀ IN YOUR JOURNAL

Write down two more facts about yourself that even an acquaintance might know. For example, "I play violin." Or "I won the talent competition by singing while juggling six coffee mugs at camp last summer."

CAPSULE 2

FAMILY FACTS

 For most of us, our family is one of the most significant influences on our lives. We spend most of our time—at least the first 18 years—with them. They know more about us than anyone else in the world. Many of the experiences we have directly relate to our families in some way.

When we begin to think about writing autobiography, we must consider our families. It's very possible that a family member or two will show up in your autobiographical essay. So in this lesson, while we're collecting our "on paper" facts, we want you to answer a few questions about each family member.

Right now, what you'll be doing is mainly listing. However, as you think about your family members, it's a good time to begin considering your life experiences too. What important incidents have you shared with various family members? What adventures or stories do you share with family members? How have they helped to make you the person you are? What have they taught you?

In this unit, we're moving toward an autobiographical essay. The autobiographical essay you write will tell a story about your life. So along with the facts, in CWJ for this lesson, we want you to begin thinking of experiences you shared with each family member and how they are important to the story of you.

CWJ

IN YOUR JOURNAL ▶

For each member of your family, answer the following questions:

Name/Nickname:

Age:

Occupation or grade in school:

Description of their appearance:

An important experience you've shared with this family member:

(Another way to say this is "a story that involves both of you.")

This CWJ requires students to list as their primary form of brainstorming. Some students may not generate ideas from listing. Instead, they may wish to draw or "map" ideas.

Mapping is a graphic form of listing. Students write down ideas on a large piece of paper and then link related ideas with circles and lines. The linking—drawing of connecting lines—only happens after the student has exhausted their brainstorming. In the past, we've watched students be very creative in their mapping: they've used multiple colors, shapes, and even drawings.

How your student composes the map is up to them. One student may choose to start writing ideas concerning their brother and find stories that link the brother to their backyard. Another student may start with a list of people who visit their mother on a weekly basis to build stories of events they remember from their childhood.

COMMUNITIES

 To begin today, you'll need a sheet of paper. It doesn't have to be big or fancy—the back of an old envelope will do. Across the top, list the days of the week, like this:

Sunday　Monday　Tuesday　Wednesday　Thursday　Friday　Saturday

Now, under each day list the scheduled activities you have on that day—schooling, music lessons, sports, clubs, church worship and activities, volunteer work, and so on.

After you've finished making this chart, think about the activities and interests that fill up your days. Can you add anything that you do occasionally but not every week, like babysitting for a neighbor or going to the movies with friends? Don't forget activities that are seasonal—like swimming at the pool in the summer or performing in the drama last spring.

Often we think of our community as being the place where we live. And that's true—our place of residence is one community to which we belong. The place where we grow up plays an important role in the person we become. The traditions we think are important, the clothes we wear, and even our accents and the words we use are shaped by our local communities. In Texas, where we live, it's hard to get along without a pair of cowboy boots. Here, you can wear cowboy boots almost anywhere and with a wider variety of outfits than someone in New England could. It's part of the culture—men can wear cowboy boots with nice suits, and women can wear boots with short dresses. On the other hand, it's pretty difficult to find a lobster boil in Texas, but in Maine, they're part of the culture.

Where we reside isn't the only community we're part of: most of us belong to several. Look back at your list of weekly events. How many of those events have a community—a group of people who share the same interest and activity—that goes along with it? Remember, the group need not be large . . . sometimes three people can share an intense interest and form a community.

Look back over your list and circle all the events you listed that have particular communities that go with them. For instance your church and your soccer team would be communities, while your music lessons may or may not have a community that goes with them..

CWJ

How many communities did you circle on your list? Was it surprising to you to discover how many different communities include you as a member?

◀ IN YOUR JOURNAL

Students should spend a good deal of time on this capsule and CWJ. Much of what they write in the rest of this book—and even into the next one—will come from this brainstorming exercise. It's fine for the student to begin on her own, but at some point, sit down and try to elicit more communities/activities that the student may be forgetting. Once she chooses her top three to five communities, talk through important events with her. Try to help her identify some interesting events she might later write about.

Carefully consider your list. Which groups do you spend the most time with? Where do you feel most "at home"? Which communities would you have the most difficult time living without? Which have had the greatest influence on your life?

After asking these questions, choose the top three to five and list them in your journal. For TWO of these, think of an important event in your life that has taken place in that community. For example: "broke my leg during a soccer game last year." Or "went on a mission trip with my church youth group."

CAPSULE 4

3.1.4

EVENTS THAT DEFINE YOU

THE PROFESSOR'S OFFICE:

Autobiographical essays are often the most fun to write. They give me the chance to reflect and to tell stories that are interesting and meaningful. When I teach autobiographical essays, I encourage students to tell small stories that carry big meaning. Most students try to tell big stories. They want to write about their three-month summer vacation, a 60-minute soccer game in which they played a major role, or their trip to Hawaii. These are huge events that would need to be covered in a book or very long essay. Ultimately, students get confused and lost when they try to write these huge essays.

The key to writing a great autobiographical essay is to develop a focus and purpose (a reason) for telling the story. What was memorable about the summer vacation? What was unique or challenging about the soccer game? How was your trip different from other people's trips to Hawaii? One of my students wrote an autobiographical essay about her summer vacation, but she began the essay with these lines:

> *This past summer my family visited China for two months. We saw The Great Wall of China, mountains, Tiananmen Square, and the Forbidden City. I ate lots of Chinese food and met many people, but none of these are what made my summer trip to China memorable. My summer vacation was less about seeing China and more about meeting and bringing my new sister to the United States.*

This student was very smart: she focused on an event she could write about in a few pages, an event she knew was important to her. The rest of the essay talked about walking into the room to meet her new sister for the first time, trying to play with her, and ultimately bringing her new sister to her new home in the United States. The essay was specific and focused—the writer had a personal reason for telling this story.

While this example of an autobiographical story is serious and moving, they can sometimes be funny. I am often asked by friends and family to share one of my autobiographical essays titled "The Story of the

This is a big question for young students to answer. And yet, it is an important question for them to consider when choosing the best topic. Feel free to help your writer reflect on this question.

If your student writes in a spiral-bound notebook, leave an extra page or two after this CWJ entry, as it is likely he will visit it again. The communities he identified here (and others he may remember or become a member of along the way) serve as the source for much of the writing he will do in *Write with WORLD*. You may even want to use a post-it tab to mark this page so that it is easy to find.

Wooden Shoes." It is nothing more than an account of my family's summer vacation to Michigan—a vacation where my brother and I lost our new tennis shoes and had to walk around Michigan and Indiana wearing wooden Dutch shoes. We'll save that story for a later date! Needless to say, writing autobiographical essays that start with small ideas can grow into essays capable of helping readers understand you better. And in some rare cases, a good autobiographical essay can persuade readers to invite you to their next dinner party . . . where they'll expect you to share a story.*

When you look back over the course of your life so far, what events stand out? Are there any specific events that have changed you? Are there any you wish you could go back and do over? Are some so **mortifying** they made you want to go hide under a rock somewhere?

Grab another sheet of scrap paper and put these headings at the top:

> Funny   Exciting   Happy   Sad   Scary   Embarrassing   Other

Spread them as far apart as possible so that you can jot some key words or phrases in each column.

Don't think too hard—just start listing anything that comes to mind. Some events may overlap—an event might be both funny and embarrassing, for instance. Don't spend too much time in **deliberation** about where to put it. The key words are to help **stimulate** ideas—we won't need the ideas in categories later.

After you've made your list, set it aside for a while—go do something else. When you come back to it, read through it. You might have something on your list that would make a good autobiographical essay, but it's too sad or embarrassing to write about. Cross those off, but don't scribble them out. Pencil through them lightly. You may use them in the next unit.

Now look again, considering each event: is this event something I can tell a personal story about? Sitting in the stands at a Cardinals game may have been one of the more important events in your life. However, if nothing really happened except that you ate a hot dog and got a sunburn, cross it out. For your autobiography, we want you to tell a story of your life that has a beginning, middle, and end. Choose an event where you have plenty to write about. It should also be interesting enough that other people would want to read about it.

CWJ

Congratulations! You've already done a lot of the work for today, and you haven't written one word in your CWJ. Today's task is easy. Look at your scrap paper list. Write down all the events you listed that both:

> Were important to you
> Have an interesting story that goes with them

Once you've defined today's words in bold in *The Right Word* section of your journal, you're finished.

◄ IN YOUR JOURNAL

Help your student understand the concept of time for this exercise. Some students will list for five minutes, run outside and play for awhile, and return to quickly make their choice of story.

Do not let your students rush this significant moment. This listing exercise could go on for two days or more. Encourage your student to list every possible story. Help them by talking about stories you or other family members remember. This could be a family brainstorming exercise.

THE ON-PAPER ME

WORLD WISDOM

We began this unit by examining the kind of basic facts that make up one piece of a person – the "on-paper" person. That's a good start, and you can learn a lot about someone that way. For example, let's look at some of the facts we know about Dr. Marvin Olasky, the Editor-in-Chief of World News Group. Later, we'll learn some interesting things that very few people know about the "real" Marvin Olasky.

"Here's my on-paper self, according to the beginning of a Wikipedia article: 'Marvin Olasky (born June 12, 1950) is editor-in-chief of WORLD Magazine and the author of more than 20 books, including The Tragedy of American Compassion. He is married to writer Susan Olasky. Olasky was born in Boston, Massachusetts to a Russian-Jewish family...'

That's a start. It's factually accurate and it notes the most important fact, my marriage. But then the Wikipedia entry gets to some crucial changes in me from middle school to the middle of my 20s: 'He became an atheist in adolescence and a Marxist in college.' Later it tells how God changed me: '...became a Christian after reading the New Testament and a number of Christian authors.' That transition in belief was crucial: From Judaism to atheism to Marxism to Christ."

— Marvin Olasky

CWJ

IN YOUR JOURNAL ▶

Today, for your autobiography project, we don't want you to write anything. You first need to look back through your CWJ for 3.1.1-4. Then, to distance yourself from the on-paper you, have your parent or teacher read out loud what you wrote. When you hear all the facts about yourself, does it sound like the person being described is you? Or could it just as easily be someone else? Does it capture who you are? What is missing? Discuss with your parent or teacher.

STYLE TIME:
To, Too, Two

Today's lesson is an easy one. You probably already know when to use to, too, and two. But if you're like most writers, sometimes when you start writing fast, you use a wrong word. That's especially easy to do when two words are pronounced exactly the same as in the case of to, two, and too. Just so there's no confusion, I'm going to explain when to use each.

Look ahead to the next unit lesson to see the limitations of what students have engaged in this lesson. Brainstorming can only capture a small part of the person—it can only produce a listing of qualities and a mere suggestion of what makes your student interesting.

To can be used two ways:

1. As a preposition:

   I am going *to* the store.

   I tied the balloons *to* the mailbox.

2. As an infinitive (a verb with the word "to" before it which acts as another part of speech—noun, adjective, adverb):

   My dog likes *to* eat Legos.

   I brought a raincoat *to* wear in case the weather gets bad.

Too can also be used to mean two different things (Wow! Look—we used all three in one sentence!):

1. Too can mean very or excessively:

   I put *too* much ketchup on my hot dog.

   I was *too* exhausted to watch the movie, so I went to bed instead.

2. Another meaning for too is also:

   Charis is going to camp *too*.

   I got an A on the test *too*.

Two is easy—it's the number (2) that comes between one and three:

   I ate *two* donuts for breakfast.

   Two tornadoes touched down in Missouri yesterday.

That's it! We'll practice looking for *to, two*, and *too* once you've written a draft of your autobiographical essay.

THE RIGHT WORD

Below are the five vocabulary words in context for this week. You should already have defined them in your journal as you found them in the reading.

▶ That may sound **daunting**, but relax.
▶ Later on we'll **delve** more deeply into your character.
▶ Are any so **mortifying** that they made you want to go hide under a rock somewhere?

▶ Don't spend too much time in **deliberation** about where to put it.

▶ The key words are to help **stimulate** ideas—we won't need the ideas in categories later.

Using your thesaurus, try to find the BEST word to replace the bold word in the sentence. If you aren't familiar with the meanings of all the synonyms for each word in the thesaurus, you may need to use your dictionary to look them up. That way you can choose the word that best fits the sentence.

Write with WORLD

WRITING AUTOBIOGRAPHY

CREATING CHARACTER

CAPSULE 1 · 3.2.1

WORLD WISDOM—THE REAL ME

In this lesson, we'll look at another **aspect** of who you are. We'll call this part the "real" you. You are more than just a list of facts on paper. You have personality and character. God made you a spiritual being. You have ideas and passions. You are unique. This is the part of you that we want to learn about in this lesson.

In the last capsule World News Group Editor-in-Chief Marvin Olasky showed you his "on-paper" self. In this capsule, Marvin Olasky shows another side of himself:.

WORLD WISDOM

"That Wikipedia entry [capsule 3.1.5] isn't bad: A biographer can capture a lot about a person. But can facts capture my real self? It depends on who is doing the writing. If God were writing my biography, he'd know all the facts and exactly which ones to emphasize. He knows my innermost secrets – things that I don't even know. No human biographer can ever write that kind of biography. We don't truly know our own hearts (see Jeremiah 17:9), so how can any human biographer really know what makes us tick?

That being said, some biographies do a better job than others of describing the essence of Marvin Olasky. Wikipedia focuses on easy-to-discover details: when I was born, where I went to college, who I married, and where I work. A more diligent biographer might paint in more details by interviewing my teachers, friends, or critics. Maybe he'd read my emails or follow me around for a day or a week to see how I spend my time. A close friend might be able to reveal even more of who I am – that I'm a Boston Red Sox fan. That I like to take walks with my wife. That this week I melded the words of the Doxology and Great is Thy Faithfulness with the music of a popular Russian melody.

Nobody but God can know the real me, but a good biographer can use words to capture a recognizable likeness."

— Marvin Olasky

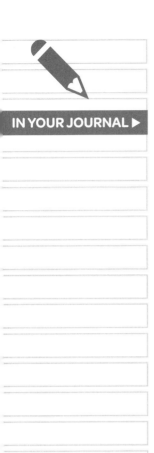

CWJ

Read back through 3.1.5 and compare it to today's reading. Answer these questions:

What is one thing you learned about Marvin Olasky today that you couldn't have figured out from reading facts about him/her?

What were you surprised to learn about the "real" Marvin Olasky?

Look back over the facts about yourself in Lesson 1 Capsule 1. What is one important thing about you that someone wouldn't figure out from merely reading facts about you?

CAPSULE 2
3.2.2

WHAT MAKES YOU YOU?

Are you a neat freak? Or a disorganized mess? Do you love to help? Or do you head out the back door when you smell a big project coming?

Questions like these help reveal character and personality, the parts that most lists of facts about you don't include. What we want to learn in this lesson is the part of you that your friends and family think about when they think of you. What makes you laugh? Who was your imaginary friend when you were three years old? What's your favorite food? What do people love about you? What annoys them?

Today, you will spend some time analyzing yourself. We don't want you to make lists. Revealing who you really are takes more than facts and one-word answers. Answer the questions in your journal with full sentences. We want to learn about the **nuances** of your personality, not just the broad outlines.

For instance, the first question asks, "Are you shy or outgoing?" Instead of a one-word answer, we want you to explain using some specifics. A weak answer would be, "I'm shy." The type of answer that will help you define the real you might look more like this: "I'm shy when I first meet people, but once I get to know them it's hard to get me to stop talking!" or "I'm shy with people one-on-one, but I love performing in front of an audience."

The point is, "shy" tells us very little. It's vague. Most real people aren't fully shy or always outgoing. They have aspects of both. Your answers should help readers understand what you're really like. Give us the details.

This is the big question. Too often students will say "there is nothing very surprising about me" or "I'm boring." We know these responses are false, for God made all of us unique and for an express purpose.

If students have trouble discovering the important thing not revealed in the list of facts, encourage them to share the paper with a peer or family member. Sometimes an audience will recognize this quality more quickly.

Students will want to give one-word answers because some of these questions are yes-no questions. If a student answers "yes," your follow-up should be "why" or "give me an example."

CWJ

This CWJ gives you an excellent opportunity. Answer in detail, modeling thoroughness for your student. Even if her answers are short and weak, when you compare notes, your more detailed answers will spark a discussion. Encourage her to keep a pencil in her hand and add to her CWJ as you discuss both sets of answers.

Today, you get to give your parent a writing assignment! At the same time as you are answering these questions about yourself, have your parent answer the questions about you on a separate sheet of paper. No talking until you have both finished.

◄ IN YOUR JOURNAL

Take some time and think about these questions. Make sure your answers reveal more about you than just facts.

1. Are you shy or are you outgoing (the kind of person who never met a stranger you couldn't talk to)? Make sure you include at least one example to help show the degree to which you are shy or outgoing, or situations in which you are shy or outgoing, etc.)

2. When you think about yourself, what activity, interest, or aspect comes to mind first? In other words, what defines you? Faith? Good character? Honesty? Work ethic? Athleticism? Sense of humor? Academics? Physical characteristic? Something else? Explain why, giving at least one detailed example.

3. What are you passionate about? In other words, what do you care deeply about? If you can't think of something right off hand, here are some questions that might help you discover the answer:

▶ If you had an hour to spend doing anything, what would it be?
▶ When you read, what do you enjoy reading about?
▶ What do you think you'd like to do when you grow up?
▶ What subjects do you enjoy talking about? (Hint: if your family gets tired of hearing you talk about something, you may be passionate about it)

When you're done, compare and discuss answers. Were they similar or very different? Why? (Make sure to save both sets of answers)

THE PROFESSOR'S OFFICE:

This unit teaches you how to brainstorm. Brainstorming may be the most important and over-looked step of the writing process. Some of my students believe they can write a successful five-page paper in one or two days; a few believe they can write the same paper in one night . . . the night before the paper is due. None of them brainstorm: they immediately start writing with ideas in their head . . . and most of the papers they turn in to me have major flaws and need much work.

We don't want you to become one of the writers described in the previous paragraph. That's why this unit asks you to brainstorm so much. Eventually you will write an essay, but we want you to think a lot about the ideas that will go into that essay before writing it.

Good writers think about and write down ideas before they start writing. Whether they write their ideas in a computer file or on a napkin at a restaurant, good writers need to start somewhere . . . and they don't typically start with the assignment. When writers have nothing, feel "blank," or need to start an assignment, they brainstorm. They make lists, answer questions, draw pictures, make idea maps; they do anything they can to develop ideas and gain inspiration.

Brainstorming often leads to great results: you may find an incredible topic, figure out how to discuss and organize a topic, or understand a topic much better.

CAPSULE 3

INSIDE EVENTS

Read the following incident:

> When I was nine, I fell off my bike and had to go to the hospital. I was riding down a steep hill and I lost control and wiped out. I couldn't get up off the ground, so my brother went and got my mom. My leg hurt really bad. My mom had to help me get in the car. I was crying. When we got to the hospital we had to wait in the emergency room for a long time. When we finally saw the doctor, he sent me for an X-ray. Sure enough, my leg was broken. They put a cast on it which I had to wear for eight weeks. It pretty much ruined my summer.

What did you learn about the writer from that story about him? Let's make a list:

- He's older than 9

- He broke his leg riding his bike

- It hurt

- He went to the hospital

- Doctors took an X-ray of his leg

- He got a cast and had to wear it for 8 weeks

- His summer was ruined

Those are almost all facts an across-the-street neighbor could have found out without ever really knowing anything about the writer. Readers don't really learn anything specific about who the writer is from that story.

Remember, the autobiographical essay is supposed to tell us about you. In the story above, the writer just told us the facts of the bike wreck. That's a little boring, and we don't know the writer any better after we've finished it. Here are some questions that we wish the writer would have answered in his story:

Why were you on a bike ride? Did you ride all the time? Did you like to ride bikes?

What were you thinking about as you rode? Did you get distracted? Or did something else cause you to wipe out?

What were you thinking and feeling as you fell? How intense was the pain?

What were you thinking and feeling as you waited at the hospital?

What conversations did you have (or hear between your mom and the doctor)?

How did having a cast ruin your summer? What kinds of things were you unable to do that you enjoy doing?

In the last lesson, we listed facts about important incidents. This time, we want you to take those same incidents and tell us about them as if we could read your mind. Here's an example of what we mean. The "inside story" of the bike wreck you just read about might look like this:

> I was small for my age and I was tired of getting beaten in everything by my brother. He was a year younger but an inch taller and several pounds heavier. People were always asking if I was the younger brother, which really annoyed me. One day when I was nine years old, we were racing on our bikes. For once, I was ahead. We were right at the top of a big hill. I glanced over my shoulder and saw that he was catching up fast, so I swerved into his path to cut him off. Smack! I heard his tire hit my back tire the same time as I felt the jolt. My front tire skidded in the gravel on the edge of the road as my back tire swung up even with the front tire. I hit my brakes, but the hill was steep, and I was moving too fast to stop. The next thing I remember is hearing a loud SNAP! and feeling the worst pain I'd ever felt. It was coming from my leg.

This tells us about the wreck, but we also learn about the writer and what led up to the bike wreck (small for his age, annoyed at being smaller than his younger brother, competitive, etc.).

Today, we'd like you to explore one incident from the list you made in 3.1.4 and give us the "inside story" on what you were thinking and feeling during those events.

Take a moment to discuss the two paragraphs. Here are some questions to get you started:

Which paragraph did you think was more interesting? Why?

Which one could you picture better in your mind? Why?

What do you think is the biggest difference between the two paragraphs?

The difference here is between a listing of qualities (an on-paper persona) and a story that has character, personality, and voice.

IN YOUR JOURNAL ▶

CWJ

Choose one incident from the list you made in 3.1.4. Choose an important "moment" or "scene" from that incident. (For example, the moment you arrived at what you thought was a costume party only to find out it was NOT a costume party.)

    1. What were you thinking at that moment?
    2. What were you feeling at that moment?

Now, write it up as a short paragraph. Here's an example.

> I rang the doorbell and waited. When John opened the door, I noticed that his costume didn't really look any different than his regular clothes. ***That's funny***, I thought to myself. ***I wonder who he's supposed to be?*** As I walked through the door, I looked around and suddenly realized that everyone's costumes looked like his or her regular clothes. Then it hit me: This wasn't a costume party at all. Suddenly my face felt like it was on fire. I backed toward the door. I wanted to run. But it was too late. Everyone had already seen me.

CAPSULE 4   3.2.4

THE YOU OF YESTERDAY

Today we want you to look at family photographs. You can look at them alone or with family members. Don't rush. Take time to notice details about yourself in the past. Really look at the other people and places in the pictures. You'll find you remember lots of details about your earlier life that you had forgotten.

We hope you'll have conversations (or memories if you're looking at the pictures alone) like these: "Look at that awful haircut you had when you were five! That's the "fix-it" haircut we had to do after you tried to cut it yourself." Or, "Oh, look, there's Benny, your first puppy." Or, "Do you remember that tree house we built together in the backyard? You and your friends spent hours playing up there."

Enjoy the pictures. No doubt you'll remember an incident or two that you've forgotten. If you discover a good one, it's not too late to add it to the list.

What we hope the pictures will help you realize is that as a person, you are not **static**. You are constantly changing. Even when you write about yourself, you're creating a character on paper. That's because the you in your story is slightly different than the you of today. Even if it was just last year, you've grown since then. You know more. You've had more experiences. You have the benefit of distance from the incident to think about it and understand it better.

Students may find writing about this material difficult. Instead, they may prefer talking about it. This is fine.

It is not unusual for great writers to talk through their ideas and record them. They then return to transcribe or take notes on what they discussed. Go ahead and introduce this idea to students who are having difficulty putting words down on the page.

CWJ

Look back over your list from 3.1.4. Now think about the photographs of yourself you just looked through. Match 1) an incident with 2) a snapshot that was taken around the same time as the incident occurred.

◄ IN YOUR JOURNAL

Quickly jot down as much information as you can about the picture. Let's see how much information can you learn about yourself from these pictures?

1. What are you wearing?
2. How is your hair cut?
3. Are you happy or sad?
4. Do you remember when the picture was taken? What was the occasion? Where were you?
5. Do you remember what you were thinking?
6. What is in the picture with you?
7. Who is in the picture with you?
8. How are you the same person you were in the picture? How are you different now?

When you look back at yourself in the picture, do you feel a sense of **nostalgia**? (Okay, we admit that we just threw that last question in because nostalgia is a great vocabulary word.)

Help students choose stories that are interesting, have a clear chronology, and present interesting characters/actions.

We once had a student who was given a prompt similar to this one. Her story turned into a comical farce that covered 15 pages, seven years, and four cities. Painful is a nice description of what we were feeling.

An event that is focused on a short period of time will produce better writing. You may need to help students see this by asking questions. In the example above, I wish the author would have chosen one-two days, one city, and four or five pages.

Choosing the right topic will play a huge role in your student writer's happiness and success. Do not let them rush this process.

CAPSULE 5   3.2.5

CONSIDERING POSSIBILITIES

As you've looked back through your list of important incidents (3.1.4), are you more drawn to some incidents than others? Which ones make the most **compelling** stories? Which reveal the most about who you are as a person? In the next lesson, we'll narrow in on two possible incidents for your autobiographical essay. Take a little time today to think about which stories you are most interested in telling about yourself and why.

CWJ

1. Examine your list of important incidents and consider which two you like most.
2. Complete *Style Time* and *The Right Word*.

◄ IN YOUR JOURNAL

STYLE TIME:

● **Tense**

As I walked by the dock, I decide to sit on the edge and put my feet in.

What's wrong with this sentence? Look at the verbs:

As I ***walked*** by the dock, I ***decide*** to sit on the edge and put my feet in.

The writer starts out in the past tense but then changes to the present. Especially as you begin writing longer pieces, you need to remember to stay in the same tense for the whole essay. For the most part when you are telling a story about your past, you will stay in the past tense:

As I **rode** my bike down the hill, I **fell** off.

One exception is dialogue. It's in the present tense because those are the words you used at the time:

"I'm going to the Wilsons!" I shouted as I ran out the back door.

Another exception is for style. Sometimes a writer will tell a whole story in the present tense to give it a sense of immediacy, as if it is happening as you read. That type of writing would look something like this:

I grab an apple as I run through the kitchen. I hear the slam of the screen door as I dash through. "I'm going to the Wilsons!" I shout.

Look at the paragraph you wrote in 3.2.3 and underline all your verbs. Are they all in the same tense? If not, choose a tense (past or present) and make the tense consistent throughout the paragraph.

THE RIGHT WORD

Below are the five vocabulary words in context for this week. You should already have defined them in your journal as you found them in the reading.

▶ In this lesson, we'll look at another **aspect** of who you are.
▶ We want to learn about the **nuances** of your personality, not just the broad outlines.
▶ What we hope the pictures will help you to realize is that as a person, you are not **static**.
▶ When you look back at yourself in the picture, do you feel a sense of **nostalgia**?
▶ Which ones make the most **compelling** stories?

Using your thesaurus, try to find the BEST word to replace the bold word in the sentence. If you aren't familiar with the meanings of all the synonyms for each word in the thesaurus, you may need to use your dictionary to look them up. That way you can choose the word that best fits the sentence.

Write with WORLD

WRITING AUTOBIOGRAPHY

DEVELOPING IDEAS

CAPSULE 1

3.3.1

WHAT STORY SHOULD YOU TELL?

In the last capsule, we asked you to think about which two stories you would most like to tell about yourself. Because you are writing an autobiographical essay, it shouldn't merely be a good story. It should reveal something about you as a person.

In this lesson, we want you to lay out two stories that you could tell. Why two? Because sometimes a story seems like it will really work well while it's still in your head, but when you get it on paper, it's a dud. Maybe you can't remember many details. Or it's not as funny as you thought. Or it really doesn't have any point.

Today, you will answer a few questions about the two stories you chose in the last capsule. If you can't give good answers to these questions, you might want to look at your list again and choose another incident.

CWJ

Answer these questions two times, once for each story:

1. Does this story have a beginning, middle, and end? Write one sentence summarizing each part.
   How does the story begin?
   What happens in the story?
   How does it end?
2. Why is this story important to you or why do you want to tell it?
3. What does the story reveal about your personality or character at the time of the incident?
4. Did the incident change you in any way?
5. In a sentence or two, explain what you learned from this experience in your life.

If writing the answers to this on paper is making your writer freeze up, talk through the answers with her. Or, as we've suggested before, have the student record the answers and transcribe them later.

You might have your student read ahead to the next capsule if he's not sure what his answers should look like in the CWJ for 3.3.1.

◀ IN YOUR JOURNAL

INCLUDING THE RIGHT DETAILS

Read this paragraph from the last lesson, noting the added details in bold:

> I was small for my age and I was tired of getting beaten in everything by my brother. He was a year younger but an inch taller and several pounds heavier. People were always asking if I was the youngest, which really annoyed me. One day when I was nine years old, we were racing on our bikes. **The sky was azure blue. Cottony white clouds dotted the sky.** For once, I was ahead. We were right at the top of a big hill.

Do the added details in bold **enhance** the paragraph? Or do they interrupt its flow?

These are not bad details. There might even be a place for them in this story. But this is not the place. The writer is writing about racing—he's probably not looking at the sky and noticing clouds while he is on the bike. In this part of the paragraph, the details are distracting, not helpful.

Sometimes writing assignments ask for students to add details after they've finished writing the essay— like sprinkles you would place on top of cupcakes after baking them. Good details are not like add-ons or decorations that make the cupcake look pretty. Instead, they are important ingredients that need to be baked into the cupcake batter.

That's why we want you to begin thinking about details right now before you actually begin writing. Good details are part of the batter, not decorations to be added at the end. The details you include should be relevant—they should connect to your story in an **integral** way.

For instance, in a story about a tidal wave ruining a perfect day at the beach, a good writer might include details about how beautiful and perfect the day was before the wave hit. Details about the beautiful day would set the scene. They would also contrast with the awful destruction that the writer would describe later in the paper.

On the other hand, a good writer would handle a story that takes place at the beach but is really about a huge argument with her sister differently. If she spent several paragraphs describing the scenery and the weather, she would write a confusing and unfocused story. In this story, pertinent details would describe and explain the relationship between the sisters—not the weather.

Let's look at an example to better explain what we mean. In this example of an autobiographical essay, let's imagine that the writer has decided to share an incident that occurred on a mission trip. Before we can determine what type of details she might need, we need to know the point of her story. So let's see

We keep discussing this point because young writers are prone to making this mistake. They tend to use details without reason, and we want them to consider why certain details are more important than others.

A nice exercise for teachers is to randomly choose an adjective from a draft—one that they like. Tell the student you thought their word choice was interesting. Then ask the student why they chose that adjective.

It is good for students to explain word choices and phrasings. Doing so will help them become more conscientious writers.

how she might have answered the questions from the last capsule:

1. Does this story have a beginning, middle, and end? Write one sentence summarizing each part.
How does the story begin?
I do not want to go on a mission trip to Mexico, but my parents force me.

What happens in the story?
I get there and am feeling sorry for myself at first until I meet a little girl named Lupe whose joy and thankfulness make me aware of how privileged, selfish, and ungrateful I am.

How does it end?
I don't want to leave Mexico. I resolve to go back again as soon as I can to help.

2. Why is this story important to you or why do you want to tell it?
Because it showed me what a selfish person I was and it made me want to change. It made me grateful to God for the blessings he has given me.

3. What does the story reveal about your personality or character at the time of the incident?
I was self-centered and lacking awareness of how blessed I am.

4. Did the incident change you in any way?
Yes, after my mission trip I changed from being so selfish to focusing on helping others and sharing the gospel.

5. In a sentence or two, explain what you learned from this experience in your life.
I learned that compared to most of the world, a majority of Americans have it easy. We take food, health insurance, comfortable homes, and cars to drive for granted. I learned to be grateful for all that I have.

From the answers to these questions, we could say that the central point or theme of this autobiographical story is the writer's growth from self-centeredness to caring, selfless devotion to helping others.

Immediately, we can think of three types of details that would be important to the story:

1. Examples showing how selfish the writer is at the beginning of the story.

2. Examples showing the contrast between the luxury of her life in the United States and the poverty in Mexico.

3. Details about Lupe and how observing and getting to know her changed the writer.

So what might some of those details look like? If the writer were to make a list, it might look like this:

1. Selfish:
- complained about having to go on the trip
- mad that I couldn't take my blow dryer and makeup
- pouted at the airport when dad wouldn't buy me Starbucks

2. U.S. luxury vs. Mexico's poverty
- houses are shacks, no air conditioning
- kids are hungry, few toys
- many can't afford school, must work to help family survive

3. Lupe
- mother is dead
- takes care of younger siblings though just 8 years old
- happy despite her circumstances, thrilled with the small gifts we gave her

We hope you are beginning to see that the best, most effective stories *show* more than they *tell*. If the writer just tells us that she went on a mission trip and learned to be grateful, we don't really know much more about her at the end of the story than we did before. We learn about the writer through the details of *how* she was selfish. Relevant details are a key ingredient of good writing. If you can learn to include the right details in your writing, you're on the path to becoming a real writer.

THE PROFESSOR'S OFFICE:

This capsule makes two key points that my best student writers understand. First, great writers understand the purpose of description. Second, great writers use details to show rather than tell. Learning these two lessons can turn an average writer into a great one.

I have already discussed this in the first point in 1.2.1-5, but it merits revisiting. Description works when it has a purpose, when it helps make your point. I once worked with a student who had a knack for writing long sentences . . . very long, long sentences. Sometimes, his sentences would cover 15 lines. Unfortunately, his sentences were not good; they were hard to follow and full of too much detail—detail that did not help make his point. Here's an example:

The young, preteen, girl wearing a sleeveless pencil dress with a yellow-green belt and matching mid-heel shoes, walked gracefully down the burgundy red, 500-meter carpet to the delight of crazy-haired, pompous paparazzi flashing blindingly bright light bulbs every millisecond and smiled at her bulky, bearded and hunky male host in the rainy, windswept green park just west of downtown Los Angeles.

What's the point of the sentence? Here it is: a young girl who is likely a celebrity walked down the red carpet and smiled at her host. I was able to write the idea in one line. The issue is one of economy: to be eloquent, an economical use of description is key.

Some of the details in the sentence help make the point. Other details are not important. Do I need to know the park was rainy, green, and windswept to understand the key point? Do I need to know the paparazzi are crazy-haired (I'm not even sure what crazy-haired means!). Do I need to know the girl is wearing mid-heel shoes that match her belt? The answer to all of these questions is NO! All these details cause me, the reader, to lose concentration and not understand the writer's point.

At the same time, great authors use descriptive details in their writings. Their details have a purpose: they help the reader understand the important points. These details show the reader the point rather than tell them. When drafting, writers tend to not use many details and make general statements like, "The look of the diving board made me nervous." This sentence tells me the writer was nervous, and I am left to wonder why. When I read a sentence like this one, I usually ask the writer a few questions. In this instance, I might ask what about the diving board's look made you nervous? Was it the rusty springs, a broken ladder, the height of the board? Then I might ask about the writer's nervousness: how nervous were you? Were you shaking? Did you not want to jump? After answering these relevant questions, the author can write a better sentence, one that uses details to show me the point. Here's the revision: "The diving board's rusty springs and cracked surface made me so nervous that I wanted to throw up." I love this revision—I can see the board and understand how nervous the writer became when they saw the diving board.

CWJ

Today, we want you to look back over your answers to the questions in the last capsule. Following the example we worked through in today's capsule, write down the main point or theme for each of the two stories you are considering for your autobiographical essay.

◄ IN YOUR JOURNAL

Now, based on your answers, come up with two types of details that will help you get your point across. Do this for each incident. (Use the example from the mission trip as a guide.)

Finally, under each type of detail, give two examples. (See the mission trip example.)

CAPSULE 3
3.3.3

CLICK. CLICK. CLICK. YOUR STORY IN PICTURES

In your memory, go back to the day that one of the two autobiographical incidents you are considering occurred. If a photographer had been following you, what pictures would he have taken? In other words, if you were telling the story through pictures, what pictures would you include?

 Thinking through a story using pictures is a method that has been in use for almost 80 years. It began in Walt Disney's studios in the 1930s. One of Disney's **animators** would pin sketches of characters and scenes on a board to help demonstrate the cartoon story he wanted to tell. Walt Disney liked this manner of storytelling so much that he turned it into a method called storyboarding. Other studios quickly adopted Disney's method. Today, many moviemakers storyboard every shot in the movies they make before they begin filming. Storyboarding actually saves money in the long run if it's done well. It helps to make sure the ideas are clear before filming starts.

People in other fields such as theater and business have **adapted** storyboarding as a tool in their professions, as well. Other types of writers, such as comic book makers and novelists also frequently use storyboarding to help organize ideas. One benefit of storyboarding is that it allows you to move ideas around and to consider telling your story using a different organization.

For instance, in our paragraph about the boy who fell off his bike, the writer could begin on the ground with pain shooting through his leg for dramatic effect. He could then flash back in time to let readers know how the accident occurred.

So today, your first task is to make a "storyboard." Create a picture for each important scene in one of the two stories you are considering. For each scene use one of the notecards (on your list of supplies for this lesson). If your event is physical (like a bike wreck) it might be helpful to think of that photographer perched on a hill above you watching the events. What would he see?

Now draw each important moment on a separate card. Don't worry about how good the drawing is—the storyboard is for you—not for anyone else. If you like to draw and being more detailed helps you think about the event, that's wonderful. Spend as much time as you'd like drawing. If you're not an artist, stick figures work just fine, too. Make lots of cards—you may decide that you don't need all of them. But it's better to have too many than too few.

CWJ

IN YOUR JOURNAL ▶

By the end of the next capsule, you should have collected enough information about each of your two stories to choose which you'd like to write your autobiographical essay about. Here are a few more questions. Think of these as a written version of the storyboard scenes you just made. Keep your cards close at hand. Use them to help you—especially on number five, as you describe the event in detail. If you find you've left out an important storyboard card, add it now.

1. How old were you when the event occurred?
2. Where were you when the event occurred?
3. Why were you there?
4. What activities or actions led up to the event?
5. Describe the event in detail.
6. What happened afterward (what were the consequences)?
7. How were you feeling during this event?
8. What were you thinking?

Some students will prefer using simple stick pictures and few words in their storyboards. Other students may want to depend on more words and minimalist drawing. Either option is fine.

The key is that the students do the drawing. On this point you may experience some resistance, for savvy students may want to use images found on a computer. Actual drawing is better for this exercise.

Students who complete the drawing themselves are thinking about the incident and likely recalling details. Drawing forces them to remember, while a computer image records someone else's memory. Putting pencil to paper and making images—either symbols or words—will help their ideas grow specifically. Storyboarding, then, is about recording details and meaning-making.

9. How did you react?

10. What did you say? What did the other people involved say?

CAPSULE 4 3.3.4

IMAGES AND STORYBOARDING

WORLD WISDOM

 When you write a story using words you're really using pictures, too—pictures that appear first in your mind and then in the mind of your reader. Picturing your story will help you select more descriptive words and active verbs. Of course, some day you may write a story that will include photos or illustrations along with your text. That is an exciting mix that helps you use the particular strengths of both words and pictures, a skill that Rich Bishop, *God's World News* Creative Director, appreciates.

" 'Words rule.'

There. I said it. The artist has finally humbly bowed to the writer. But it didn't come easily. After all, so much in my experience wants to argue for the preeminence of the visual image.

Zebra. 'Click,' your brain just delivered a picture.

Ask someone for driving directions. 'Turn left at the large white barn.' Click, another image.

You've heard teachers say that some students are visual learners? I've never met someone who is not a visual learner.

We constantly soak up images and digest them into brain food—information. It's the way God made us. So yes, words may rule—the word may be king, but the picture is queen.

In my work as an art director I try to find ways to make images serve, complement and enhance the written word. And pictures can accomplish those things in different ways.

Images can be objective. That is, they can deliver clear and definite facts to the viewer. A photo shows that the space shuttle is white with black tiles. Maps, info-graphics, or charts can efficiently deliver facts and figures that would otherwise require lengthy and dull descriptions in writing. As an art director I value images that fill in the details of a story.

Images can be interpretive. They can set the tone for a story by delivering a mood or emotion. A story about a war-torn African nation might best be introduced with a close-up news photo of a young refugee child.

Images can be artistic. An illustrator can capture the theme of a story or essay with a drawing through the use of symbols or metaphors.

The king rules, but the queen is in the house, and she's quite the picture."

— Rich Bishop

IN YOUR JOURNAL ▶

CWJ

Today, we want you to storyboard your second autobiographical essay idea. Remember, the pictures can be as simple or detailed as you like. Use cartoon bubbles if you want to include dialogue. Create enough storyboards that someone looking at the pictures could make sense of your story.

When you've finished, answer the same questions about the story as you did last time:

1. How old were you when the event occurred?
2. Where were you when the event occurred?
3. Why were you there?
4. What activities or actions led up to the event?
5. Describe the event in detail.
6. What happened afterward (what were the consequences)?
7. How were you feeling during this event?
8. What were you thinking?
9. How did you react?
10. What did you say? What did the other people involved say?

CAPSULE 5
3.3.5

MAKING A CHOICE

Today, look back through 3.3.3 and 3.3.4. Lay out both storyboards and see which one you like better. You might find it helpful to have a parent or teacher look at them with you. Based on your storyboards, which autobiographical story do you think is better? Which would you rather tell? If you answer both questions with the same story, you've chosen your story. If they're different, look at your storyboards again. Would it help to add more scenes to the story you want to tell? Could you change the organization to make the story more interesting?

Students may rebel at doing this big task all over again for another possible autobiographical narrative. Perhaps your student is certain she wants to write about the incident she storyboarded about in the previous capsule. There's a good chance she's right—at least 50 percent. However sure she feels, have her storyboard the second narrative. It may jog some memories and remind her to add cards to her first storyboard. She may surprise herself and discover that this incident actually has more substance and makes a better story. She may also choose to use this storyboard as the basis for her fiction project in the next unit.

Regardless, practicing the new skill of storyboarding is helping her think through the details of a story. This is not wasted time.

Students must make this decision—doing so is key to their owning the story.

They are not required to make this decision in a vacuum. They can and should seek the counsel of people they know and trust.

Don't be surprised if this decision causes anxiety. Your student may feel confused and torn by their excitement over both topics. The key for a student who has thought deeply about the choice and is still unable to choose is to get on with it. Once the student makes a choice, they will probably feel excited (that is until they have to start writing!).

Ultimately you must make the decision. The good news is, even if your chosen story is a flop, you have another one ready to write. So it's okay to take a risk. I'm sure any professional writer could tell you more than one tale about a piece of writing that just didn't work. But real writers don't let that discourage them—they regroup and start over.

CWJ

Today, work on *Style Time* and *The Right Word.* Take a little break from thinking about your story.

STYLE TIME

 The lesson for today is a difficult one—good writers frequently make this grammar error. Why? Because it's a shortcut. Almost everyone makes this mistake when they talk. See, we just made the mistake right there. Did you notice? See if you can find my mistake.

The mistake is lack of agreement between a pronoun (in this case, *they*) and its antecedent (in this case, *everyone*). Corrected, this sentence would read:

Almost everyone makes this mistake when he or she talks.

So why is this such a common mistake? Sometimes it's because people don't realize that the indefinite pronouns everyone, everybody, anyone, anybody, no one, nobody, someone, and somebody are singular. So a correct use of an indefinite pronoun in a sentence looks like this:

Somebody forgot to put his or her dishes in the dishwasher.

However, repeated sentences like this one become **tedious**. If you keep saying "his or her" over and over again it starts to pull the focus away from what you're saying and onto the repeated use of "his or her."

People often make this same mistake with singular nouns:

Each participant should bring their own lunch.

When possible, use plural nouns to avoid this problem. In this case, we could fix the sentence like this:

Participants should bring *their* own lunches.

Here is another example. Though the first sentence is correct, the second is preferable. Change:

Each student should hang his or her coat on his or her hook outside the door.

To:

Students should hang *their* coats on the hooks outside the door.

Now, look back through your journal entries for this lesson. Circle each use of they and their. Find the antecedent—the word the pronoun refers back to. If it's singular, change either the pronoun or its antecedent so both agree (both plural or both singular).

THE RIGHT WORD

Below are the five vocabulary words in context for this week. You should already have defined them in your journal as you found them in the reading.

▶ Do the added details **enhance** the paragraph?
▶ The details you include should be relevant—they should connect to your story in an **integral** way.
▶ One of Disney's **animators** would pin sketches of characters and scenes on a board to help demonstrate the cartoon story he wanted to tell.
▶ People in other fields—such as theater and business—have **adapted** storyboarding as a tool in their profession, as well.
▶ However, repeated sentences like this one become **tedious**.

Using your thesaurus, try to find the BEST word to replace the bold word in the sentence. If you aren't familiar with the meanings of all the synonyms for each word in the thesaurus, you may need to use your dictionary to look them up. That way you can choose the word that best fits the sentence.

Before students turn in a document, they should use their word processor's search feature to find every instance where they use they or their.

Each time, they should look for the antecedent—the word that the pronoun refers to in the sentence. If the antecedent is singular, have the student change either the pronoun or the antecedent so both agree (both should be plural or both should be singular).

Write with WORLD

CAPSULE 1   3.4.1

WRITING A BEGINNING

The time to write has arrived! In this lesson, we'll help you figure out how to get your autobiographical story down on paper. The good news is much of the work is already done. The very first thing you should do today is go back through and tab the pertinent pages in your journal where you've already gathered information that may help you write. Using Post-its or Post-it flags, tab these sections in your journal:

Lesson 2

    3.2.3: Capsule 3 (paragraph on an important moment from the incident where you tell what you were thinking and feeling)

    3.2.4: Capsule 4 (questions about a picture taken around the time the incident occurred)

Lesson 3

    3.3.1: Capsule 1 (Summary of the incident and why it is important to you)

    3.3.2: Capsule 2 (Main point or theme of your story, types of details that get your point across, two examples of details you could use)

    3.3.3 or 3.3.4: (Questions, including describing the event in detail for the incident you've decided to write about)

As you look back through your responses to these lessons and capsules, you should see that the framework of your story has already been written. That's a huge accomplishment! Now you need to think about how you want to tell your story. Here are some questions to consider:

    What order do you want to use to tell the story? Do you want to start at the beginning? Or would you rather start in the middle to help capture your reader's interest? What about starting at the end when the event has already occurred?

Take a moment to examine all of the work your student writer has produced. Your writer should have produced an extensive collection of brainstorming and idea development. They've created significant content for the essay and started to organize that content.

Your writer has engaged a process of meaning making, and they are ready to write this essay. Congratulate them on this achievement!

What tone will you take? Humorous? Serious? Playful? You're telling this story, so you want your voice to come through. (By voice, we mean your own unique way of "talking" on paper.) If you're known for your sense of humor, you may want to try to carry that over into your writing. Of course, you want your voice to match the subject of the story.

How will you capture your readers' interest so that they want to keep reading? If you begin with a long explanation, they may quit before the second paragraph. Some good attention-grabbers are beginning with dialogue or starting in the middle of things so readers want to find out more.

God's World News Editor Dr. Jenny Pitcock will write an autobiographical essay along with you. That way you will have examples to help illustrate possible ways of writing your essay. Here are two examples of how she could begin her essay:

1

I barely noticed the signs anymore. We had been at Virginia Beach for almost two weeks, and nothing had happened. When we first arrived, Larry, Jill, Missy, and I couldn't get into our swimsuits fast enough. We raced each other down to the beach. As my brother, sisters, and I ran into the surf, my father made us stop and look at a small wooden sign at the water's edge: Beware of Undertow. "The undertow is really strong here," he said.

"What's an undertow?" My sister Missy asked. She looked hard at the sign. At five, she was just learning to read.

"After the waves hit the beach, the water heads back out to sea," my dad explained. "If you get caught in the undertow, you can get pulled out with it. Every year, a few people get caught in the undertow. Some of them get sucked far out into the ocean and drown."

I was a cautious kid by nature, so at first I stayed close to the shore, playing in the waves. But as the days wore on, I began to lose my fear. My parents bought us rafts and we spent hours each day running out into the waves with the rafts, jumping on, and riding them back in to the beach. **How could something so fun possibly be dangerous?**

2

I sat up as high as I could on my raft, hoping someone would see me. For a while I thought maybe I was drifting back toward shore, but now I was sure: the people on the beach definitely looked smaller. I could see two lifeguard chairs rising six feet or so above the beach, but apparently, no lifeguard could see me. The worry I had been feeling was rapidly morphing into panic: **I was caught in the undertow, and I was being sucked out into the open ocean. I had never been more terrified in my life.**

Notice that I've highlighted the final sentence of each beginning. Remember that you need to reveal the main point or central focus of your story for the readers at some point in the beginning section.

In older days, many of us wrote drafts on paper and, when we had perfected them, copied them nicely on clean paper. Once word processors entered the picture, writing changed. At first, we continued to draft on paper and then typed the final copy for presentation sake.

Today's young writers are typing everything—from brainstorming to drafts to final versions. Word processing systems are designed to perform the real work of good writing. Students can cut text, paste it somewhere else, play with arrangement, and then rewrite transitions to fit. At some point students need to know what their processing system can do to support them.

It might help your student to think of this part of writing like one of those Russian dolls—you open it up, and there's a smaller doll inside. That's kind of what we're doing here. The first doll, or layer, is the big facts—the key events in the story. But as you open it up and go deeper inside, more and more dolls (or details) emerge. Help your student to keep opening up each event in the story to see what details he can find inside.

You might want to read through the example together with your student. Then discuss what you notice. How

CWJ

◀ IN YOUR JOURNAL

Look at the two possible introductions above. Which one do you think works better? Why?

What strategy will you use to get your readers' attention at the beginning of your essay?

Now look back through the sections you tabbed in your writer's journal. Once you decide how you want to start, take your storyboard cards and lay them out in the order you will tell the story.

On your computer or on a clean sheet of paper, write a beginning to your story. There's no set length, but generally you should be able to lay the groundwork and create the setting for your story in 1-3 paragraphs.

In laying the background for your story, your beginning should tell where the event occurred (in my story, the beach) and it should prepare readers for the story (in both possible introductions, I show what will drive the action of the story—that there is a dangerous undertow). You may also include other information such as important characters in the story, your age at the time, or what you looked like if this information helps to set up your story.

When you have finished, underline the theme or main point of your story revealed in your beginning section.

CAPSULE 2   3.4.2

AVOIDING A MESS IN THE MIDDLE

Congratulations! You've taken the first step—writing a beginning to your story. If it's not perfect, don't worry. Real writers draft. A rough draft—what you're writing right now—is an early version of your story. It doesn't have to be perfect. You can change it later as you realize you left something out or as you think of a better way to phrase something. Just getting started is a huge accomplishment.

Today, we're going to write the biggest part of your story—the middle section that tells exactly what happened. The good news is that you've already got the skeleton of this part done—twice. Remember your storyboard cards? You should have the key events on your cards. Now flip back to 3.3.4. In your writer's journal you should have answered the question: **Describe the event in detail**. Dr. Jenny Pitcock's list looks like this:

> When I was a kid, my dad was in the Naval Reserve. He spent two weeks each summer training at Virginia Beach.
>
> The summer when I was seven, he took our whole family with him. We lived in an apartment on

the U.S. Navy base and played on the beach all day while he was in training.

My parents bought us rafts. We loved running out as far as we could with the rafts, jumping on, and riding the waves back to shore.

Near the end of the second week, I got a little too brave. Virginia Beach had a serious undertow—there were signs everywhere. Despite all the warnings, I went out too far and the waves began pulling me out to sea instead of pushing me back to the beach.

I sat on my raft for what felt like a very long time hoping someone would see me. I prayed that God would help someone to see me. Finally, just as I was about to get off my raft and try to swim back to shore, two lifeguards arrived in a boat and took me back to the beach.

They instructed me not to go out any deeper than chest level.

I went and sat on my mom's towel and didn't say anything. She had no idea what had happened.

Soon my brother came up and told my mom that he had seen me way out in the ocean by myself. He had alerted the lifeguards who came and got me.

is the middle of the story organized? What details help to make the story interesting? Describe the little girl in the story. What do you know about her by the time you finish this section?

Use this discussion to bring up your student's story. What strategies does he see in the model that he might use in his story? What ideas does it give him that he can include in his piece?

If we had just given you the instruction, "Write an autobiography," you might think your list WAS an autobiography. But you know better. In the last three lessons you've thought about and even researched (through pictures) your own life. This is the place to include those details—what you looked like at the time of the event, how you felt, what you were thinking, and what people in your story said.

It's okay to change the order of events on your list if you need to—but remember that your list provides the "bones" for your story. You may have a great story, but if your readers can't follow it, they will quickly lose interest.

One thing you might want to do is look back through the capsules you tabbed with Post-its. In these capsules, you've already gathered some valuable information—don't let it go to waste. You also may want to jot down a few specific examples, thoughts, and feelings for each item on your detailed list of events. Here's what one of the items on the author's list looks like after she adds some details:

ITEM:
I sat on my raft for what felt like a very long time hoping someone would see me. I prayed that God would help someone to see me. Finally, just as I was about to get off my raft and try to swim back to shore, two lifeguards arrived in a boat and took me back to the beach.

DETAILS:
1. I said "Help!" and screamed a few times but I was a little embarrassed and besides, no one could hear me.

2. As I looked back at the beach, I could see a strip of people in the water playing on rafts, bodysurfing, swimming and standing. The noise they made was loud, but over the water noise sounded different than it did on land. The sound hung in the air over them like a ceiling of noise.

3. I was drifting further and further away from the noise and I was beginning to worry that I would never get back.

4. The canvas raft I sat on was orange on one side, turquoise on the other.

We are not going to assign any more prewriting. If you feel ready to write, it is okay to jump right in and get started. If you talked to five professional writers and asked them how they begin writing, you'd probably get five different answers. Some writers do lots of organizing first. Charts and outlines help this type of writer. Others just like to jump in and begin writing and see where the story takes them. Our advice is, if you're stuck and don't feel quite ready to write, go ahead and do a little more prewriting first. If you CAN get started, go ahead and begin.

You will notice Dr. Jenny Pitcock chose her second beginning. We think it is a better attention grabber and it gets to the story's point faster. We think the theme of her story is clearer in this version, as well.

> I sat up as high as I could on my raft, hoping someone would see me. For a while I thought maybe I was drifting back toward shore, but now I was sure: the people on the beach definitely looked smaller. I could see two lifeguard chairs rising high six feet or so above the beach, but apparently, no lifeguard could see me. The worry I had been feeling was rapidly morphing into panic: **I was caught in the undertow, and I was being sucked out into the open ocean. I had never been more terrified in my life**.

Here's the middle part of her story:

> How had this happened? When we had first arrived at Virginia Beach nearly two weeks before, Larry, Jill, Missy, and I couldn't get into our swimsuits fast enough. We raced each other down to the ocean. As my brother, sisters and I ran into the surf, my father made us stop and look at a small wooden sign at the water's edge: Beware of Undertow. "The undertow is really strong here," he said.
>
> "What's an undertow?" My sister Missy asked. She looked hard at the sign. At five, she was just learning to read.
>
> "After the waves hit the beach, the water heads back out to sea," my dad explained. "If you get caught in the undertow, you can get pulled out with it. Every year, a few people get caught in the undertow. Some of them get sucked far out into the ocean and drown."
>
> I was a cautious child, and the signs scared me. At first, I played in the waves close to the beach. While my dad—a commander in the Navy—went to training each day, the rest of the family

Notice that Dr. Jenny Pitcock uses a lot of the material from her first introduction in the middle part of the story. Here's some free advice: NEVER THROW ANYTHING AWAY. Don't delete it either. Good writers usually keep a second file open called "Extra" when they are writing on the computer. When they write something that doesn't work, good writers cut and paste it into that file. Sometimes they go back and get the material in the "Extra" file and use it later.

spent eight or ten hours on the beach. After a couple of days, I began to get braver. Soon I was splashing out a little further into the ocean. My older brother Larry taught Missy and me a fun trick: If you jumped up just as a wave came in from the ocean, it would carry you up to the beach. Sometimes you'd have a nice smooth ride, but other times, the wave would flip you over and tumble you around and you'd end up with a mouth full of sand and saltwater. Either way, it was a fun ride.

Soon we were borrowing other kids' rafts to ride the waves. With rafts, we could wade out deeper and ride the waves longer, making the game even more fun.

One night my dad came home from the navy base store with a surprise for us: Four rubberized canvas rafts, bright orange on one side and turquoise on the other with ropes on the front that we could hold onto as we dragged the rafts out into the ocean.

My parents were not the type to buy us things—no ice cream at the beach or hot dogs when we went shopping at the mall. We got presents on our birthdays, but with four kids, money was tight and my parents didn't waste it on frivolous gifts. Normally if we did get something, it would be to share.

So the rafts were a real surprise. We watched as my brother and father blew up the rafts—with their mouths and not a pump. "This one's mine!" I said as I claimed one and jumped on it, landing flat on my stomach. I pretended to paddle with my hands. Before bed, we stacked them along the wall in the living room of the small apartment where all four of us kids slept each night in sleeping bags—the two big kids on a foldout couch and Missy and I in chairs pushed together into makeshift beds. Even with the lights out, I could see the bright orange of the rafts in light that came under the bottom of the hall door. I went to sleep imagining how fun it would be to play on my own raft the next day.

And for the next few days, I had the most fun I'd had in my life. I—the kid who was too afraid to ride anything but the merry-go-round at the state fair—became quite an expert on raft-surfing. I'd run out into the waves dragging my raft by its rope until I saw a big wave coming. Then I'd jump into the wave and onto the raft stomach-down at the same time, turning the raft with the rope so that my head was facing the beach, then ride the wave in.

I'd do this for hours on end. My brother, sisters, and I would start the day together, but soon would get separated. Sometimes, after a couple of hours of raft-surfing, I'd find myself several hundred yards down the beach from where I'd started.

As the second week wore on, I got braver, venturing out deeper and deeper into the water to catch bigger waves. I wasn't a particularly strong swimmer, but on my orange and turquoise raft I felt safe.

The wave that took me the wrong direction didn't look any different than the hundreds I'd ridden safely into shore. I jumped on, expecting to ride in to the beach as usual, but soon I noticed I was being pushed away from the beach instead of toward it.

By the time I recognized that I was in trouble, the beach looked quite far away. I realized no one was out as deep as I was. As far as I could see in either direction, a strip of people played in the waves close to shore, swimming, laughing, jumping. I was beyond that safe margin of people—I was the only one I could see outside that safe line.

I tried to yell, "Help!" a few times, but I was too far out for anyone to hear me over the sound of the waves and the strange noise of so many people talking, laughing, and yelling. The further I drifted, the weirder it sounded. The voices of the crowd seemed to go straight up above their heads, creating a ceiling of noise over them. As I continued to drift, I realized just how far from that group and their collective noise I was. With a sinking feeling I realized that no matter how loud I hollered, no one would ever hear me over the hundreds of voices amplified into a roar as the sound bounced off the water.

As the minutes ticked by, I began to panic. Out here, the waves were just bumps—they knocked me around a bit, but they didn't seem to be heading toward shore. My hope of riding a wave in quickly vanished.

In my blue bathing suit with a shoelace tied across the straps in the back to keep it from falling off, I looked young for my age. But even though I was just out of first grade, I was old beyond my years. I often glanced over the newspaper as I ate breakfast. Terrified, the realization hit me that I could become a newspaper headline: "Indiana Girl, 7, Swept Out to Sea, Drowns." A refrain of "Jesus, please help me," had been running through my head, but now I began to pray in earnest. "God, please help someone to see me," I prayed. "Please don't let me die."

Feebly, I tried to yell a few more times, and even managed a slight scream. But I knew it was no use. No one could hear me way out here. In the midst of my panic, I knew that the right thing to do was to stay on the raft, but fear made me reckless. I had to try to get back to shore. I was just about to slide off the raft and try to swim back toward the beach when I saw a canoe coming rapidly in my direction, two lifeguards inside.

"You okay?" one said as they got near me. The other reached out and grabbed the rope on my raft. "You're pretty far out."

I don't remember my response—if I said anything at all. I was horrified and embarrassed to have to be rescued. But mostly I was relieved.

With the boat pulling me, the ride back to shallow waters seemed to take only seconds. When we got to shore, one of the men turned to me, his hand at chest level. "Don't go out any deeper than this," he said. "We don't want to have to come rescue you again."

I slunk up the beach and sat quietly on the edge of my mom's towel. I listened as she talked to one of the navy wives she'd befriended during the long days on the beach. While I was glad to be alive, I was humiliated and silenced by my experience.

I'm not sure how long I sat there before my 13-year-old brother ran up. "Did you see the lifeguards bring Jenny in?" he said to my mom.

For the first time, since I'd come up, my mom really looked at me. "I thought she was awfully quiet," she said. "What happened?"

My brother laughed. "I looked out and saw Jenny on her raft, way out there," he pointed. "So I told the lifeguards and they got in a boat and rescued her."

My mom looked skeptical. "Is that true? How did I miss it?" she said. I sat there quietly, mortified as they discussed my experience, wishing they would quit talking about it. Scared though I was, I quickly got back in the water so I wouldn't have to answer any more questions about my near-death experience.

This time though, I stayed close to shore.

CWJ

IN YOUR JOURNAL ▶

Using the directions from today's capsule and instructions from past lessons, write the middle part of your story. If you can type, we highly recommend drafting on the computer. In later capsules it will be much easier to revise your draft if you don't have to rewrite the whole thing. In any case, write this section OUTSIDE of your journal. Today you'll be using the tabbed sections of your journal to help keep you on track with your organization. Also, in 3.2.3, you may have already written a paragraph you can use.

Happy writing!

CAPSULE 3   3.4.3

DRAWING A CONCLUSION

One meaning of the word conclusion is "the end." This section is the last one of your essay—the ending. But that's not the only meaning of conclusion. Another meaning is a judgment reached after lots of thought and deliberation. And that's what I want you to think about as you end your essay.

Writing like this is not likely to happen in one sitting. Motivate your student to sit down and write, to take breaks only after they have drafted significantly.

Writer's block may become an issue. In some of these instances, the student may be more worried about how they sound. We call these student writers "perfectionist drafters."

The point of drafting is to get ideas, words, sentences, and paragraphs down on the page. In short, the writing does not have to be polished; writers often have writer's block because they worry about the quality of their writing.

Take pressure off of your student by reminding them that drafts are not graded on quality of writing. Draft grades rest only on quantity and seriousness of effort. Repeat this mantra to your student writer: "Get words on the page first; then worry about how they look and sound."

Flip back through your journal to 3.3.1. Look at your answers to questions 2 and 5.

> 2. Why is this story important to you or why do you want to tell it?
> 5. Explain what you learned from this experience in your life.

Now read back through your autobiographical essay so far. After reading the essay, are your answers to these questions still the same? If not, how have they changed?

These answers should inform (provide shape or form, give vital material to) your conclusion. However, just copying the above sentences will compromise all the hard work you've done so far. What you learned is important, but it's not the only reason you wrote this story. Your autobiographical story also reveals lots of other information about you. It's more than just a fable with a moral at the end.

So be subtle. Don't hit people over the head with the lesson.

Let us show you what we mean:

Here's an awkward, forced ending to Dr. Jenny Pitcock's essay.

> That day at the beach, I learned to stay close to the shore when swimming in the ocean. I also learned that God hears me and answers my prayers.

Here's a more thoughtful summing up or conclusion that explains why her "lost at sea" experience was an important event in her life:

> After we got back home to Indiana and life got back to normal, I nearly forgot about the day I was almost lost at sea. But sometimes at night, as I drifted off to sleep, the image of myself, far out in the ocean, sitting on my knees on that raft would flash before my eyes. A feeling of terror would wash over me, startling me awake.

> But in a strange way, when I saw myself in my mind's eye on that raft, it also brought me peace. For the first time in my life on that raft, I had prayed with real desperation. And I knew without a doubt God had heard me and answered my prayer.

Can you see the difference? The section you have to write today is short. So as you write your conclusion, take your time and really consider what the experience you chose has meant in your life.

CWJ

Using the directions from today's capsule, write a conclusion to your autobiographical essay on a separate sheet of paper or on the computer. Like the introduction, there's no set length. In general, it takes 1-3 paragraphs to sum up your story.

◄ IN YOUR JOURNAL

Excitement and adrenaline will cause some students to write a conclusion as quickly as possible. They'll put little thought into what they are saying—they just want to finish.

One way around this dilemma is have students write two conclusions. Then, with two drafts in hand, students are asked to choose the better conclusion and explain why it has more potential than the other choice. Once a decision has been made and explained, the student then rewrites the conclusion they chose, adding more thought and substance.

CAPSULE 4

3.4.4

MAKING YOUR AUTOBIOGRAPHICAL ESSAY EVEN BETTER

Congratulations! You now have a complete draft of your essay. Notice that we didn't say you were finished. A rough draft is the first stage in developing an essay. All the parts are there, but it can still use some polish and cleaning up before you have a final draft of the essay. Depending on what type of writer you are, it may be a very rough draft that still needs lots of improvement, or it could be nearly finished.

Are you a writer who does lots of planning in advance? Do you keep reading back through as you write and making changes when you notice something is confusing or is missing? If so, you may be almost finished. But if you are the type of writer who writes to discover what you have to say and likes to get your ideas down on paper quickly, you may have lots of work remaining. Some people need only two drafts to get to a final version. Others may take many more.

So how will you know when you are done? When both you and your teacher are satisfied with what you've achieved, you can turn in your final draft and move on to the next unit. Even then, you might not be fully finished. As professional writers and teachers, we believe that writing is a process. If you haven't already, we advise you to get some sort of folder, three ringed binder, or even just a large envelope. Here, you should store all the various drafts of papers you write for this course. A few months from now when you've learned more and developed as a writer, you may return to this essay again and revise it once more. As your skills grow, your essays can grow and change with them.

CWJ

IN YOUR JOURNAL ▶

Before you finish this unit, we want you to spend at least a couple of days on revision. In this capsule, we want you to do two exercises that will help you improve your essay. For the first, you'll need a copy of your essay, the help of a parent or teacher, and a box of colored pencils. For the second, you'll need a copy of your essay, recording device, and your journal.

Give a copy of your essay to a parent or teacher. Ask him or her to mark the following things using the colored pencils:

RED—underline a favorite sentence in the essay. This might be a great description, good dialogue, a great image, or some other particularly well-phrased sentence.

ORANGE—underline good word choices—strong verbs, descriptive nouns, interesting adjectives.

BLUE—underline all sentences that you find confusing or hard to understand. In the margin,

So as a teacher, how do you know when an piece of writing is done? This will differ from student to student. They key is a balance between their effort and their attention span for this type of work. We're working to get students excited about writing. Making them work endlessly on revisions will kill any love or joy they've found in writing. If they've made a strong effort and they feel finished, you might have them revise a single paragraph that is representative of issues you see throughout.

A student who wants to get it perfect may desire more revision work. This is fine too.

The most difficult student is the one that's just phoning it in. If you feel like he's not really putting the effort in, don't let him move on. If necessary, work through a paragraph or two with him, helping to engage him in the writing process. Be firm about continuing to revise until he's showing real effort.

The pencils are as much for you as they are for the student. They help you to limit the scope of what you're trying to correct in a single piece of writing. You'll notice that our focus here is entirely on content (blue helps them to see confusing content and green asks them to provide more detail). At this point in the process, focusing on word and sentence-level errors can shut a student down. We want them focused on getting interesting, detailed ideas down on paper in a way that it can be understood. Errors can be fixed later.

please write some questions or comments to help the writer understand what's missing or what got you confused.

GREEN—circle sections or paragraphs that need more detail or description. In the margin, write questions that you'd like to have answered with more details.

Once your reader has given you comments, rewrite your essay to include the new information and clarifications your reader noted on your rough draft. (If you drafted on the computer, this step will be much easier!)

After you've made the changes, have someone else read your revised essay aloud and record it. Though you can read it yourself, we suggest having another reader help you get as much distance from the essay as possible. This helps keep you from mentally filling in the details since you already KNOW what happens.

As you play the recorded essay, take notes in your journal. (You can stop the recorder when you need to write.) Did any parts seem confusing to either you or the reader? Note where in your journal. Could you use more detail? Note the places where you need more details. Did you remember anything else you think you should include in your story? Note it in your journal.

Using your notes, make final revisions.

CAPSULE 5

3.4.5

WRITING AUTOBIOGRAPHY

WORLD WISDOM:

You've come a long way and learned a lot about how to plan, arrange, and write an autobiographical essay. While it may seem like a complicated process at times, you'll discover that the more you write the more automatic it becomes. You will still be very thoughtful and deliberate about your approach, but the steps will be obvious to you and the whole process very logical and natural. Someone who writes this way all the time is Amy Henry, a writer with *WORLD Magazine*. Let's hear how she has learned to take stories from her life and make them relevant and appealing to a wide audience of people.

"Since I'm a mom, when I have a blog post or an essay due, the logical place to find subject matter is inside my four walls. Readers, however, usually don't want to hear that tonight I am making pot roast for dinner or how two of my kids got into a fight over the Xbox. Personal stories add depth to your writing, yes, but what readers want to know is how my story connects to their stories, how my experience fits into the bigger

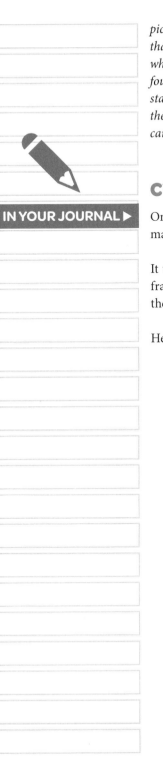

picture. To do this, once I get an idea about what I may want to write about, I scan the news for something that ties my experience in with what is going on in the world and build my piece accordingly. For example, when I wanted to write a post about my daughter getting married at seventeen, I googled around and found research on teenagers' top priorities, if couples that marry young are happy with their decision, and statistics showing the success rates of early marriages. I then wove my story in with the research to produce the post. Be open, be honest, be vulnerable, but don't just write about the pot roast. Only your mother will care about that."

- Amy Henry

CWJ

IN YOUR JOURNAL ▶

Once you've got your story's content as perfect as possible, the next step is working on correctness—making sure your essay is neat, well-formatted, and as grammatically correct as possible.

It would be a good idea to go back and check for ALL the grammar issues we've worked on so far—fragments, run-ons, it's/its, and so on. However, we especially want you to work on putting into practice the things we've emphasized in Unit 3.

Here are tips to help you check for the errors noted in this unit:

1. Consistency of verb tense: use the same tense throughout your entire essay. Usually because the event happened in the past you will use PAST tense throughout. The one exception is dialogue. Since you are repeating the words you said at that time, you'll use present tense in dialogue.

To check for proper tense, underline all verbs in your essay and check each to make sure it's in the proper tense (present for dialogue, past for everything else).

2. Pronoun antecedent agreement: pronouns and their antecedents (the words they refer back to) must agree. The easiest way to check for this is to underline each use of *they* and *their* in your paper. If you've written on a word processor, you can search for these words. Each time you find *they* or *their* locate the noun the pronoun refers back to. If it is an indefinite pronoun (everyone, everybody, anyone, anybody, no one, nobody, someone, somebody), you need to use a singular pronoun (his/her) because indefinite pronouns are singular.

This mistake is so common, people often make it with regular singular nouns (Example: Each person should bring their own lunch). So if you find you've used they or their with a singular noun, when possible, change to a plural noun (Example: People should bring their own lunches.)

3. To, Too, Two: This is an easy one. *To* is an infinitive (Example: I like to eat peaches) or a preposition (Example: I walked to the store). *Too* means very (Example: I ate too much pizza) or also (Example: I liked the movie too). And *two* is the number between one and three (Example: I ate two bananas.).

Underline each use of two, too, or two, and check to make sure you've used the right one in each place. Or if you typed your essay on a word processor, do a search for each of these words, checking each usage to make sure you've chosen the proper *to, too,* or *two* for the sentence.

THE RIGHT WORD

Rather than have you do a new batch of words in this lesson, we'll be reviewing the 15 words you learned in this unit. Below, choose the best SYNONYM for each word:

1. aspect
   a) position   b) size   c) characteristic

2. nuances
   a) subtleties   b) pictures   c) nuisances

3. static
   a) unchanging   b) flighty   c) heavy

4. nostalgia
   a) fun   b) boredom   c) wistful remembering

5. compelling
   a) relaxing   b) captivating   c) silent

6. enhance
   a) grow   b) enjoy   c) strengthen

7. integral
   a) essential   b) smart   c) unimportant

8. animators
   a) paratroopers   b) writers   c) cartoonists

9. adapted
   a) chose   b) changed   c) carried

10. tedious
    a) boring   b) fascinating   c) solemn

11. daunting
    a) lacking   b) ugly   c) discouraging

12. delve
   a) lose   (b) search)   c) wash

13. mortifying
   (a) embarrassing) b) hilarious   c) sad

14. deliberation
   a) silence   (b) thought)   c) recklessness

15. stimulate
   a) deaden   (b) encourage)   c) discover

Write with WORLD

GENERAL OVERVIEW

By the time your student finishes Unit 4, he will have completed half of the *Write with WORLD* curriculum. In the second half, your student will experience a variety of writing types; we will begin to move faster and take on more writing tasks in each unit.

But before we speed up, we want to solidify what we've been teaching in the first three units. In Unit 4, the assignment follows a similar pattern to the autobiographical incident from Unit 3. In fact, some students may choose to use the same event as the basis for their fictional narrative.

Your student will continue to work on building strong sentences and paragraphs, and on organizing these building blocks into a strong narrative. Focusing again on a moment from the student's life encourages him to take ownership of the piece and continue to develop his narrative voice.

Though the student will be doing some fictionalizing in Unit 4, we firmly believe that for young writers, sticking close to experience helps create strong, authentic writing. Choosing a moment from his life grounds the story in real emotion. Though the student may not yet have particularly strong word choice or perfect sentence structure, a story with real feeling behind it will ring true and help him create a piece that he feels connected to and can be proud of.

We've kept the pattern of development similar. The student writes a narrative that is organized chronologically and approached in similar ways as in the last unit—brainstorming questions, practice writing, storyboarding, and so on. These familiar elements should help make the student comfortable so that he can work on mastering several important new elements we'll introduce in Unit 4.

The first is point of view. Being able to examine a situation from a variety of perspectives is essential to good writing. Trying to understand how another person might see the same situation will eventually help your student craft strong arguments. If she can't understand what another person is thinking or feeling, it's unlikely she will be able to persuade him to her side in an argument—or even get him to listen to her viewpoint.

In this unit, we challenge your student to move away from telling his own story from the first-person perspective. He can tell his story from another person's point of view, or he may choose to use a third-person narrator. In either case, thinking from another perspective will begin to develop the ability to look at a situation or issue from all sides.

Another emphasis in Unit 4 is using *showing* in writing. One of the key skills we want your student to take away from this course is providing relevant, specific details in her writing. Whether she's writing a financial report or a novel, we want the question, "How can I demonstrate the point I'm making?" to always be in her mind. In a fictional narrative, specificity is created through recreating scenes and showing the readers what happened. This attention to detail is an important skill that we will continue to develop in various ways throughout the course.

We also expand on something we touched on in Unit 3: Developing purpose. We want your student to understand that all writing communicates a message. He needs to know what message he wants readers to take away from his writing. Everything from the scenes he chooses to the details he includes should help communicate his message.

DETAILED OVERVIEW

4.1.1-5: In this lesson, we jump right into point of view. After explaining what point of view is and how it works in written language, we begin experimenting. First, we have your student rewrite a short section from his autobiography from the perspective of another person in the story. Second-person perspective is difficult to use in a story, but we want your student to experience writing from this perspective as well. We ask him to write a letter or email to a person who shared an autobiographical experience he is considering for his fictional narrative. This exercise serves as research and also provides the student with an audience for writing. The student also experiments with various third-person viewpoints. By the end of this lesson, the student should begin to get outside of his own perspective and see how others might have different thoughts and concerns even though they share an experience.

4.2.1-5: Narrative writing requires both showing and telling. In this lesson, our purpose is to help the student see the difference between showing and telling and when to use each. We begin by having her identify and copy an example of showing and an example of telling from a favorite book. We then have her answer a series of questions that help draw out the level of detail—both of the event and of her feelings during that event—that she will need to recreate specific scenes for the readers. Using the answers to these questions, the student will sketch a scene. In the final capsule, she will work on adding and improving details at the sentence level. She will also look for clichés in her writing.

4.3.1-5: One of the emphases of *Write with WORLD* is thoughtful writing. We want students to spend a good deal of time thinking before they write each essay. Before a student begins a draft, he should have a clear purpose in mind. That purpose may change as he writes and learns more about his subject. However, he should always have a reason for writing and know what that reason is. In this lesson, the student tests a couple of potential narratives by answering a series of questions about them. If your student doesn't have a reason for wanting to share a particular story, it may not be right for this assignment. The student then chooses which scenes he wants to include in his narrative based on that purpose. He's also encouraged to fictionalize to enhance the story and make its purpose stronger. Storyboarding once again helps him to organize and focus his ideas in preparation for writing.

4.4.1-5: In this lesson, students will write the narrative they've been preparing in this unit. A model fictionalized narrative written by a student serves as an example. (This student has built upon her autobiographical incident; comparing the two can help students understand how they can modify their real-life experience to make it into a work of fiction.) In the second capsule, your student begins writing, focusing on opening with a strong attention-grabbing strategy and foreshadowing her theme. In the third capsule, the student is encouraged to write using her storyboard cards. The cards help to keep the idea of the visual—showing—in mind. They also remind the student to pay attention to organization. In capsule 4, the student writes a conclusion that points back to the story's theme in some way. The unit wraps up with a capsule on revision, in which you will provide specific comments to help your student improve her fictionalized narrative.

HELPING YOUR STUDENT THROUGH EFFECTIVE FEEDBACK

In Unit 1, we encouraged you to use low-stakes grading to let your student know how he is doing without discouraging him. If this has been working for you, you may still be using low-stakes grading. One reason we wanted to create this course is that you and your student can focus on writing without getting hung up on grades. This doesn't go on a college transcript; that gives you freedom to evaluate your student in a way that best encourages him.

Some of you may already be using a traditional grading system. This is fine too. Some students are highly motivated by grades.

If you haven't introduced graded assignments yet, you may want to consider doing so. Your student has completed one long assignment. He has developed some new skills and increased confidence in his writing abilities. Through more targeted conferencing and high stakes grading, now may be a good time to begin giving your student more specific feedback.

EFFECTIVE CONFERENCING

1. How often should you conference? If you are following a two-year plan for this two-part course, the five capsules in each lesson will be completed in a two-week period. If you work on writing three days per week, that gives one built-in day for conferencing every two weeks. At minimum, plan on devoting this one day per lesson to conferencing. Even confident, motivated students benefit from a conference to share potential topics and organizational strategies before they draft. They also profit from another in preparation for revision.

Some students may need substantially more. For these students, you might begin each capsule with a short conference. If your student has trouble getting started, you may need to read the capsule together and ask leading questions to help him get going. You may need to look over what he's done when he finishes to ensure he's on track. As his confidence rises, you can gradually decrease your involvement.

As you see your student's abilities improve, put more of the responsibility for the conference on him. Have him come to the conference with a specific purpose in mind. (e.g., "I want to talk to you about two ideas I have for my story so you can help me see which one works best." Or "I'm having trouble with my organization. I'd like to talk to you about it.") The ideal is for your student to schedule time to meet with you as needed—but the likelihood is that you will need to initiate conferences and help your student determine in what areas they need help.

2. What should you be conferencing about? Once again, it depends on the student. For a reluctant writer, you may need to conference each capsule about each mini-assignment to help her get started. For average students, checking in daily to make sure they know what they're supposed to do and conferencing once or twice each lesson is probably about right. For instance, in Lesson 1 of this unit, you might ask to see all the paragraphs your student wrote on point of view. Then at 4.1.5., you would sit down with your student. Ask her which of her paragraphs she enjoyed writing the most. Tell her what you like about each and why. Spend some time talking about what story she might like to use for her fictionalized narrative and what point of view she's considering. In the next lesson, two spots seem appropriate for conferencing. After she's completed capsule 2, discuss her answers to the questions. Use your own questions to help her fill in missing parts and draw out more details. The more vivid her descriptions here, the better material she'll have to write her paragraph in the next capsule. For instance, if she's struggling to remember what other sense experiences she may have heard, felt, or smelled during the incident, you can use a conference to help her develop her answers.

> Parent: I like your answer about how you felt after Grandma yelled at you in Walmart. I think you capture how frustrated you felt. That's good. But it looks like you are having a little trouble telling what was going on around you.
>
> Student: I don't really remember.
>
> Parent: I can see how it would be hard to remember that specific day. But we go to Walmart every week. What are some sounds you always hear there?
>
> Student: It's loud.
>
> Parent: Right. What are some of the things that make it loud?
>
> Student: Well, sometimes I hear people making announcements.
>
> Parent: That's good. Write that down. Is there music or anything?
>
> Student: Um, I don't think so. But when we walk in, there are always people messing with the carts.
>
> Parent: that's another good sound. How would you describe it?

Student: Clanking. Clattering.

Parent: Great. Write that down too. What about the smell? There's a Subway right by the door.

Student: Yeah, they're always baking bread and cookies.

Parent: That's good too. Why don't you add that to the question about smells?

And so on. You get the idea. Another place for a conference would be after Capsule 4 when she's made her four specific changes. (Or before, if she's having trouble understanding what the questions are asking her to do.) You can examine the changes she's made so far and help her see what she's doing well. Together, work through the questions one more time and add in another strong verb, adjective, additional sense description, and revise out another cliché.

Here are some other points in this unit where a conference might be helpful:

4.3.3—Before the conference, look back through the writing he's done for this lesson. Do the stories he's chosen have a clear purpose that he can identify? If not, use the conference to help him see what the purpose for each story might be through leading questions. Once you've accomplished that, use questions once again to help him think about what kinds of details might best demonstrate the purpose.

4.3.5—Prepare for the conference by looking through each stack of storyboard cards. Can you get the story's basic plot from the cards? Are any key points missing? If so, begin the conference by talking about where you get confused and why. Have the student jot down headings on cards to fill in gaps. (He can complete the cards later on his own.) After that, talk through the questions in the CWJ for capsule 5.

4.4.1.—Prepare for conference by reading through the whole student example included in 4.4. Have your student read through it too. Ask your student what he likes about the piece. Talk about some things the student is doing well. Ask how he's planning to organize his essay—talk through his plan with you.

4.4.2.-4.4.4—If your student wants to discuss each day's work with you, that's fine. Leave this up to the student.

4.4.5.—After you've read the essay and made your comments, schedule a conference. Some students will benefit from reading through your comments first and having some time to absorb and think about them. For others, explaining your comments right when you give the essay back is helpful. In either case, use the conference to make sure your student understands what you've written. Another possibility is to use the conference to work through revisions. Do one of each type together to ensure your student knows how to incorporate the revisions you've suggested.

3. How long should a conference last? Don't overdo it—anywhere from 5-20 minutes is fine. Remember, you don't have to hit everything each conference. Specific, targeted conferences are better than conferences with a laundry list of items to cover.

EFFECTIVE GRADING

At the beginning of this section, we suggested it might be a good time to introduce high-stakes grading. All students may not be ready—we're not trying to rush you into this change if low-stakes grading is working well for you. You want to make sure your student is well-grounded and beginning to feel comfortable and confident before you begin quantifying her achievements. You need to do what is best for your student.

If you feel your student is ready for graded writing, there are various ways to accomplish this. You can decide to give a numeric percentage grade. In that case, you assign a weight to each element. Your categories might look something like this:
▶ Content-50%
▶ Language/style-20%
▶ Grammar-10%
▶ Clarity-10%
▶ Point of view-10%

We think this is a difficult way to grade—you will probably end up quibbling over points—"If you just gave me a 90 instead of an 89 on content, this would have been an A!" The categories tend to work together, anyway. Clarity and grammar have something to do with each other. So do content and language. It's very difficult to divide these things apart. If you do go with this method of grading, you will need to create some sort of a rubric defining what you are looking for in each category (see below). For example, what exactly are you evaluating in the content section?

You can use letter grades—probably the system you and your student are most familiar with. We've provided a rubric for this assignment to help you see what we think makes A, B, C, and D writing:

A Overall well-organized. Flows smoothly and uses good transitions. Paragraphs are well-developed and student uses a wide variety of sentence types. Easy to follow and interesting to read. Very little confusion/missing information. Good use of action verbs and descriptive language throughout. More showing than telling. Few grammar problems. Interesting introduction that grabs attention and foreshadows theme. Consistent point of view. Conclusion has a subtle reiteration of the theme or message—in some way shows how the student has grown or learned. Story is clearly based on a theme and the story is structured to bear out the theme. (The student sample we include in Lesson 4 is an example of A writing.)

B Well-organized with occasional lapses. Fairly smooth, uses some transitions, though it may be a bit choppy. Paragraphs are developed and the student uses some compound and complex sentences. Language may be a little less precise, but still should include all the information to make the story fairly easy to follow. Verbs are fairly strong, but could be improved, as could descriptive language. Student tends to tell a little too much—could show more. May have a few grammar problems. Introduction is solid, but could be a little more interesting/ attention grabbing. Point of view should be clear. Conclusion should in some way point out the story's theme. Theme is clear in the story.

C Story is organized so that you can follow it, though you may have to struggle a bit. Lacks strong transitions. Sentences do not flow into each other—paragraphs are choppy. Student uses mostly simple sentences. Student has a few strong verbs, but needs to work on exchanging being verbs for stronger verbs. Also needs to use descriptive nouns, adjectives and adverbs. Student tells much more than he shows. Some persistent grammar problems. All elements are present, but minimal—story has an introduction, but it may not clearly foreshadow theme and does not show much effort to draw the reader in. Point of view may lapse. Conclusion is present but may not tie to story's theme. Theme is present in the story in some way.

D and below — Story is hard to follow, lacks organization. Transitions are minimal or absent. Student may have difficulty composing sentences—fragments and run-ons are frequent. Student relies on weak verbs. Few descriptive nouns, adjectives or adverbs. Student does not grasp the concept of showing—all or almost all telling. Grammar problems abound. Point of view is unclear. May be missing introduction and/or conclusion. No clear theme.

General note: Reward risk-taking. A student who tries something a little more complex when it comes to vocabulary, organization, or sentence structure should be rewarded for taking a risk even if it isn't perfect. (This type of risk-taking might raise otherwise B-level work to B+ or A-, or average work to C+ or B-.)

Letter grading can be a good way to give your student feedback. But our preference is something slightly different that gives feedback while still allowing for growth and change throughout the course of the year: benchmark grading with a final graded portfolio. What does that mean?

After this unit, for her final year-end project, have your student select two projects to revise. This would include 1) one of the paragraphs she wrote in Units 1 and 2, and 2) either the autobiography or the fictional narrative she wrote in units 3 and 4.

When she returns to these projects, she will discover room for improvement. You can work together to help her see where she might make revisions. Once she has revised the assignments and perfected each as best she can, assign each a letter grade. Average these grades to create a portfolio grade. If you've already been giving letter grades, the portfolio grade will make up the remaining 10 to 20 percent of the student's course grade.

If you've chosen to use a combination of low-stakes and high-stakes grading, we recommend that most of the course grade (around 80-90 percent) be based on effort and completion (low-stakes). We believe focusing on effort and completion is appropriate for students at this developmental level. (If they've given their best effort and completed the work, their low-stakes grades should be in the A-range.)

For those who feel your students are not ready for letter grades, use the portfolio as an opportunity to encourage your student. Write comments that specifically note the improvements you observe between final portfolio pieces and earlier drafts. Comment on improvements you've observed in his writing overall, as well.

Implementing portfolios—whether graded or not—gives students the opportunity to continue to improve their writing over the course of the entire year.

Note: If we were assigning grades in the course, we might break down the final grade like this:

Low-stakes grading (assignments leading up to this unit): 80%

Fictional narrative: 5%

Portfolio: 15%

CAPSULE 1
4.1.1

WRITING FROM A FIRST-PERSON PERSPECTIVE

 Have you ever had an argument with a brother or sister? Chances are you both thought you were right. You were both in the same situation, but you were looking at the situation from different points of view. Let's say for instance that your sister is watching television. You walk into the room, sit down, and watch the rest of the program. When it ends, you pick up the television controller and change the channel. From your point of view, she's gotten to watch one program and now it's your turn. How do you think she might see the situation from her point of view? Here's my guess as to what she might say: "Hey, I was here first! I was watching that channel. Change it back!"

Both of you probably think you're right, and both cases have merit. Taking turns is fair. At the same time, it's rude to walk in and change the channel without asking. It all depends on your point of view.

If each of you were to tell your side of the story to a parent, your point of view would color your story. You would tell the story as you saw it, not from your sister's point of view. Imagine how shocked your mom would be if you said, "Janey was watching TV, and I came in and rudely changed the channel right in the middle of a "Shrug the Ladybug" marathon. I know it's her favorite show, and that was really inconsiderate of me."

No, your story is going to be influenced by the way you saw the situation. It would probably sound more like this: "Janey is being so selfish! She's been watching TV all morning. I just wanted to watch one little show, and she threw a fit! She really needs to learn to share!"

You can't help but see the story from your point of view. Even shared experiences where two people AGREE on an event are going to be experienced slightly differently. If you and your sister both observe a car accident, depending on where you're standing, you might see different things. Quite literally, your point of view (point from which you are viewing the accident) will never be exactly the same.

In this lesson, we're going to show you how point of view can affect a story. We will examine various points of view you might choose to employ when you write your fictional narrative later in this unit.

The topic of point of view offers a great opportunity for discussion. Here's one idea. Observe an event together. (This should be something short—perhaps even something you ask another family member to do, such as enter a room wearing a funny costume or have a silly conversation with another family member.) Immediately after the event, both you and the student should jot down your impressions. Compare notes. What is the same? What is different? This is a good discussion-starter.

We'll show you how a slight change in perspective can add new meaning and create new understanding for readers.

Let's begin by looking at the point of view you used in writing your autobiographical narrative. It's the same perspective we demonstrated above in the argument between you and your pretend sister Janey. When you tell a story from your point of view, you're telling it in *the first person*. You're telling what you saw, the thoughts that ran through your head, what you felt, and what you learned from the experience.

Why do we call this perspective "the first person"? Think back to the grammar lessons you've had in the past. The chart for personal pronouns looks like this:

	Singular	Plural
First Person	I	We
Second Person	You	You
Third person	He, She, It	They

When a story is told, someone has to do the telling. Since these are all the possible "persons" in English, any story will be told from one of these perspectives or some combination of them.

Any time a story is told from the perspective of "I" it's being told in the first person, whether it's a true story or not. Sometimes fiction writers tell a story in the first person to make the story seem more personal and real. These writers use the first person to help readers relate more closely to the story. For instance, in *The Adventures of Huckleberry Finn*, author Mark Twain tells the story using a first person narrator. (The narrator is the person who narrates or tells the story.) Here's the first paragraph of the book as told by the character of Huck Finn:

You don't know about me without you have read a book by the name of *The Adventures of Tom Sawyer*; but that ain't no matter. That book was made by Mr. Mark Twain, and he told the truth, mainly. There was things which he stretched, but mainly he told the truth. That is nothing. I never seen anybody but lied one time or another, without it was Aunt Polly, or the widow, or maybe Mary. Aunt Polly—Tom's Aunt Polly, she is—and Mary, and the Widow Douglas is all told about in that book, which is mostly a true book, with some stretchers, as I said before.

Already, after one paragraph of Mark Twain's story, you've learned some vital information about Huck Finn. What does his language tell you about him? You can infer that he's not very educated. He repeats himself—he doesn't seem like a terribly organized person. And Huck tells you that he's featured in a book by Mark Twain called *The Adventures of Tom Sawyer*.

As you try to decide what kind of narrator you want to tell your story in your fictional narrative, this example shows one of the advantages of a first-person narrator. You can reveal aspects of the main character through his manner of speaking. One of the disadvantages—which comes to light as you read more of *Huckleberry Finn*—is that a first person narrator is not always reliable. Just like the "you" in the argument with your sister at the beginning of the capsule, a first-person narrator sees the story only from his own **biased** perspective.

WORLD WISDOM

Writing in the first person may be the perfect voice for your story, but it can create problems depending on the type of writing you are doing. As you just learned, a first person narrator has only his perspective to report, so it may not be reliable. That is why first person is rarely used in journalistic writing. Someone who knows the strengths and the potential pitfalls of first person writing is Joel Belz, the founder of *God's World News* and *WORLD Magazine*.

"It's a little dangerous for a journalist to choose to write from a first person perspective. Aren't journalists committed to objectivity?* And doesn't objectivity suggest the need to scrub away any personal touch on subjects a journalist writes about?

Yet if it's truthful, what beats a first-hand experience? The serious reader, very much like a careful juror, appreciates being able to hear the witness say: 'I saw this for myself.' And whenever you are able to do that in an honest way, you serve your reader well.

What also serves your reader well is modesty on your part. No arrogance. No superiority. No flaunting of credentials. No 'Pay attention to me because I'm so smart.' Modesty puts all the emphasis on the evidence being presented rather than on the person offering that evidence. 'I,' by itself, is just a tad self-centered. If you have to end up as a key witness, go ahead and take the witness stand. But keep the focus on the facts, more than the fact-teller."

—Joel Belz

*Objectivity means not allowing biases, personal feelings, or opinions to show.

CWJ

You've already written your narrative in the first person. But as we begin to think about writing fiction, we would like for you to try to see a situation from another person's point of view.

Today, we want you to take another person from your narrative and write a first-person account from their perspective. You don't have to retell your whole story—just a paragraph or so. For instance, in Dr. Jenny Pitcock's narrative about drifting away from the beach on a raft, she could tell the story from the perspective of the lifeguard:

"Hey!" I heard a voice say. A boy of about twelve years old stood below the lifeguard chair on

---

Question for discussion: Do you like to read articles and stories that have a first-person narrator? Why or why not?

◀ **IN YOUR JOURNAL**

the sand. He pointed. "See that little girl way out there on that raft? That's my little sister. I think she might need some help."

I looked in the direction he was pointing. I spotted the raft first, an orange rectangle bobbing on the waves. I grabbed my binoculars. Sure enough, a small girl sat perched on top. I couldn't see her face, but she sat stiff and still, as if she feared any movement might cause her to topple off. "Thanks, Buddy," I said to the kid as I climbed quickly down the chair's built-in ladder. I wondered where these kids' parents were. We were supposed to be lifeguards, not babysitters. "Hey, Jimmy!" I yelled as I headed for the rescue boat. "We got a kid stuck on a raft. Let's go!"

Now it's your turn. Don't forget to include the thoughts and feelings of your chosen character.

CAPSULE 2

4.1.2

WRITING FROM A SECOND-PERSON PERSPECTIVE

 "Would you grab some spoons and put them on the table?" your mother might ask you before dinner. "r u going to swim practice?" a friend might text you on your phone. Most of the conversations we have on a daily basis—whether in person, through email, letters, or texts—require use of the second person, the personal pronoun you.

But of all the points of view, it's the most rarely used in narrative writing. Think about it. You requires a response. Writers can keep a one-sided conversation going without seeming too strange in a short story, especially with a very **garrulous** first-person narrator. However, using a second-person narrator is difficult to sustain in a novel or other longer work.

One exception is epistolary novels. You're probably familiar with the term "epistle" from the Bible. The books called "epistles" are the letters church leaders such as Paul wrote to the churches. Epistolary novels tell a story through letters. Using letters, a writer can allow readers to see inside the mind of one or more characters as they share their thoughts and feelings with another character or characters.

Sometimes journals or diaries can be used in a similar way. For instance, Anne Frank, a young Jewish girl who went into hiding to escape the Nazis during World War II, recorded in her diary her experience in hiding. Shortly before her family was discovered and sent to a concentration camp, she began preparing her diary. Anne wanted to publish it after the war. She started the editing process, creating a fictional friend named Kitty with whom she shared her thoughts in her diary entries. Though Anne died of illness in a concentration camp, her diary has lived on, becoming one of the most widely read books in history.

The danger of the first-person perspective is that students will stop thinking about strong actors and use only *I* as their subject.

Some people respond to this problem by outlawing the use of *I*. Too often we've worked with students who believe they cannot use I in a paper.

We prefer a different response—one we touch on here. If students use *I* as the subject of their sentence, they need to know why. Are they using *I* because it is essential to the first-person perspective they are developing? Or, are they using *I* because it is truly the best subject?

If students can provide a reason for using *I* as their subject—a reason that moves beyond convenience—we would be willing to let them use it. Just make sure that they don't overuse *I*.

The second-person perspective is tricky for a few reasons. First, this perspective lends an informality that is uncommon in many essays. The second-person perspective actually works best for how-to types of writing—mostly instructional materials.

The biggest danger of writing from the second-person perspective is maintaining it and being consistent. Writers who start with the second-person often switch to the third-person perspective.

Students are looking for a narrative that has good parts. Do not disqualify a story if it is incomplete or if the student does not remember many details. In fact, this type of story may work best. Because we are working toward a fictional piece, your student writer will eventually fill in the details—and hopefully enjoy the process.

As you consider points of view you might use in your fictional narrative, the second-person perspective is a possibility. You could tell your story through a series of letters or emails between characters. However, we would advise you to proceed with caution, as this is a tricky perspective. In the next lesson, we will discuss further the value of *showing* rather than *telling* your readers in a story. If you choose to use the second person, you ARE telling because you're talking directly to your reader. Therefore, you immediately make the task of showing rather than telling more difficult.

CWJ

◀ IN YOUR JOURNAL

Today, to practice writing in the second person, we want you to write an email or a letter. Its purpose is to gather information for the fictional narrative you'll write later in this unit.

First, we want you to look back at the list you made in 3.1.4. You listed various events that happened to you under categories like *funny, sad*, and *scary*. Is there an event here that you would have liked to write about, but felt a little uncomfortable sharing it as a personal narrative? This unit might be a good place to explore that story further as a fictional story.

What about the story you had as a "backup" for your personal narrative? You've already done a lot of research and thinking about that story, so this unit might be a good place to tell it.

If you liked your personal narrative and would like to continue on with that story, that's fine, too.

You don't need to make a firm decision on your topic for your fictional narrative today, but it's a good idea to start thinking about it.

Right now, choose an experience from your life that you might want to write about. Remember that this piece will be based on true events and feelings, but you can change parts as well. The event you're considering may already be on your list, but it may not. Perhaps you've had a new experience since you made this list that you think would make a good story.

For the purposes of this assignment, the event you choose must include another person who is still living. That person must have shared the experience with you in some way. Write the person a letter or email asking him/her what he/she remembers about the event. For instance, Dr. Jenny Pitcock's email to her brother looks like this:

> Dear Larry,
>
> Do you remember when we went to Virginia Beach as kids and I got stuck on a raft and you sent the lifeguards out to get me? I'm writing a story about it, and I'd love for you to write back and tell me what you remember about that day.

Thank you in advance for any memories you can share.

Love,

Jenny

Copy the letter or email into your journal. If you get a response, include it in your journal as well.

Here is the response Dr. Jenny Pitcock received:

Our father was a College Professor and Chairman of his department. He was also a Captain in the Naval Reserve. Every summer he would "get his orders" and "ship out" to Training Duty. This was almost always at a Navy Base on the ocean somewhere. Most of the time we went along and had a wonderful family vacation.

Twice he was stationed in Virginia Beach and we stayed with him in a two-room apartment which was literally on the beach. Jenny was six the first time we visited and eight the second. I'm pretty sure the episode I am describing happened when she was eight. Either way, she was my little sister, and I was a teenager.

When we stayed in Virginia Beach, we must have done many things, but honestly all I remember is being just a few steps from the beach. We would walk out of the BOQ and cross a little wood bridge and step onto the beach.

We played in the surf all day, every day—that's my memory.

There are four kids in our family. Jenny and Missy are the two youngest and are closest in age, being just over a year apart. Jill and I are the older two and were able to go off more on our own deeper into the water.

We had inflatable boogie boards which we used to surf the waves with. We had perfected the skill. We learned that if we went out beyond where the waves started to break we could catch them perfectly and ride them all the way in on top and not be rolled under.

We were both strong swimmers and had these inflatable rafts which we called boogie boards and we were only up to our shoulders in the water so we were fine.

Our mom was generally with Jenny and Missy because they were much younger and smaller. They also had a raft that they were using in the knee deep water.

Jill and I wanted to share the real thing with Jenny so we put her on the raft and floated her out to our spot beyond where the waves broke.

Now keep in mind – we had spent time at different beaches almost every summer. We had heard repeated warnings about undertow and riptides.

What I recall is Jill and I standing in the ocean up to her chin and my shoulders watching Jenny shoot straight out to sea. She was moving faster and farther than we could swim. I honestly do not recall if we had let go so she could ride a wave or if it was pulled from our hands.

We were absolutely terrified and horrified. She wasn't able to hear us. Or if she did we couldn't see any acknowledgement.

Jenny was one of those kids who could sit on the floor with her knees together straight out in front and her feet alongside her hips. That's how she was sitting on this tiny floating raft. We wanted her to lie down and paddle with her arms to offset the pull of the riptide. We were well versed in the theory of swimming sideways out of the fast riptide. We were also terrified that if she started moving around she would fall off and possibly not hang on. At least we could see her.

It probably wasn't very long before we made our way to the dreaded lifeguard chair. I don't remember if my mom was even there. She may have taken Missy inside which would explain why we didn't run to her and why Jenny was "entrusted" to us.

We got the lifeguard's attention and pointed to the tiny fading dot on the horizon that was our sister and our responsibility.

The lifeguard was a young woman. She never said a word. She just climbed down, trotted into the ocean, swam out and towed Jenny back. She may have said something when she climbed back up to her chair. Something about being more careful.

All I remember is quietly building sand castles as far from the water as I could for awhile.

Did you notice all the differences between the brother's version and Dr. Jenny Pitcock's version of the same incident? In this case, the story happened over 35 years ago, so we're not surprised the memories don't match up exactly. However, even we were surprised that the two remembrances of the same event had so many significant differences!

What does this extreme example of two points of view show us? First, that no matter how hard we try to honestly portray an autobiographical event, our minds fail us. Our perception of the event and our memories of them are not perfect. Unless we happen to have photographic memories, we'll get some of the details wrong.

Second, it shows us the value of different perspectives. Both Larry and his sister were terrified, but their reasons for the terror and the feelings were not identical. Part of his terror stemmed from a responsibility he felt as an older brother for his sister's safety. If the story were to be rewritten as a fictional narrative

This is a great lesson for students to return to when writing their narrative. Student writers worry about making up material or changing the "real" narrative. These two different perspectives of the same event reveal the space student writers have to play, and to make up material. The perspectives also reveal limitations: whatever they add or change in a story needs to be realistic.

from Larry's point of view, we could use his perspective to help the author see the story through his eyes.

CAPSULE 3 4.1.3

WRITING FROM A THIRD-PERSON PERSPECTIVE

 In speech, when we use the third person, we're talking about someone not directly involved in the conversation. For example, if your mom walked into the house and asked, "Where are your brothers?" You might say, "They went for a bike ride." In this case, you're relaying information about your brothers because they're not available to answer the question themselves.

That's typical usage of the third person in speech. In fact, with the possible exception of babies and small children, it's considered rude to talk in the third person right in front of someone. No one likes to be talked about as if they are not there.

In writing fiction, the third-person perspective is used most of the time. Why? Third-person narrators are the least **intrusive** type. Since they play no part in the story, we hardly notice them. And often, they know everything and see everything, so we can trust that we're getting an accurate story. They are very different from first-person narrators. As we mentioned before, a first-person narrator such as Huck Finn adds a lot of interesting color to a story. However, when the story is told through the mouth of one of the characters in the story, we know that his or her biases influence what they say.

There are three types of third-person narrators: omniscient, limited, and objective. Today, we'll look at the first type, omniscient. You've probably heard this word before. We sometimes call God an omniscient God, meaning that he's all-knowing (Latin: *omni* = all, *scientia* = knowledge).

When we say a narrator is omniscient, we mean that the narrator is all-knowing in the context of the story. He doesn't just observe what the characters do. He knows what's going on in characters' minds and what motivates their actions. An omniscient narrator knows more about the characters than they themselves do.

Historically, the third person omniscient is the most common type of narrator in fictional stories. Especially in long stories with lots of characters, this type of narrator helps keep the story moving and the plot clear. And, of all the narrators, the third-person omniscient offers readers the most confidence that they're getting the true story. A third-person omniscient narrator's knowledge is so far beyond the characters' that they often **foreshadow** or even outright tell readers in advance things that the characters don't know. A third-person omniscient narrator might make a statement like this one: "Though she didn't know it yet, this was the last time Lisa would see her sister alive."

As a writer, you might decide to choose a third-person omniscient narrator because it gives you the ability to reveal details about each of your characters that other types of narrators would not know. You can relay more information quickly and easily because you have access to the thoughts and feelings of everyone in the story, as well as advance knowledge of what will happen next.

CWJ

Today, we will practice writing from a third-person omniscient point of view. You can either work with a moment from your autobiographical essay or, if you already know what experience about which you will write your fictional story, you can choose a moment from that event.

Because we want you to show an omniscient viewpoint, you should choose a moment that involves at least two characters. To demonstrate, we've created an example of how we could transform a scene from Dr. Jenny Pitcock's personal narrative into fictional narrative by telling it from a third-person omniscient point of view.

Here's the original scene from the autobiographical essay:

> Feebly, I tried to yell a few more times, and even managed a slight scream. But I knew it was no use. No one could hear me way out here. In the midst of my panic, I knew that the right thing to do was to stay on the raft, but fear made me reckless. I had to try to get back to shore. I was just about to slide off the raft and try to swim back toward the beach when I saw a canoe coming rapidly in my direction, two lifeguards inside.
>
> "You okay?" one said as they got near me. The other reached out and grabbed the rope on my raft. "You're pretty far out."
>
> I don't remember my response—if I said anything at all. I was horrified and embarrassed to have to be rescued. But mostly I was relieved.

Here's the same incident from a third-person omniscient perspective:

> "Help!" the little girl feebly yelled. "Help!" But it was no use. No one could hear her. She could feel her eyes beginning to fill with tears. She struggled to hold them back, along with the rising panic she was beginning to feel. As the minutes ticked by, it became harder to sit on the raft and wait. What if no one ever saw her and she was swept out into the open ocean? She remembered her father's lectures. Even strong swimmers can't swim against the undertow, he had warned. She knew she wasn't a very good swimmer. But as she drifted further from shore, she began to think maybe she should risk it. She might not be able to hang on if the waves got very high. And what if there were sharks?

Use this CWJ to help your student become comfortable with the idea of adding fictional details. Note for her some of the details that are different from the autobiography—the eyes filling with tears, the sharks, and so on.

Once she chooses the incident she's going to write about in her CWJ, ask some questions like these.

How might a person feel in that situation (e.g. if they were lost)?

How would his or her face look?

How might a person who is lost act?

Encourage her to use at least one fictional detail in her writing for today.

◄ IN YOUR JOURNAL

The lifeguards paddled up just as she began to slide off the raft. "Need some help?" the one in the front asked. He had a feeling they'd arrived just in time. The little girl looked even smaller up close. She couldn't be more than six or seven years old. Even in the midday sun, her face looked pale. Clearly, she was terrified. She nodded. He grabbed the rope and began towing the raft toward shore as the other lifeguard continued to paddle. The child still had a death-grip on the raft, but as they neared the beach, her breathing returned to normal and she no longer looked as if she were about to burst into tears.

Now you try it. Make sure you include the thoughts and/or feelings of at least two characters.

CAPSULE 4 4.1.4

MORE THIRD-PERSON NARRATORS

There are two other types of third-person narrators. One is third-person limited. In this case, the information the narrator provides is limited to the senses and thoughts of a single character. In some ways, it's like having a first-person narrator because you only see things through the eyes of one character in the story. So why might an author choose this type of narrator? Even though the narrator's viewpoint is limited, as readers, we can trust that the information we're being provided is reliable, not biased like a first-person narrator's information.

Glance back at the example from 4.1.3. The whole first paragraph would work in a story with a third-person limited narrator. However, the second paragraph would need to be from the little girl's perspective too:

> The lifeguards paddled up just as she began to slide off the raft. "Need some help?" the one in the front asked. She was too embarrassed to look him in the eye, but she nodded. She climbed back up on the raft. The lifeguard who had spoken to her grabbed the rope and began towing the raft toward shore as the other lifeguard continued to paddle. She still had a death-grip on the raft, but as they neared the beach, relief washed over her. *We're almost there.* She thought. *I'm safe.*

The final type of third-person narrator is the third-person objective. This narrator is like a cameraman. A third-person objective narrator can't see inside any of the characters' minds; he functions as an observer who only records what he can see. Seeing from the perspective of a third-person narrator is similar to watching a movie or observing the family sitting next to you on a blanket at the beach. The information you have is what you see and hear and nothing more.

If we rewrote our sample paragraph from a third-person objective point of view, this is how it might look:

The two paragraphs above model a strategy you might incorporate into your teaching third-person omniscient.

If a student is experiencing difficulty writing a third-person omniscient section, have them write a story where they are one of the characters and allow them to use I. Then they can revise the I to a character with a name.

As we mention in the lesson, third person objective can be helpful in working with students who are not describing well. If you find your student is telling instead of showing, have him write first from this "cameraman" perspective. He can always go back in and add thoughts and feelings. Using this perspective encourages him to visualize the events on the paper, which in turn helps his readers to better visualize what he's writing about.

"Help!" the little girl feebly yelled. "Help!" No one was close enough to hear. Her eyes began to fill with tears. She clenched her jaw and closed her eyes. She sat that way for a while, almost motionless, *as if* afraid any movement might cause her to topple in.

When she opened her eyes again, she had drifted even further from shore. She waved one arm and made a sound that might have been a scream, but then stopped, *apparently* giving up. Then, still holding the rope, she cautiously lay down on the raft, being careful not to tip it as she changed positions.

Two lifeguards paddled up just as she began to slide off the raft. "Need some help?" the one in the front asked. The little girl nodded, eyes downcast. Even in the midday sun, she *looked* pale and terrified. He grabbed the rope and began towing the raft toward shore as the other lifeguard continued to paddle. The child still had a death-grip on the raft, but as they neared the beach, her breathing returned to normal and she no longer *looked* as if she were about to burst into tears.

The third-person objective point of view can be a good choice for beginning writers. It forces writers to show more than they tell, since they don't have access to the characters' thoughts. Whether or not you choose to write your fictional narrative using the third-person objective viewpoint, it might be a good idea to start out using the third-person objective as you draft.

CWJ

Today, we'd like you to practice writing from the third-person objective point of view. Once again, if you have a good idea which autobiographical incident you will write about, choose a moment from that story. If you wish, you may revise the third-person omniscient moment that you wrote for 4.1.3. If you do so, make sure to remove all thoughts and feelings expressed by the characters.

Notice the italicized words in the example of an objective third-person narrator in today's capsule—*as if, apparently, looked*. These words let readers know that the narrator cannot see into the character's mind; the narrator is merely reporting what he observes.

◄ IN YOUR JOURNAL

CHOOSING A POINT OF VIEW

As you begin considering which story you will tell, you should already be thinking about your readers. How can you make your story interesting? What message or point would you like them to get from reading your story?

Point of view can take a story that might otherwise be a little dull and make it interesting. For instance, a story about a visit to the zoo might be a little boring. But if you told the story through the viewpoint of your four-year-old sister, it might be a very entertaining fictional narrative.

Also, the point or message of the story may shift depending on who tells it. If Dr. Jenny Pitcock were telling the story of being swept out to sea from her brother's perspective, the message would be quite different. If she were writing that fictional narrative, the story might be about her brother realizing how fragile life is and how easily it could be swept away.

IN YOUR JOURNAL ▶

CWJ

Today, we want you to begin considering what point of view you might use in your fictional narrative. There are just a couple of ground rules:

1. If you use a first-person narrator, YOU cannot be the character doing the narration. The first-person narrator must be someone else in your story.

2. You must have your teacher's approval if you choose to use a second-person narrator. As we discussed in 4.1.2, this is a very tricky perspective. It's very difficult to SHOW more than TELL using this perspective. If you have a good reason for wanting to use this point of view, you need to make a strong case for your choice of a second-person narrator.

In 4.1.2, you looked back at your list of autobiographical incidents and began considering which you might use for your fictional narrative. Today, we want you to look at the list again, this time considering point of view. A story that seems a little bland when you tell it might be much more interesting when told from the point of view and in the voice of a younger brother or sister. Are there some things they say in a funny way (or used to when they were smaller?) Remember, this is fiction, so you can **embellish** the story to make it even funnier, sadder, or more embarrassing than it was when it actually happened.

You need to choose THREE incidents from your list that you might consider writing a fictional narrative about. For each, answer these questions:

This is a good moment for a discussion with your student. While you should let your student make the decision for herself regarding what story she will tell and what point of view she will use, offer your opinion. You might suggest a particular point of view your student hasn't considered that would work well for a story. Or you might look through her lists with her to help her find an incident that you think might make a good basis for her fictional piece. By talking through assignments at the choice stage, you can help your student start down a path that will likely bear fruit instead of becoming a dead end.

1. What happened in the story? Write one sentence each summarizing the beginning, middle, and end of the story.

▶ Beginning—

▶ Middle—

▶ End—

2. From whose point of view are you considering telling this story? What type of narrator will you use (first person, second person, third person omniscient, limited, or objective)?

3. How will the point of view you chose add interest or meaning to the story?

STYLE TIME: I OR ME?

Are you afraid of *me*? We don't mean me, the person writing this. We are talking about the personal pronoun *me*. When parents and teachers correct kids' speech, one of the big things they correct is improper usage of the word me.

If you started a sentence with "Me and Sarah . . ." you probably didn't ever get to finish the sentence. Your parent or teacher probably made you start over again: "Say, Sarah and I." Over time, you got the message. In fact, you may have thought that it was improper to use *me* when you spoke of yourself and someone else doing something together. Saying "Sarah and me" sounds like you don't have good grammar, right?

Well, some of the time that's true. When you are the subject of the sentence, that's true. You wouldn't say, "Sarah and me like to bowl." That would be incorrect.

But what about this sentence:

David gave Sarah and I his cookies at lunch.

That looks good, right? Actually, it's wrong. The personal pronoun you should use is determined by how it's being used in the sentence. In this situation, David is the subject of the sentence. Cookies is the direct object. *Sarah and me* function as the indirect object.

Are you more confused than ever? We're going to give you a few quick tips to make it easy to know when to use I and when to use me:

1. Always use I in the subject of the sentence.

2. Look at the verb. If it's a being (linking) verb, use I in the predicate of the sentence (that's the verb and everything that follows it.)

Here's a list of the being verbs:
- ▶ am
- ▶ was
- ▶ being
- ▶ is
- ▶ were
- ▶ been
- ▶ are
- ▶ be

Example:
> The MVPs of the game were Sarah and I.

3. In the predicate of the sentence after an action verb, use me, not I. Action verbs are ALL verbs that are not on the list of being verbs above.

Example:
> The teacher asked Sarah and me to collect the papers.

That's it. With these three rules, you should know exactly when to use *I* and when to use *me*.

Grammar Tip: Most of the time if you get confused, it's because you've got a compound subject or object—such as *Sarah and I or Sarah and me*. A quick way to check and see if you are right is to leave the other person out and see if it sounds right. For instance, you would never say, "The teacher asked I to collect the papers," so you would know that the sentence "The teacher asked Sarah and me to collect the papers" is correct.

THE RIGHT WORD

 Below are the five vocabulary words in context for this week. You should already have defined them in your journal as you found them in the reading.

▶ Just like the "you" in the argument at the beginning of the capsule, a first-person narrator sees the story only from his own **biased** perspective.
▶ Writers can keep that going without it seeming too strange for a short story, especially with a very **garrulous** first-person narrator.
▶ Third-person narrators are the least **intrusive** type.
▶ Third-person omniscient narrators' knowledge is so far beyond the characters' that they often **foreshadow** or even outright tell readers in advance things that the characters don't know.
▶ Remember, this is fiction, so you can **embellish** the story to make it even funnier, sadder, or more embarrassing than it was when it actually happened.

Using your thesaurus, try to find the BEST word to replace the bold word in the sentence. If you aren't familiar with the meanings of all the synonyms for each word in the thesaurus, you may need to use your dictionary to look them up. That way you can choose the word that best fits the sentence.

Write with WORLD

CAPSULE 1

SHOWING VERSUS TELLING: WHAT DOES IT MEAN?

Which one of these scenarios better **piques** your interest?

— I —

Amanda was a painfully shy child. She always hated it when her mother introduced her, especially to adults. She knew exactly what she was supposed to do, but somehow it seemed impossible. Her mother expected Amanda to look the adult in the eye and say, "Hello," or "Nice to meet you." But no matter how hard she wanted to comply, she felt physically frozen. Just today when they were at the grocery store, her mother had wanted Amanda to say hello to Mrs. Stillwell from the club. Amanda had been humiliated once again. She couldn't force herself to raise her eyes from the floor. She'd try to make her voice work, but barely a whisper came out.

— II —

"Well, Jennifer Jones!" a loud voice sang out. "Where have you been keeping yourself? I haven't seen you at the club all summer!"

Amanda felt her face flush. She glanced around quickly. *Could I make it to that aisle without drawing attention to myself?* she wondered. She stared hard at the ugly white linoleum tiles on the floor in front of her, willing them to open up so that she could crawl underneath.

Her mother squealed and the two women hugged. "We just got back in town. I was going to call you. We'll be up to the club later today or tomorrow. We've been in Boston. Jack had an assignment there, so we all decided to tag along and make a vacation of it."

Amanda hunched behind the grocery cart, trying to make herself invisible. She could see her mother looking around, trying to catch her eye. She looked down quickly and pretended not to see.

To enhance the information in this capsule, read the two paragraphs together and discuss. Which does he like better? Which is more interesting? In which does he feel he knows more about the character? Use the opportunity to demonstrate to your student the differences between showing and telling using these model paragraphs.

"Amanda, honey, you know Mrs. Stillwell, from the club," she heard her mother say. "Come over here and say hello."

Amanda shuffled over. "Hi," she croaked out, her eyes still glued to the floor tiles, her voice barely a whisper. Her palms felt sweaty and her mouth was dry. She was certain her face was as red as the tomatoes in the grocery cart. She fought back tears of frustration. What's wrong with me? she thought. *Why can't I just talk to people like a normal person?*

Both of these scenarios reveal that the character, Amanda, is painfully shy. In fact, the first one tells readers so in the first sentence. Notice that in the second scenario, the word shy doesn't even occur. Yet I would argue that the second scenario gives readers a better sense of exactly how shy Amanda is. Why? It doesn't simply tell us. It gives us a specific example and lets us figure it out.

Part of the enjoyment of a story is piecing together what's going on. It would be no fun to get to know a new friend by reading a report about them, and it's not a fun way get to know a character in a story, either. Getting to know them through "watching" them respond to situations and "hearing" how they talk is much more engaging.

In this lesson, we will demonstrate the difference between showing and telling. We'll give you opportunities to sharpen your "showing" skills. You can't show all the time, though. As the scenarios from today's capsule demonstrate, showing takes a lot more words. So we'll also help you determine when to show and when to tell.

CWJ

IN YOUR JOURNAL ▶

The first step in learning to show more than tell in writing is recognizing the difference between the two. Even good writers do some of both. Today, we want you to find an example of telling and an example of showing and copy each into your journal.

Choose a novel by one of your favorite authors. Find one passage where the author TELLS readers something about the character and copy it into your journal. Now choose another passage where the author reveals or SHOWS something about the character without directly telling readers and copy it into your journal too. For the second passage, answer the question, "What does the author show about the character in this passage?" (In our example above, the answer would be, "Amanda is painfully shy.")

PREPARING TO SHOW

If you enjoy reading, we will bet you've read some stories full of events that could never happen—for instance a futuristic science fiction novel. Even so, you found yourself drawn into the story. You were so fully absorbed in the events on the page that you couldn't put the book down. When the main character's life was in danger, you felt your palms get sweaty. Your heart was beating so loudly you could hear it in your head. You found yourself reading faster and faster because you just had to know what would happen next. Even though the story was based on an impossible **premise**, it *felt* real. You could see the story's action in your mind. You could feel what the characters were feeling. They seemed like real people.

You've probably read other books that actually could have happened. The stories should have been interesting, but you never really connected with the characters. What makes the difference? In most cases, it's how the story is told.

When a writer creates vivid images, reading a story can be like having front-row seats to a blockbuster movie. You feel like you're up close watching the action. On the other hand, reading the work of a less-skilled writer can be like having your friend tell you about a great movie she just saw—it might be mildly interesting, but her retelling of the story probably doesn't have you on the edge of your seat.

So as a writer, how do you get your readers' hearts racing instead of putting them to sleep? There is no perfect formula. Your best friend's favorite author might be your least favorite, and vice versa. But even bearing differences of opinion in mind, there are a few qualities of good writing most experts agree on. We could write a book on them—and, in fact, many people have. However, in this lesson, we'll start small. Let's look at two:

1. Draw upon real emotions *and your reactions to them.*
Let's look at the statement, "Alex was angry." Anybody can be angry. What draws readers into the story is not the emotion itself, but rather how the character reacts to it. What did Alex's anger drive him to do? Punch a wall? Burst into tears? Pray for the person who angered him? It's in their response to emotions and situations that we learn about characters in a story. Authentic reactions make for much more believable characters. That's one reason we're having you base your fictional narrative on something that really happened. We want you to be able to remember and use real feelings to inform your story.

2. Recreate important scenes in the story for your readers.
Often, writers are told, "Show, don't tell." But that's impossible to do all the time. Unless you want your short story to be longer than this textbook, you'll need to show some things and tell others. Showing generally means including lots of details. Then—as we demonstrated in the second "shy Amanda" example—good writing lets the reader add up those details to figure out something about the character.

IN YOUR JOURNAL ▶

Choosing to show certain moments in the story in great detail is key to getting your readers to care about the characters and the story.

CWJ

In today's capsule, we've given you two targets to shoot for in your fictional narrative: (1) creating realistic reactions to emotion and (2) recreating important scenes instead of just telling readers about those scenes.

In your journal today, we're going to have you answer some questions about a moment in an autobiographical incident. We'll use this incident to help you work on portraying emotion and recreating scenes. Once again, flip back to 3.1.4.

Look through the incidents you listed. Find one that **elicits** strong emotions in you. Does one in particular bring up memories of fear, anger, sadness, or elation? When you find an incident that does, answer the following questions:

▶ In a sentence or two, describe the incident you chose to write about in your journal today.
▶ What strong emotion(s) did you feel when this happened?
▶ What physical reactions did you have? (Think big and small—your leg might have begun twitching, but maybe you also shouted out loud.) Be as specific as possible and include as many details as you can.
▶ Did you say anything? If so, what was it?
▶ How did you feel immediately afterwards? How do you feel when you think back on the incident now?

Think about the moment again—but this time, instead of considering what was going on in your mind and how you felt about it, think about what was going on around you.

▶ When you play the scene in your mind, what exactly do you see yourself and the other people doing?
▶ Where were you? Describe the setting.
▶ What do you remember hearing? (Example: an air conditioner whining in the background, the sounds of bowling balls crashing into pins)
▶ Any significant smells? (Example: smoke from a campfire, your mother's lasagna in the oven)
▶ Any tastes? (not limited to food—could be tears, sea water, etc.)

Warning: If you focused on each sense in every scene, you would end up with no focus and a lot of **irrelevant** details. However, often people only think about what they saw. Sometimes another sense is just as important. These questions may help you remember other important things you experienced through various senses.

Before your student answers these questions, you might discuss the incident with them. Have the student tell you about the experience. In addition to listening, your role is to ask follow-up questions. This brainstorming will help them answer the CWJ questions.

STRATEGIES FOR SHOWING—SKETCHING A SCENE

 Have you ever been to a museum with walls full of great art? Even if you've seen pictures of famous paintings, seeing them up close is a whole different experience. For one thing, they are often much bigger than you imagined. Dr. Jenny Pitcock remembers one such experience:

A few years back, I visited the Art Institute of Chicago. I remember my surprise when I happened upon Georges Seurat's painting A Sunday Afternoon on the Island of La Grand Jatte. I'd seen pictures of it in textbooks, but it didn't prepare me for what the painting really looked like. It was almost seven feet tall and over 10 feet wide. Even more amazing, the whole painting was created using tiny dots of color!

Often, we're caught up in the beauty the artists have captured in their masterpieces. Sometimes we might even wish we had their talent so that we could whip up some paintings like these. Because obviously, it takes talent to be a great artist, right?

Of course. But just as important (maybe even more so), it takes dedication and lots of hard work. Seurat spent over two years creating A Sunday Afternoon. He sat in the park and sketched. He did lots of preliminary drawings. He made oil sketches. And even after he had the painting on the canvas, he continued to rework it.

We don't expect you to spend two years writing your fictional narrative, but you get the idea. Like a great work of art, good writing isn't generally dashed off in an afternoon without any forethought or revision later. It takes time and effort to get it right.

In previous units, you've practiced some of the skills you'll need to create vivid mental images for your readers. Today in your journal, we'll work on sketching out a scene. In the next capsule, we'll begin adding in elements such as strong verbs, well-placed phrases, and interesting adjectives. Think of today's writing like sketching on a canvas before you begin adding the "paint" that turns it into a work of art.

CWJ

Look back at your last journal entry. In question number 6, you described the scene. You told about it. But in the questions that followed, you generated a lot more details. In today's journal entry:

1. Read back through your answers to questions 6 through 10. Quickly use words to "sketch the scene" on the page.

◀ IN YOUR JOURNAL

We cannot overemphasize the importance of students knowing this. Good writing takes much thought, practice, and time. Some students will be ready to go; others will have difficulty writing an official paper.

The key for both groups is to realize that they are writing a draft—not the final product. For students who are ready to go, this is a draft that will require revision—they will have to dedicate more time than they expect. For students having difficulty starting, this draft should free them. They are not producing anything that cannot be changed. In fact, they are throwing ideas up against the wall to see what works and what does not.

Effective writers work at different paces, but all of them put great effort, thought, and time into their writing.

2. Give yourself another name and write in the third person to begin practice writing as fiction.

3. Remember, let the readers figure out for themselves what you're writing about—don't tell them.

Read through this example before you begin:

In a sentence or two, describe the incident you chose to write about in your journal today.

I was taking care of my grandma who was losing her memory. When I realized she had shoplifted a picture frame from Walmart, I had to try to keep her from getting angry and upset while also making sure we gave the picture frame back.

What strong emotion(s) did you feel when this happened?

At first I felt panic when I realized my grandma was shoplifting. Then I felt worried about how I would get her to take the picture frame back when she was convinced it was hers. Then I felt angry that I had been left to deal with this situation. I was humiliated by the greeter's pity for me and embarrassed to find myself in this situation.

What physical reactions did you have? (Think big and small—your leg might have begun twitching, but maybe you also shouted out loud.) Be as specific as possible and include as many details as you can.

My face turned red and I could feel tears standing in my eyes. When other people started watching, I felt hot all over, like my skin was on fire. Tears ran down my face as I fled from the store.

Did you say anything? If so, what was it?

"Grandma, if you want the picture frame, we'll have to pay for it."

How did you feel afterwards? How do you feel when you think back on the incident now?

I felt like I couldn't win. I was trying to do the right thing, but by doing so, I was just making her madder. At the same time, I felt sad because it was more like I was the grownup than her, even though I was 12 and she was in her 70s. Now I think I realize a little more that Grandma wasn't trying to be stubborn and mean. The way she was acting was the disease, not the grandma I used to know and love.

Think about the moment again—but this time, instead of considering what was going on in your mind and how you felt about it, think about what was going on around you.

When you play the scene in your mind, what exactly do you see yourself and the other people doing?

I'm walking toward the door of Walmart with my grandma. My mom is pulling the car around. My grandma starts to put her jacket on, and as she does, a picture frame falls to the floor. I pick it up and turn to take it back, but she grabs it out of my hand, insisting it's hers. When she yells, the lady at the front of the store notices us and comes over. I see her look of pity as I ask her to wait with my grandmother while I go get my mom. I see myself running out toward my car, tears streaming down my face.

Where were you? Describe the setting.

The entrance/exit to a Walmart store. The checkout lanes are to our left as we walk toward the door. There's a nail salon, a bank, and a Subway Restaurant on the right. We're headed toward the door where there's a greeter watching people come and go.

What do you remember hearing? (Example: an air conditioner whining in the background, the sounds of bowling balls crashing into pins)

The beeps of the registers, the loudspeaker announcements, "Attention, shoppers . . ."the clack of carts and their loud clatter against the floor. People talking. How quiet it got when my grandma yelled at me.

Any significant smells? (Example: smoke from a campfire, your mother's lasagna in the oven)

cookies, bread from Subway

Any tastes? (not limited to food—could be tears, sea water, etc.)

no

As they hurried toward the door, Grandma pulled her red fleece from Alice's hands and stopped to put it on.

"You don't need that, Grandma," said Alice. "It's a hundred degrees outside. And we need to hurry. My mom is going to be worried about us."

But already, Grandma was shaking it open. Alice slowed her pace but didn't stop. Maybe if she kept moving, Grandma would too. They were in front of the Subway Restaurant right by the store's front door. At the rate Grandma was moving, Alice could sit down and eat a sandwich and still beat Grandma outside, where she was sure her mother was impatiently waiting.

Crash! Something dropped from the red fleece to the floor. A gold picture frame, price tag still on the front, lay on the white tile in front of her. Grabbing it quickly, Alice flipped it over.

"Oh, good. It's not broken. Grandma, stay here for a second." *No harm done,* she thought as she turned to run the picture back to the cashier stand.

"Wait one minute!" She felt the picture jerked from her hand. "You can't have that! It's mine!"

Oh, no. Not now. Alice thought. *Not in front of all these people.*

"If you want it, we have to pay for it," Alice said, trying to sound pleasant and calm. Nothing set Grandma off faster than having a child tell her what to do.

"Nonsense! I've had this picture for 30 years. It's mine!" Now Alice had to hurry to catch up with Grandma. For someone who was almost 80, she could move fast—when she wanted to.

Alice grabbed for the picture, but Grandma held it close to her chest and elbowed her out.

"Look Grandma," she pleaded. "It still has the price tag on it. And look at the picture. There's no one you know in it."

As they neared the greeter's stand, she caught Grandma's arm. "If we go past her and she sees you with that picture, she'll call the police on us for shoplifting," said Alice, pointing to the elderly lady in the blue vest.

"Young lady, don't accuse me of stealing!" Grandma was almost shouting now. "This picture is mine!"

Out of the corner of her eye, Alice could see the greeter moving toward them. Heat flooded her face. She fought back tears.

"Is something the matter?" the greeter asked kindly.

"This little girl is trying to steal my picture," said Grandma, clutching the picture to her chest.

Alice struggled to hold back tears. "Could my grandma wait here with you while I go get my mom? I'm sure she'll be able to straighten this out."

She didn't wait for an answer but ran toward the door, tears streaming down her face.

CAPSULE 4

SHOWING MORE THAN TELLING

How do we make our writing show more than it tells? Whether you realize it or not, you've been practicing since the very first lesson of this book. Including specific details and using descriptive language help readers see your story.

WORLD WISDOM

You may be surprised by someone who really values using specific details and descriptive language. Let's hear from Krieg Barrie. He isn't a writer. He is an illustrator for *WORLD Magazine* who depends on a writer's vivid language to guide his pen and brush strokes. That's how he makes his illustrations convey the writer's meaning.

"When I am assigned to illustrate a particular story or article for WORLD *I begin by carefully reading through the story, looking for the author's central idea or message. I also look for the specific details that the author uses to convey that idea. The details are what really tell the story, clarify the idea and make it an interesting read along the way.*

In the illustration I try to take the author's idea and turn it into a visual picture. I want the idea in the picture to be clear so I rely on the details. Even a little detail like the angle of an eyebrow on a face makes all the difference between happy, curious, angry or frightened. I also want the picture to be interesting to look at. Since details are information, the more details that are included, the more informative and interesting the picture will be. To tell a story well in words or in pictures requires information, the more interesting the better, and details are the key!"

—Krieg Barrie

In Unit 1, we spent a good deal of time examining images. Our reason for doing so was to help you to begin considering how to create images using words. Compare these two sentences:

I had an interesting day.

I spent the day fighting off wolves.

The second sentence is definitely more specific. In Units 1 and 2, we showed you how changing verbs and adding adjectives, adverbs, and phrases can take a sentence that doesn't really say anything and turn it into one that makes a picture pop into your head. Let's review a bit.

The second sentence is better, but by providing more information, we can add even more detail to the picture.

First, let's add a strong verb:

I devoted the day to fighting off wolves.

That's interesting, but I'd like to know how he did it, wouldn't you? So let's add an adverbial phrase that tells us:

I devoted the day to fighting off wolves armed only with a baseball bat and pocket knife.

We're not finished yet. What kind of wolves were they? Can you tell us any more about the weapons? Adding some adjectives can give us an even clearer picture:

I devoted the day to fighting off hungry wolves armed only with a wooden baseball bat and rusty pocket knife.

You get the idea—a few additional well-placed adjectives and adverbs can really improve the picture you're creating for readers.

Another way to make sure your language shows more than tells is to try to capture in words the exact way you felt when the experience happened. Avoid clichéd descriptions. Clichés are phrases that get overused such as "all's well that ends well." Similarly, clichéd descriptions are phrases that get used over and over in writing to the point where they lose their meaning. For instance, the first time someone said, "Her eyes were big as saucers" or "He was as strong as an ox," these descriptions might have been interesting, but over time, they became clichés.

It's particularly easy to fall into clichéd language when describing emotions. As you read back through your sketch from yesterday, make sure you're not relying on clichés to share your emotions. Try to remember how you really felt.

CWJ

IN YOUR JOURNAL ▶

Today, we want you to take another look at the scene you sketched out in 4.2.3. Now it's time to add color. By choosing words carefully and thoughtfully, we can create strong images for our readers.

Since this is fiction, it's okay to embellish. You can add dialogue or change what characters said to make the words more effective. If you don't remember *exactly* what happened, draw on other experiences that occurred at the same place if you can. For instance, we've been to Walmart a number of times. So we could draw on other experiences from our many trips to Walmart to help add details to the fictional story.

How can you add color to the scene you sketched yesterday? We'd like you to make four specific changes.

Clichés appear often in the writing of students. When looking at your student's writing, question any comparison or image they use. Clichés often sneak into their writing—particularly when they try to show instead of tell. Typically clichés that appear in student writing are either common similes or phrases that appear in media and advertising.

Some students will err in the other direction. Instead of using clichés, they will use the thesaurus in creative ways—more or less replacing a cliché with a synonym found in the thesaurus. Unfortunately, the chosen synonym doesn't quite fit the meaning they want.

1. Circle all your verbs. Choose two that you can strengthen by making them more specific. (Hint: if you have being verbs, try changing them to action verbs.)

2. Choose one sentence and make it more specific by adding an adjective, adverb, or phrase.

3. Add a sense other than sight to your story. Don't just say what you saw, add in something you smelled, heard, or felt.

4. Change a clichéd description. Describe how it really felt, looked, sounded. Don't just repeat what you've read or heard people say.

CAPSULE 5   4.2.5

WHEN TO SHOW, WHEN TO TELL

 We've spent most of this lesson demonstrating how to show. Showing takes more brain power than telling. You have to think hard to remember how you really felt when an event occurred so that your language isn't full of clichés. To effectively show, you must remember what people said—or invent some dialogue to carry the story along. Remember, the idea is to let the reader "watch" a scene unfold and try to figure out what's going on.

But there are times you need to tell. For instance, if there is more than one important scene in your fictional narrative, telling what happened between them is a good choice. As the writer, using mostly telling for the unimportant parts helps the reader know which scenes are most important when you switch to showing. IF EVERYTHING IS GIVEN THE SAME EMPHASIS, IT'S KIND OF LIKE WRITING IN ALL CAPITALS. You don't know which part of the story to focus on.

Even within your showing sections, there are places that you'll need to tell to keep the story moving. For instance, in Alice's story, here's a moment when the writer tells:

> Something dropped from the red fleece to the floor. A gold picture frame, price tag still on the front, lay on the white tile in front of her. Grabbing it quickly, Alice flipped it over.

This is a good spot to tell because the stolen picture frame is not the puzzle that the reader is trying to figure out. The reader is trying to tease out the relationship between the girl and her grandma and figure out why the grandma is stealing.

This is the kind of telling you don't want to do:

> Alice's grandmother sometimes stole stuff. She didn't mean to do it, but she had Alzheimer's and sometimes she got confused. Alice found it scary and embarrassing.

Here, the narrator has told the readers the central point of the story. Can you see the difference? Tell to move the plot along, not to ruin it.

CWJ

IN YOUR JOURNAL ▶

Read through the scene you wrote in capsule 3. Using a colored pencil, <u>underline</u> all the places where you tell instead of show. Did you find any "telling" moments that reveal plot information that should be shown instead? If so, choose ONE underlined section and rewrite it so that it shows instead of tells.

STYLE TIME: WHO OWNS WHAT?

i If you aren't sure when to use apostrophes, they can seem like a secret code—little tiny marks that seem to cluster around the letter -s. But what do they do? In this lesson, we'll begin to **demystify** apostrophes. We'll show you one reason you need to use them: To show who owns what.

Compare these two sentences:

> My aunt's millions will be my sister's millions now.

> My aunt's millions will be my sisters' millions now.

Depending on where you put the apostrophe, you can make one sister rich or all your sisters rich! In the first sentence, the apostrophe comes before the –s. That makes it singular. In the second, the apostrophe comes after, making it plural—two or more sisters.

When it comes to apostrophes that show possessions, there are three simple rules:

1. Add –'s to a singular word to show ownership:
   The basket's handle
   The dog's collar.

This includes proper nouns:
   John's puppy
   The White House's lawn

This holds true even when the word already ends in –s:

Chris's brother
Dr. Jones's house

2. When a plural word ends in –s, just add an apostrophe to show ownership:

The monkeys' cage
The Joneses' house

3. When a plural word does not end in –s, add an –'s:

The children's breakfast

That's it! If you understand how to use apostrophes to show possession, you've taken a big step toward cracking the code.

Grammar Tip:
If you have difficulty knowing when to use possessives, here's a tip for checking: circle or underline all the words that end in –s. Now look at the word that follows it. If you wrote Johns book, could you change it *to the book belonging to John*? Yes. If you can reverse the words and add "belonging to" between them, you've got a possessive and you need an apostrophe.

THE RIGHT WORD

 Below are the five vocabulary words in context for this week. You should already have defined them in your journal as you found them in the reading.

▶ Which one of these scenarios better **piques** your interest?
▶ Even though the story's **premise** was impossible, it felt real.
▶ Find one that **elicits** strong emotions in you.
▶ If you focused on each sense in every scene, you would end up with no focus and a lot of **irrelevant** details.
▶ In this lesson, we'll begin to **demystify** apostrophes.

Using your thesaurus, try to find the BEST word to replace the bold word in the sentence. If you aren't familiar with the meanings of all the synonyms for each word in the thesaurus, you may need to use your dictionary to look them up. That way you can choose the word that best fits the sentence.

Write with WORLD

CAPSULE 1

WHAT STORY DO YOU WANT TO TELL?

Do you know any good storytellers? It's fun to listen to them talk. A good storyteller can take an ordinary situation—a visit to the doctor, an encounter with the neighbor's dog, a case of the hiccups—and make you laugh so hard tears roll down your cheeks. Good storytellers know how to make a story enjoyable for listeners.

That's because these natural storytellers are thinking about YOU as they craft their stories. They want to make you laugh. When they create stories, they choose details that will keep their listeners interested. They probably even embellish the story a little. They instinctively understand that one purpose of a good story is to entertain.

Knowing your audience and what will entertain them is an important part of being a good writer. That's part of what we want you to think about as you determine what story you want to tell in your fictional narrative.

However, good stories usually have other purposes too. They make us think. They focus on **universal** themes that we can relate to because we've felt the same way or had a similar experience ourselves. Perhaps we even come to new understanding about human nature by reading a good story. In this lesson, we'll show you how to craft a narrative with a purpose.

Have you ever heard the old proverb, "You can't make a silk purse out of a sow's ear?" That's true with a story, too. You can't create a story with meaning if there's none in the story to begin with. The most important part of crafting a narrative with purpose is choosing the right material.

So as you look at your story, it's important to choose one with some depth to it. That doesn't mean it has to be terribly detailed or involved. It probably means that something happened, and as a result, you learned something or changed in some way. Often, it's an experience that made you grow up a little or become wiser as a result.

Students will understand the concept of depth more as they learn to reflect on what they read. Have a student choose a favorite story or book. Ask the student two questions.

First, what about the writing did they enjoy? Was it the author's use of details, the way they developed character, or the way they made the story seem real? Second, what did the student learn from the story? Did they learn how to handle difficult situations?

More mature readers typically become effective writers. There is a reason for this: a reader's ability to answer questions like those above teach valuable lessons about depth, showing vs. telling, character development, and style.

WORLD WISDOM

Susan Olasky, a writer for *WORLD Magazine*, is someone who appreciates the value of good fiction stories, whether she is reading or writing them. The emphasis, however, is on *good* stories. As you become a better writer you will also develop more discernment as a reader, so you'll get more out of the reading you do.

"I write fiction and read fiction for the same reason: I love stories. Some people think stories are untrue, so why should we waste our precious time reading them? But a good story allows me to experience life from someone else's perspective. What would it be like to be an immigrant or orphan, a slave or someone unjustly accused of a crime? Fiction helps make my heart tender towards people who are different from me. Good fiction touches the heart because it dives down below the brain's rational defenses. When Nathan confronted David about his sin with Bathsheba, he used a story.

Not all stories are good ones. Some are like junk food. Digest too much of them and you'll get sick. Others are like poison, they'll eat away at you from the inside out. Discerning readers have to learn to tell the good ones from the bad."

—Susan Olasky

CWJ

IN YOUR JOURNAL ▶

Today, in your journal, we want you to write about two experiences you're considering for your fictional narrative.

For each incident, answer the following questions. Be as specific as possible.

1. Why is this story important to you?

2. Why do you want to tell this story?

3. What does the story reveal about you?

4. What does it reveal about the other characters?

5. Did you (or anyone else in the story) change in any way from this incident?

6. In a sentence or two, explain what you learned from this experience in your life.

PROS AND CONS OF FICTIONALIZING YOUR PERSONAL NARRATIVE

You've already created one narrative with purpose—your autobiographical essay. You researched the story you chose through photographs. You thought about what it means to you. In short, you've put a lot of work and time into that essay. Should you continue with the same story for this essay, your fictional narrative?

We don't know. Some students probably should, and others shouldn't. So how do you know which kind of student you are? If you were tired of your narrative by the end of the last unit, going forward with the same story probably isn't for you. Or if you're thinking, "All I have to do if I stick with my story is go in and change *I* to *she* and I'm done," sticking with the same story isn't for you, either.

But if you're the type of student who enjoys reworking your writing—searching for just the right word, just the right scene, and the perfect description—you may enjoy continuing with the same story. Perhaps seeing it from a different perspective—like a different first person narrator or a third person narrator—would bring something new to the story.

Today we want you to experiment with your autobiographical essay to help you determine whether turning it into a fictionalized narrative is a good choice for you.

CWJ

Reread the final draft of your autobiographical essay. When you finish, choose one paragraph and rewrite it. Be sure to:

◀ IN YOUR JOURNAL

1. Rewrite from a different point of view (third person narrator or first person narrator from another character's point of view).

2. Include some additional dialogue to make your narrative different from your story. (If used properly, dialogue can also help you show more than tell.)

3. Rewrite a different section than you wrote in 4.1.1.

Before you begin writing, read this real student's autobiographical essay. Pay close attention to the paragraph in bold:

Challenge your student to produce dialogue that is realistic. Take them to a public setting to listen to everyday conversation surrounding them. As they do this, they will become aware of phrasing, words, and actions people employ in daily conversations. Great writers often take time to observe people—their actions and words.

"Madeline, you need to be careful of pickpockets. Italy is infamous for having them. They will either come up to you in groups and bump and jostle you, or they will try to make you pity them by acting weak and asking for money." These were the first words my dad said to me as we got off the train from Germany to Bologna, Italy. I went to Europe with my dad when I was ten. We had just gotten off our train and were standing in a train station waiting for transportation to Florence. I was excited because standing in this train station marked the first time I had ever set foot in Italy. When we got off our train I took a look around the train station, thinking that this dirty, grungy place was amazing merely because it was Italy.

When my dad warned me about the pickpockets, suddenly, in my mind, the station was transformed from a great Italian landmark to a pickpocket convention. Everyone looked fishy. The little children who had looked cute earlier suddenly were distractions used by pickpockets so they could steal from us vulnerable tourists. Everyone looked like a pickpocket, and I was terrified. As I sat on my hard metal bench in the summer heat of the train station, I must have looked very vulnerable, because a lady came up to my father and me, and croaked "Water, please. Spare me some money for water." I was terrified. I started looking around frantically for other pickpockets to come up and steal our money while we were distracted, as if a mob of thieves was going to descend upon us. But luckily, nothing happened.

I sat with my dad for a few minutes peacefully but warily looking for pickpockets. My dad nudged my shoulder and said "Look, Madeline, that girl we saw a minute ago asking us for money just got money from that man and actually went to buy water. I guess she really wasn't a thief after all."

I was relieved that she hadn't actually been a thief, and for the first time since we arrived at the train station, I let myself relax. I closed my eyes and rested. I vaguely heard some men talking behind us in Italian and the sounds of the train station and the lady at the Intercom talking in a soothing Italian voice. I found that I was too excited for Italy to be tired at all though, so I turned around and watched the men talking behind us. One of them was a young man with short, spiky hair, and the other was an old bearded man who looked creepy and kind of like a hobo. As I watched them, the young man started to raise his voice and then started yelling at the top of his lungs. The old man didn't yell but kept his voice fairly calm and even. At the time, I thought the old man was the rational one of the two. However, that was far from the truth. The old man slowly reached into his back pocket.

I didn't see what the old man pulled out, but I heard my dad yell "Run!" and so I ran in the other direction without even thinking about it. I looked back to where we had been sitting, and I saw the old man walking around the station with a large butcher knife held out in front of him. Then I realized my dad wasn't there, and I looked around fearfully for him, until I saw him walking toward me. "Dad did you see his knife?—It was huge—Do you think he would have hurt us?—That was so scary—Are you okay?—What do you think will happen to the man he was fighting with?"

My dad was obviously bewildered by the number of questions I threw at him, but he patiently answered them," Yes, it was a very big knife. No, I think the knife was just a threat. I'm fine. Are you? I think the man he was fighting with is probably scared but okay."

Lo and behold, the train I had been so desperately awaiting finally showed up, right when I stopped needing it. How frustrating!

My father and I then boarded our "late" train, my father worrying about our safety in Italy. I immediately fell asleep, no longer as excited about Italy and its wonders, but instead dreaming of good old America.

Now read her fictionalized paragraph and compare to the paragraph in bold above. Notice her change of narrator from first person to third person omniscient. Also note her addition of dialogue:

A woman lounging under the station sign looked very suspicious. Every which way the poor girl turned, she saw a pickpocket.

"I'm scared," she whispered to her father. "When does our train to Florence come?"

Her father looked at his watch. "About half an hour."

Inwardly, the child groaned. Thirty whole minutes of being scared out of her skin?

Looking around, the girl saw a group of ladies whispering. One of them left the group and approached the girl and her father.

"Water," she croaked. "Water."

Despite the numbing fear that gripped her, the girl wondered why the woman was speaking English. Even after the woman left to rejoin her group, the girl still couldn't open her mouth to ask her father the question.

CAPSULE 3 4.3.3

DETAILS THAT CONVEY YOUR PURPOSE

In 4.3.1 and 4.3.2 of this lesson, you explored some possible autobiographical stories you could turn into fictional stories. In 4.3.1, you chose two possible stories and answered questions to help you determine whether or not the stories' purpose was strong enough to make a good fictional narrative. In 4.3.2, you practiced fictionalizing part of the autobiographical narrative you wrote in the last unit.

Today, we will move a step closer to choosing the experience you will write about for your fictional narrative. We would like you to narrow your choices down to the final two you are considering writing about. Today we'll examine the purpose for each of these stories and demonstrate how including the right details is essential in getting your story's purpose across to your readers.

In Unit 3, you practiced including details that convey your story's purpose. When writing fiction, the purpose remains the same. However, you need to be even more particular about the details you choose and how you present them. Readers expect a certain amount of telling in an autobiography. After all, you are the writer, so they expect you to include some of the things you know about yourself or that you've learned. But in fiction, part of the readers' enjoyment of the **genre** is figuring out the story for themselves. So you need to choose "telling" details—details that point back to the story's purpose.

Let's look at an example. Here's how our student writer answered the questions from capsule 1:

Why is this story important to you?
   Because it gave me *different expectations and showed me a different side of Italy than I expected to see, especially on my first day*

Why do you want to tell this story?
   to show how my innocence and hopefulness about Italy changed to worry and doubt

What does the story reveal about you?
   that I am too trusting and that I don't expect bad things to happen

What does it reveal about the other characters?
   My dad's protectiveness

Did you (or anyone else in the story) change in any way from this incident?
   My view of Italy and my expectations for the trip changed drastically once I had seen how dangerous it could be.

In a sentence or two, explain what you learned from this experience in your life.
   I learned that the world can be a dangerous place. You can't always anticipate and be prepared for the bad things that are going to happen to you.

Based on her answers to these questions, when turning this experience into a fictional story, her purpose or theme could be the central character's realization that the world can be a dangerous place and you can't always be prepared or protect yourself. This is a universal theme in literature—a character moves from innocence to experience. We can all relate to that theme. That's a good starting point for this student's story.

In order to get her point across, what types of details might the writer include?

Student writers need to identify and develop a central theme before they begin writing the story. They should be able to share their theme and tell you why the theme is important, and what it will teach the essay's readers.

Help your student writer to see opportunities where they can link or develop their theme through the thoughts, actions, and words of their characters.

Also recognize that advanced student writers know their theme from the opening line of their story. But they may wait to fully reveal the theme until the end.

If students do not develop a theme for their essay, the theme will likely lose control at the idea and organizational levels.

► Details that show her anticipation of the "perfect" Italy she imagines
► Details that show how the reality differs from what she expects
► Details that show how she is changed by the experience.

So what might those details look like specifically?

1. Perfect Italy
  ► Girl is excited about what she expects Italy to be—great food, art, famous tourist sites
  ► What she actually sees from the train window—Italy's beautiful landscapes
  ► First view of the train station—bustling, full of new sights and sounds

2. Contrast of the train station and experience there
  ► Girl doesn't know about pickpockets, but once her dad tells her about them suddenly everyone looks like a pickpocket
  ► Fear of the woman who asks them for water; assumes she's a pickpocket
  ► One man pulls a knife on another man

3. How she is changed
  ► Can't get the picture of the knife fight out of her head
  ► She reacts physically to the knife fight
  ► She is warier; she wonders if Italy will be as great as she's imagined

This student's process should look similar to your process in the last unit when you decided what details best conveyed your purpose in your autobiographical story. In both types of narratives, the writer's purpose should determine what details he or she includes in the narrative.

If this writer came up and said to you, "The world is a dangerous place," you would probably agree. But her specific experience of that danger—a knife fight in a train station in Italy—is much more memorable and persuasive.

As you continue with this course, we hope you'll begin to see a pattern. Good details are important in all types of writing, not just stories. In all good writing, details provide evidence that convinces readers and sways them to believe the truths you are telling them.

CWJ

Write down the main purpose or theme for each of the two stories you are considering for your fictional narrative. (If you look back through your journal, you have probably already answered questions that will help you determine what the purpose or theme is. Check 4.3.1.)

◄ IN YOUR JOURNAL

Under the first purpose statement, list two types of details that will help you convey your story's purpose.

(See the student example above.) Underneath each type of detail, list two specific examples of details you could use in your story.

Do the same for the second purpose statement.

CAPSULE 4

THE STORYBOARDING TEST

Uh, oh. There's that word—test. But don't worry. You'll be giving this test, not taking it. Today, we want you to test the stories you're considering. We want you to see if they possess the qualities of a good story. Grab a sheet of paper. On the left hand side, write:

Beginning

Middle

End

Do that twice. For each of your stories, write a sentence or two under each section. (You may have done this already for one or both of the stories you're considering. To save yourself some time if you've done it already, flip through your journal and copy what you have already written.)

Were you able to do this for each story? If so, they've passed the first part of the test.

Along with having a beginning, middle, and end, a good story creates images in readers' minds. In a previous lesson (4.2.2), we worked on developing imagery. We focused not just on what we saw during certain incidents. We focused on our other senses too. The more specific and real the sights, smells, emotions, and feelings you create for your reader, the stronger the sense of **immediacy** you will be able to create. The goal is for readers to forget for a minute that they are reading a story. You want them to really care about your characters.

With the goal of fully engaging your readers, grab a stack of 4 x 6 cards. Remember storyboarding? We want you to put yourself behind the camera again. Pretend you are following yourself through the experience you are considering for your fictional narrative and snapping pictures. For each major scene, you should have a card.

Students may balk at this step. It seems like a lot of extra work. But a central focus of *Write with WORLD* is its focus on images in writing. This "extra" step helps your student to both organize and visualize her story. Don't skip it. We believe she'll produce a much better story as a result of storyboarding.

Let's go back to our student narrative about the train station in Italy. The student's list of "snapshots" might look something like this:

1. On the train to Italy sitting with her father
2. Landscape view from the window
3. First view of the train station
4. Father telling her about pickpockets
5, 6, 7. Shots of people who look like pickpockets
8. Woman approaching them, asks for money for water
9. Woman buying water
10. Two men verbally arguing
11. Father pulling girl off bench, away from fight
12. Old man threatening young man with a knife
13. Girl running
14. Father finding daughter
15. The two sitting on the bench again
16. Their train arriving
17. The father and daughter boarding train

Instead of journaling today, create storyboards for each of the two stories you are considering:

1. Begin by listing a "title" at the top of each card (like those on the list of 17 cards that I've made above).

2. Now, on each card you may draw a scene OR sketch out details in *words*. What do I mean? For card 13, you could either draw a picture or write in words what happens: "The girl's father shouts, 'GO!' She runs as far and as fast as she can, not looking back." You could also include other word images that you may or may not decide to use. "As she runs, she hears people speaking Italian and wonders if they are talking about her. She sees a train pull into the station. She stops next to a bench."

As you look at each set of cards, ask yourself these questions and answer them on your cards:

1. Does your story provide vivid scenes that you can turn into a story? Explain how.

2. Do the scenes you've chosen to storyboard reveal your purpose? Explain how.
After storyboarding your two possible fictional narratives, you should have a good idea of whether or not they contain the elements of a good story. If you had a hard time seeing one of the stories in your mind or making storyboard cards for it, you should probably choose the other. If you can't see a story in your own mind, you'll probably have a hard time creating images readers can visualize.

Don't forget that this is fiction. That means you are free to add or change scenes to improve your story. With this in mind, ask yourself one more question:

What details might you add or change to strengthen your story's purpose?

CAPSULE 5

4.3.5

WHY FICTIONALIZE YOUR NARRATIVE?

After looking at your cards, you may be thinking, "I've got a pretty good story here. Why should I fictionalize it? Why not just tell it as an autobiographical story?"

Fictionalizing allows you to alter events. For instance, an event that happened over several days can be collapsed into a single day to move the story along and strengthen the dramatic effect.

Turning your story into fiction also frees you to enjoy writing more. Rather than getting caught up in whether you remembered the details perfectly, you can invent the details you don't remember. It gives you a great deal of **latitude** to enhance the story and make its purpose or theme stronger.

Two things you should use that latitude to do is (1) include more dialogue and (2) change your point of view. Making these two changes will help you to show more than tell—and that helps keep your audience interested. When the readers are thrown into the middle of your story and must piece together what's going on, they'll be more engaged.

And believe it or not, writing from a fictional perspective is good for your development as a writer and a thinker. Writing fiction forces you to get out of your own mind a little bit and examine things from another point of view. You have to consider other viewpoints—a skill that will be essential as we begin learning other types of writing.

Seeing things from another vantage point is also good for you as a believer. The Bible says we are to be conformed to Christ's image (Romans 8:29). Christ's understanding, love, and sympathy for others is written all over the New Testament. His incarnation provides the ultimate example of his ability to understand mankind. He faced human temptation and can sympathize with our weaknesses (Hebrews 4:14-15). We're following Christ's example when we empathize with others. We may not agree with others' beliefs or their worldviews, but, following Christ's example, we should be willing to listen and extend the love of Christ to them.

4.3.5—Prepare for the conference by looking through each stack of storyboard cards. Can you get the story's basic plot from the cards? Are any key points missing? If so, begin the conference by talking about where you get confused and why. Have the student jot down headings on cards to fill in gaps. (He can complete the cards later on his own.) After that, talk through the questions in the CWJ for capsule 5.

CWJ

Answer these questions in your journal:

1. Which incident have you chosen for your fictional narrative?

2. From whose viewpoint will you tell the story? What type of narrator will you use?

3. How will this viewpoint help convey the story's purpose?

◀ IN YOUR JOURNAL

STYLE TIME: SHORTCUTS

 Apostrophes do two main things:
1. Show who owns what
2. Make word "shortcuts"

"Apostrophes show who owns what and make word shortcuts." If you can remember that line, you'll have a pretty good handle on when to use apostrophes. In the last Style Time, we talked about the rules for possessive apostrophes. Today's rule is even easier. When you contract (shorten) a word, you replace the missing letters with an apostrophe.

If you listen to yourself and others around you talk, you'll hear lots of contractions. Unless you want to sound **pretentious**, you probably rarely utter a sentence like this one. "I cannot eat this toast without butter. I shall go to the refrigerator and get some more." Real language sounds more like this. "I can't eat toast without butter. I'll get some more out of the fridge." When we talk, we tend to shorten things. Some words get shortened so often they have become standard contractions:

> Cannot = can't
> I will/I shall = I'll
> did not = didn't
> do not = don't
> he is = he's
> she will = she'll

These are just a few contractions we use every day. If you look at the list though, you can see the pattern. Most contractions start as two words. To form the contraction, the two words get stuck together:

> Ihave

and the middle part gets left out:

> Ive

And the apostrophe goes where the missing letters used to be

I've— (apostrophe goes where the missing *ha* was)

That's it! With the two rules for apostrophes we've studied in 4.2.5 and 4.3.5, you've covered most of the uses of apostrophes you'll run across in your writing.

THE RIGHT WORD

Below are the five vocabulary words in context for this week. You should already have defined them in your journal as you found them in the reading.

▶ They focus on **universal** themes that we can relate to because we've felt the same way or had a similar experience ourselves.
▶ But in fiction, part of the readers' enjoyment of the **genre** is figuring out the story for themselves.
▶ The more specific and real the sights, smells, emotions, and feelings you create for your reader, the stronger the sense of **immediacy** you will be able to create.
▶ It gives you a great deal of **latitude** to enhance the story and make its purpose or theme stronger.
▶ Unless you want to sound **pretentious**, you probably, you probably rarely utter a sentence like this one.

Using your thesaurus, try to find the BEST word to replace the bold word in the sentence. If you aren't familiar with the meanings of all the synonyms for each word in the thesaurus, you may need to use your dictionary to look them up. That way you can choose the word that best fits the sentence.

Write with WORLD

CRAFTING NARRATIVES

WRITING A FICTIONAL NARRATIVE

CAPSULE 1   4.4.1

GETTING READY TO WRITE

Grab your journal and flip back through it. Whether or not you feel like a writer yet, you've done an impressive amount of writing in 15 lessons! You've written several times a week—maybe even every day.

Take a few minutes to reflect on what you've learned so far about yourself as a writer. Where do you like to write? Do you work better with complete silence, or does having music playing in the background help your creativity flow? Do you like to meticulously plan out every detail in advance, or do you prefer a loose organization that allows flexibility to change and add details as you write?

Whether your style is very controlled or more "blow where the wind takes you," you will benefit from spending a few minutes planning before you begin a larger writing project. Today, we don't want you to start writing the fictional narrative you've been preparing in this unit, but we want you to be ready to go when you begin Capsule 2.

First, find your Post-it Flags. Beginning with 4.1.1, go through your journal and tab anything you've already written that may help with your fictional narrative. For instance, in 4.1, you wrote scenes from various points of view. You may already have a paragraph that will fit into your story. You also answered questions that might be helpful (4.1.5).

Once you've tabbed relevant pages in your journal, lay out your storyboard cards. Start with your cards in numerical order. Based on what you learned in Unit 2, you know that the natural order for stories is chronological. That doesn't necessarily mean you will tell your story from start to finish. You can begin your story anywhere you choose.

Play around with the cards. What scene might make an interesting starting point? You may start in the middle, skip back to the beginning, and then go to the end. The key (as you'll also remember from Unit 2), is your transitions. The words and sentences you use to link your scenes together cue readers in to what happened first, next, and last in your story. Using phrases like, "Just moments before," and "a short while later," help lead the reader through the story's timeline.

When you think you know how you'll order your story, move on to your journal assignment for today.

IN YOUR JOURNAL ▶

CWJ

By the time you finish this journal assignment, you should be ready to write. If you think you need a more detailed outline, make one now. One possibility would be to go through and make an outline based on your card titles. For instance, our student writer could add a short outline of what she plans to write under card number 3:

3. First view of the train station:
   ▶ Lots of noise and activity
   ▶ Crowds moving to get on trains
   ▶ Lady eating sandwich
   ▶ Man speaking German

Choose ONE card and make a bullet-point outline like this one for the card in your journal. If you find the process helpful, continue with your other cards. You're only required to do one; doing more is optional.

CAPSULE 2   4.4.2

A GOOD BEGINNING

How do you decide whether or not you want to read a book? If you're like us, an interesting title grabs your attention. Then we'd probably look at the back for the "blurb" that tells a little about the story. If that sounds interesting, we might flip the book open and begin reading the first paragraph.

And that's where we'll probably ultimately decide whether we are going to check the book out of the library or put it back on the shelf and keep looking. If the author doesn't grab our attention pretty quickly, he's lost us as potential readers.

You've already planned your story. You should have a good idea of where you will begin it. However, how you begin is just as important as where you begin. Readers decide very quickly whether or not they want to spend their valuable time reading your story. You need to have a good "hook" to draw them in.

Students are more than ready to write this essay. They've spent a considerable amount of time developing ideas, characters, details, actions, and themes. Your role is give the student writer space to write. If the student wants to bounce ideas off of you, feel free to respond. If the student has questions, feel free to answer those questions.

Remember, you will likely evaluate this essay as a high-stakes assignment. You do not want to compromise this role, which requires that you assign a grade to the student's writing.

Try to not become a collaborator on this paper. Work to make sure the student owns the drafting process, revisions, and final edition.

In Unit 3, we talked about two good strategies for starting your essay—beginning with dialogue or beginning in the middle of things to grab readers' attention. Let's add one more: *A statement that raises questions for the reader and makes them want to find out more.* Here's an example:

> If I told you how I ended up on top of the city's water tower wearing a chicken costume on the coldest day ever on record in Jasper, Illinois, you probably wouldn't believe me.

As you write your introduction today, keep your audience in mind. Use one of these three strategies to get your readers interested in your story.

Now you're ready to begin writing. We're not going to tell you exactly how many paragraphs to write, but you need enough to set up your story. The two main elements we want you to include are:

▶ A strong introductory strategy
▶ Introduction or foreshadowing of your story's theme

Note that, so far, we've written most of the examples we've included in our units. However, in Unit 4, we are including writing composed by a real student writer. Let's take a look at our student writer's introduction.

> If someone had been looking around inside a Eurostar train heading to Bologna, Italy, they might have seen an American man shaking his daughter awake.
>
> "Wake up," he said. "We're almost at the train station!"
>
> The girl sat up abruptly. "Are we *finally* in Italy?" she asked.
>
> "Yes. At last we've escaped that *miserable* place, Germany." He grinned.
>
> "It was not miserable!" she protested. "It's just that —well, I wanted to come to Italy because Italy is, see—"
>
> "Italy is Italy," her father nodded understandingly. "Where everything was made. Pizza, pasta, amazing art, famous buildings . . . . You name it."
>
> The girl looked eagerly out the window. Imagine—Italy! Full of soccer, where the tower of Pisa is, not to mention the Coliseum, and don't forget the statue of David!
>
> But looking around, she saw a breathtaking sight—the country. Farms, sweeping hillsides, grassy meadows, roaming livestock. The girl had never seen anything like this. Everything was so beautiful that it overwhelmed her. Inside she felt a bubble of happiness that seemed like it

would never burst. Italy was amazing. It had everything.

Sighing, the girl laid her head back on her seat. *Perfect*, she thought. *This trip is going to be perfect.*

Does she include the two key elements? It's easy to tell that she has the first one. She quickly launches into dialogue.

The second one is a little trickier. If you look back at 4.3.3, you'll see that the student's theme is the realization the world is a dangerous place and you can't always be prepared or protect yourself. Her final sentence is the character's thought, "*This trip is going to be perfect.*"

Here, she sets up her theme. The student goes into this experience innocent, thinking she's only going to find perfection in Italy. That lays the groundwork for the story's theme of danger and imperfection she will discover as the story continues.

This student's introduction does a good job of drawing readers in and setting up the story's message or theme.

CWJ

IN YOUR JOURNAL ▶

Now it's your turn. On your computer or a separate sheet of paper, write the first part of your story. Make sure you choose a strong introductory strategy. You should also foreshadow or introduce your story's theme.

THE PROFESSOR'S OFFICE

You may have noticed that the student writer includes a few fragments in the introduction to her fictional narrative. Here they are: "Full of soccer, where the tower of Pisa is, not to mention the Coliseum, and don't forget the statue of David!" and "Farms, sweeping hillsides, grassy meadows, roaming livestock." As you read these lines, you may have said, "Aha! I've got her . . . that's a fragment." And you were correct. These are fragments, but we call these "stylistic fragments."

Especially in fiction writing, there are times that a fragment is stylistically appropriate. This student uses fragments in dialogue. It sounds natural, like real people talking. She also uses fragments to express what the character is seeing out the window, which is an effective use as well.

I'm sure this thought has crossed your mind: "Hooray . . . I can use stylistic fragments as much as I want and not worry about them being marked wrong." This is what many of my students think when we discuss stylistic errors.

Every year, I have a student who writes run-on sentences and tells me the sentence is actually not wrong— it's a "stylistic run-on." I ask the student to explain how a run-on is not incorrect, and more often than not they cite William Faulkner, the great American author. Faulkner once wrote a sentence that had over 1,800 words; the run-on sentence runs over 20 pages in the edition I own and has mechanical and grammar problems. My students who produce multiple run-ons in a paper often say they are "writing like Faulkner."

Here's the problem: they are not Faulkner. Faulkner is one of the United States' best-known writers who won a Nobel Prize for Literature. When Faulkner wrote that "stylistic run-on" he knew what he was doing: he had proven he knew how to write with correct grammar and understood that this outrageously long sentence was a run-on.

Our student writer in this essay is not Faulkner either. But she seems to know what she is doing. The rest of the paper is grammatically correct and shows a nice stylistic sense that includes simple and complex sentences. Because these fragments have a purpose (they help make the dialogue sound realistic), they are stylistically fine. The story would be different if the student turned in a paper that had many fragments.

Use fragments only when the situation deems it necessary, and remember that fragment use should be purposeful and sparing to be considered "stylistic."

CAPSULE 3

4.4.3

SHOW YOUR STORY

How did your introduction go? Did you sit right down and write it out with no problem? Or did you find yourself starting over several times and trying more than one strategy before you were satisfied with what you wrote?

If it was harder than you thought it would be, don't get discouraged. Many writers find getting started to be the hardest part of writing. Today should be a little easier.

For one thing, you should have a big stack of storyboard cards to help lead you through the story. If you did some more prewriting in Capsule 1, that will help too. Right now would also be a good time to flip back through Unit 4 and look at the journal entries you tabbed.

We hope you're encouraged by all the work you've already done to prepare for writing the middle of the story. Now it's time to dive in and get started. You should have already decided how you will order the events in your story. Remember, if you're skipping around in time, you need to use clear transitions: "The week before," or "When she was five," allow you to flash back in time without confusing your reader.

> Here, we suggest beginning from the third person limited if the student has trouble showing rather than telling. If you suspect your student will struggle, it's fine to have him begin from this point of view.

As you work today, keep the word, "cameraman" in your mind. If you're using a third- person narrator, you might begin by writing from the third person objective viewpoint. Remember, that's the point of view where the narrator sees all the events but can't see inside the characters' minds. That will help make sure your story shows instead of merely tells. You can add characters' thoughts later.

If you're using a first person narrator, it might be wise to take the same approach. Tell what the narrator sees, says, and hears. Then go back through and add what he's thinking.

Also, don't forget that your story's organization serves the same purpose as the bones in your body. Without them, you'd be a blob of flesh with nothing to hold you up. The same holds true for your story. It needs structure. Use your storyboard cards to help keep you on track.

If you keep in mind the ideas of *showing* and *organization* as you write, you should be well on your way to a good first draft of your fictional narrative.

Before you get started, look at the middle (or body) of our student writer's story:

A little while later the Eurostar train from Frankfurt, Germany to Bologna, Italy, pulled into the station. The girl and her father stepped off the train and looked around curiously.

"Wow!" breathed the girl. "Wow!"

Before the pair's eyes lay a hustle-bustle of people moving from train to train. Over there a lady was shoving an interesting-looking sandwich into her mouth. A few feet away from the lady, a man was shouting in rapid German.

"There are people everywhere!" exclaimed the girl's father. "This would be a great place for pickpockets."

"Pickpockets? What do they do?" questioned the child.

"Well, they usually travel in groups, and one might ask for money or food or water, and when you pull out your wallet, they would steal your whole wallet. Or they might crowd around you and bump you to distract you while one of them stole your money."

The girl's mood changed abruptly. She was very frightened now. Everyone seemed like a pickpocket.

A woman lounging under the station sign looked very suspicious. Every which way the poor girl turned, she saw a pickpocket.

"I'm scared," she whispered to her father. "When does our train to Florence come?"

Her father looked at his watch. "About half an hour."

Inwardly, the child groaned. Thirty whole minutes of being scared out of her skin?

Looking around, the girl saw a group of ladies whispering. One of them left the group and approached the girl and her father.

"Water," she croaked. "Water."

Despite the numbing fear that gripped her, the girl wondered why the woman was speaking English. Even after the woman left to rejoin her group, the girl still couldn't open her mouth to ask her father the question.

Her father squeezed her hand tight to show that everything was going to be alright, and that he knew his daughter thought the woman was a thief, but maybe she wasn't.

For a long time the two sat on a bench in silence watching the group of what the girl was sure were thieves. Some time later, a young man came and sat down on the other side of the bench. The girl watched him for a while out of pure boredom. Eventually, her father nudged her.

"Look, that lady that came up to us, a man gave her money for water, and she didn't steal any money. She used his coins to buy water. Maybe she was just a poor lady after all."

"Well," protested the girl, "*I* still think she was a thief."

"Your opinion isn't always right."

"Your opinion isn't always right, either," the girl shot back.

"Maybe," retorted the father. "But usually it doesn't really matter. What I say goes, even if it's wrong. What you say doesn't matter, even if what you say is right."

Scowling, the girl tried to hide a smile as her father grinned mockingly and triumphantly at her.

"Well—" she started to say, but she was cut off by sudden shouts behind the two of them. The young man that had been sitting down behind them was standing now, shouting at an old man, who was glaring and giving hostile looks in return.

Then, slowly, the older man reached into his back pocket.

The girl felt her arm being wrenched away from her body by her father. She stood up and followed him while only one thought echoed in her brain: that man's going to kill the boy. Looking behind her, the girl saw the men moving closer.

"GO!" shouted her father urgently and authoritatively. But his child needed no further urging. She dashed as far and fast as she could until her father shouted for her to stop.

"It's okay," the girl's father reassured her. "The man's leaving now, and he didn't hurt anybody. He was just trying to end his argument—very violently."

But still she could not get one picture out of her head. The picture of the man with the knife.

* * *

When he saw the man reach for his back pocket, the girl's father knew what the man was going to pull out—a knife or a gun.

Pulling his daughter's arm, he lifted her from the bench. "GO!" he cried with such urgency but calmness that he surprised even himself. When he saw his daughter run he looked back at the man. He had pulled a long, sharp butcher knife out of his pocket. Scanning the station he saw the young man who the knife-wielding man had been arguing with was alive but shaken.

Apparently, the man with the knife hadn't wanted to kill, only threaten.

The man with the knife jogged over close to where his daughter had fled. "Frightened" didn't come close to describing her.

Pale as a sheet, she looked like death had come knocking at her door.

He sprinted to his daughter. "Now that was a thief. Freaky, old, and crabby. And that humongous knife. Yep, he was definitely a thief."

CWJ

IN YOUR JOURNAL ▶

Can you see what this student is doing well? She's definitely following the order she set up in her storyboard cards. And she's using dialogue and description to show. There are still spots where she's telling too much, but this is a good draft.

Today, continue with your draft. You should write until you've completed the middle section of your story. Take us through the main action of the story before you stop.

Some students may take more than one day for this section of the story. That's fine. By this point in the course, you should have a good sense of your student's abilities. For most, just pushing through and getting a draft of the body of the fictional narrative is best. Stopping and restarting is often more difficult than doing the body in one sitting.

But if your student struggles, you should create a schedule that works better for her. One caution: Have a set number of cards to get through in one day. If you simply extend the time, she'll likely put off the writing and end up rushing through the assignment on the final day.

A STRONG FINISH

You did a lot of work in the last capsule. You've now written the biggest part of your story. You should have only a paragraph or a little more left to write. You may be tempted to scribble something quickly so you can be finished. But avoid the temptation. How you finish will either leave your readers feeling satisfied, or as if they've just wasted their time reading your story.

I'm sure you've seen movies or read books that are great right up until the end. Then they try to finish up too quickly and they fall flat. Even the ancient Greeks had this problem. You remember that they were known for drama, right? But not all of their drama was great literature. Sometimes, dramatists would conclude a play by using a *deus ex machina*. *Deus ex machina* is Latin for "a god from a machine." At the end of these plays, the Greek god would be lowered to the stage on a piece of machinery and solve all the human problems. It got things over in a hurry, but it probably didn't really satisfy the audience.

Your ending is not the place to fictionalize and make your story all wrap up neatly. Life isn't usually like that. Your conclusion should grow naturally from what happened in the story. In some way, it should subtly point your readers back to the purpose or theme of your story.

In other words, don't try to be Aesop here. Leave your readers with something to think about, but don't TELL them explicitly what the story's moral is. Stick to showing. It takes a little more time, but it will give your story a much subtler, more satisfying ending.

Before writing your conclusion, read our student writer's ending to her story:

> When his daughter smiled weakly, he felt relieved. She would be fine once they checked into their hotel and ate dinner. The two of them sat for a little while, and then their train came. And the pair left for Florence with the day's events looming over them, and doubts about Italy's wonders.

She's done a good job of remaining subtle. The last sentence reflects how her attitudes have changed from the time that she arrived at the train station. She might add a sentence or two or SHOW the change in some way, but in general, she's on the right track here.

CWJ

Read back through your draft so far. You should have finished writing all the action of the story. In your conclusion, you want to reinforce the story's theme in some way. How might your characters act that would show how they've been affected by events? What might they say? In other words, how can you subtly get your theme across without saying it outright?

◀ IN YOUR JOURNAL

When you are ready, write a conclusion to your story.

When you've finished, read your whole narrative and answer these two questions in your journal:

1. How have you communicated your story's purpose (theme) in your conclusion?

2. List two or three possible titles for your story.

CAPSULE 5

MAKING IMPROVEMENTS

The first thing you should do today is read back through your fictional narrative. How do you think it turned out? Do you like what you wrote? Do you see any things you want to change?

Take some time today and make improvements—adding relevant details to show rather than tell, rewriting transitions, and improving organization are areas where you can make a big difference. When you have finished, give it to a parent or teacher to get some feedback on what they like about your story and what they think could be improved.

Here's the final draft of our student writer's fictional narrative after she made revisions:

First Impressions

If someone had been looking around inside a Eurostar train heading to Bologna, Italy, they might have seen an American man shaking his daughter awake.

"Wake up," he said. "We're almost at the train station!"

The girl sat up abruptly. "Are we *finally* in Italy?" she asked.

"Yes. At last we've escaped that *miserable* place, Germany." He grinned.

"It was not miserable!" she protested. "It's just that—well, I wanted to come to Italy because Italy is, see—"

"Italy is Italy," her father nodded understandingly. "Where everything was made. Pizza, pasta, amazing art, famous buildings . . . . You name it."

The girl looked eagerly out the window. Imagine—Italy! Full of soccer, where the tower of Pisa is, not to mention the Coliseum, and don't forget the statue of David!

But looking around, she saw a breathtaking sight—the country. Farms, sweeping hillsides, grassy meadows, roaming livestock. The girl had never seen anything like it. Inside she felt a bubble of happiness that seemed like it would never burst. Italy was amazing. It had everything.

Sighing, the girl laid her head back on her seat. *Perfect*, she thought. *This trip is going to be perfect.*

A little while later the Eurostar train from Frankfurt, Germany to Bologna, Italy, pulled into the station. The girl and her father stepped off the train and looked around curiously.

"Wow!" breathed the girl. "Wow!"

Before the pair's eyes lay a hustle-bustle of people moving from train to train. Over there a lady was shoving an interesting-looking sandwich into her mouth. A few feet away from the lady, a man was shouting in rapid German.

"There are people everywhere!" exclaimed the girl's father. "This would be a great place for pickpockets."

"Pickpockets? What do they do?" questioned the child.

"Well, they usually travel in groups, and one might ask for money or food or water, and when you pull out your wallet, they would steal your whole wallet. Or they might crowd around you and bump you to distract you while one of them stole your money."

The girl's mood changed abruptly. Terror gripped her. Everyone seemed like a pickpocket.

A woman lounging under the station sign seemed to be watching everyone, as if plotting to steal their money. Every which way the poor girl turned, she saw a pickpocket.

Trembling, she whispered to her father, "When does our train to Florence come?"

Her father looked at his watch. "About half an hour."

Inwardly, the child groaned. Thirty whole minutes of being scared out of her skin?

Looking around, the girl saw a group of ladies whispering. One of them left the group and approached the girl and her father.

"Water," she croaked. "Water."

Despite the numbing fear that gripped her, the girl wondered why the woman was speaking

English. Even after the woman left to rejoin her group, the girl still couldn't open her mouth to ask her father the question.

Her father squeezed her hand tight. He knew his daughter thought the woman was a thief, but maybe she wasn't.

For a long time the two sat on a bench in silence watching the group of what the girl was sure were thieves. Some time later, a young man came and sat down on the other side of the bench. The girl watched him for a while out of pure boredom. Eventually, her father nudged her.

"Look, there's that lady that came up to us. A man gave her money for water, and she didn't steal any money. She used his coins to buy water. Maybe she was just a poor lady after all."

"Well," protested the girl, "*I* still think she was a thief."

"Your opinion isn't always right."

"Your opinion isn't always right, either," the girl shot back.

"Maybe," retorted the father. "But usually it doesn't really matter. What I say goes, even if it's wrong. What you say doesn't matter, even if what you say is right."

Scowling, the girl tried to hide a smile as her father grinned mockingly and triumphantly at her.

"Well—" she started to say, but she was cut off by sudden shouts behind the two of them. The young man that had been sitting down behind them was standing now, shouting at an old man, who was glaring and giving hostile looks in return.

Then, slowly, the older man reached into his back pocket.

The girl felt her arm being wrenched away from her body by her father. She stood up and followed him while only one thought echoed in her brain: that man's going to kill the boy. Looking behind her, the girl saw the men moving closer.

"GO!" shouted her father urgently and authoritatively. But his child needed no further urging. She dashed as far and fast as she could until her father shouted for her to stop.

"It's okay," the girl's father reassured her. "The man's leaving now, and he didn't hurt anybody. He was just trying to end his argument—very violently."

But still she could not get one picture out of her head. The picture of the man with the knife.

* * *

When he saw the man reach for his back pocket, the girl's father knew what the man was going to pull out—a knife or a gun.

Pulling his daughter's arm, he lifted her from the bench. "GO!" he cried with such urgency and calmness that he surprised even himself. When he saw his daughter run he looked back at the man. The filthy, bearded old man pulled a long, sharp butcher knife out of his pocket. Scanning the station he saw the young man who the knife-wielding man had been arguing with was alive but shaken.

Apparently, the man with the knife hadn't wanted to kill, only threaten.

The man with the knife jogged over close to where his daughter had fled. "Frightened" didn't come close to describing her.

Pale as a sheet, her eyes darted around frantically, searching for her father.

He sprinted to his daughter. "Now that was a thief. Freaky, old, and crabby. And that humongous knife. Yep, he was definitely a thief."

When his daughter smiled weakly, he felt relieved. She would be fine once they checked into their hotel and ate dinner. The two of them sat in silence for a little while until their train came.

The pair boarded the train, and the girl took the seat by the window. Night was beginning to fall as the train began its journey. Menacing shadows darkened the countryside which had earlier seemed so inviting and beautiful. As the train raced toward Florence, the day's events loomed over them, each of them doubtful about what awaited them on the journey ahead.

WORLD WISDOM:

How did our student writer do with her revised fictional narrative? WORLD writer Susan Olasky shares her reactions:

"The writer has good writing mechanics and often uses vivid verbs and good specific detail. She made a few small edits between the first and second drafts that improved her story. For instance, she changed "she was very frightened now" to "terror gripped her." She changed "a woman lounging under the station sign looked very suspicious" to "a woman lounging under the station sign seemed to be watching everyone, as if plotting to steal their money." Instead of telling us the woman seemed suspicious, the writer shows us what she was doing—watching everyone—that made her look suspicious to the girl in the story."
— Susan Olasky

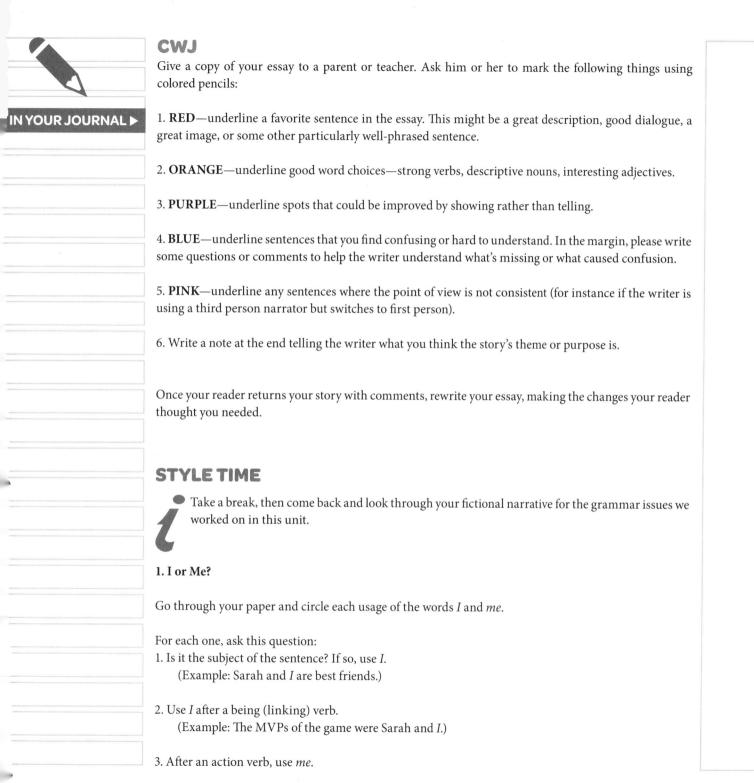

CWJ

Give a copy of your essay to a parent or teacher. Ask him or her to mark the following things using colored pencils:

1. **RED**—underline a favorite sentence in the essay. This might be a great description, good dialogue, a great image, or some other particularly well-phrased sentence.

2. **ORANGE**—underline good word choices—strong verbs, descriptive nouns, interesting adjectives.

3. **PURPLE**—underline spots that could be improved by showing rather than telling.

4. **BLUE**—underline sentences that you find confusing or hard to understand. In the margin, please write some questions or comments to help the writer understand what's missing or what caused confusion.

5. **PINK**—underline any sentences where the point of view is not consistent (for instance if the writer is using a third person narrator but switches to first person).

6. Write a note at the end telling the writer what you think the story's theme or purpose is.

Once your reader returns your story with comments, rewrite your essay, making the changes your reader thought you needed.

STYLE TIME

Take a break, then come back and look through your fictional narrative for the grammar issues we worked on in this unit.

1. I or Me?

Go through your paper and circle each usage of the words *I* and *me*.

For each one, ask this question:
1. Is it the subject of the sentence? If so, use *I*.
     (Example: Sarah and *I* are best friends.)

2. Use *I* after a being (linking) verb.
     (Example: The MVPs of the game were Sarah and *I*.)

3. After an action verb, use *me*.

(Example: The teacher asked Sarah and *me* to collect the papers.)

Reminder: To check, leave out the other person and see if it sounds right. "The teacher asked I to collect the papers" wouldn't be correct, so you know it's not right to use "Sarah and I" in this sentence, either.

2. Apostrophes

Remember that apostrophes do two things—(1) show who owns what and (2) make word shortcuts.

1. To check to see if you need an apostrophe to show who owns what, circle each –s at the end of a word in your narrative. Then look at the word that follows it. If you wrote Johns book, does it make sense if you change it to "The book belonging to John"? If your answer is yes, then you have a possessive and you need an apostrophe (John's book).

2. To make sure you are making your word "shortcuts" correctly, circle words that have apostrophes in them.

Look at the word and determine what two words it originally came from (example: don't = do + not). Put the two words together (example: donot). Put an apostrophe in place of the missing letter or letters (example: don't). If you've got the apostrophe in place of the missing letters, you've made the "shortcut" the right way.

When you've finished making all the corrections, prepare a final copy of your paper to turn in.

THE RIGHT WORD

Here are the 15 vocabulary words we studied in this unit. Match each word in the first column with the synonym from the second column that BEST expresses its meaning.

_i_ biased   a. engage

_d_ garrulous   b. predict

_n_ intrusive   c. style

_b_ foreshadow   d. talkative

_i_ embellish   e. unnecessary

_a_ pique   f. freedom

_g_ premise   g. basis

_l_ elicit   h. closeness

_e_ irrelevant   i. partial

_o_ demystify   j. adorn

_k_ universal   k. common

_c_ genre   l. evoke

_h_ immediacy   m. showy

_f_ latitude   n. interfering

_m_ pretentious   o. clarify

Congratulations! By now you have added 60 words to your vocabulary. That's quite a substantial number. In future lessons, we encourage you to put these words to work in your writing. Remember, a word isn't a working part of your vocabulary until you use it. So give it a try.